Planet Earth

VOLCANO

By The Editors of Time-Life Books

Time-Life Books, Amsterdam

PLANET EARTH

EDITOR: George G. Daniels
Editorial Staff for *Volcano*
Senior Editor: Thomas A. Lewis
Designer: Donald Komai
Chief Researcher: Pat S. Good
Picture Editor: John Conrad Weiser
Text Editor: Gus Hedberg
Writers: Jan Leslie Cook, Roger E. Herst, John Newton,
Peter Pocock, David Thiemann
Researchers: Susan S. Blair and Jane Edwin (principals),
Judith W. Shanks
Assistant Designer: Susan K. White
Copy Coordinators: Victoria Lee, Brian Miller
Picture Coordinators: Jane Martin, Donna Quaresima
Editorial Assistant: Annette T. Wilkerson

Special Contributors: Champ Clark, Paul O'Neil, Russell
Sackett, Robert Wallace (text)

Correspondents: Elisabeth Kraemer (Bonn); Margot
Hapgood, Dorothy Bacon (London); Susan Jonas, Lucy T.
Voulgaris (New York); Maria Vincenza Aloisi, Josephine
du Brusle (Paris); Ann Natanson (Rome). Valuable
assistance was also provided by: Wibo van de Linde
(Amsterdam); Helga Kohl (Bonn); Robert W. Bone
(Honolulu); Millicent Trowbridge (London); Felix
Rosenthal (Moscow); Angela Lauro, Maria Odone
(Naples); Carolyn Chubet, Miriam Hsia (New York);
M. T. Hirschkoff (Paris); Bogi Agustsson (Reykjavik);
Mimi Murphy (Rome); Janet Zich (San Francisco); Ed
Reingold, Katsuko Yamazaki (Tokyo); Traudl Lessing
(Vienna).

THE CONSULTANTS

Dr. William Melson is Curator-in-Charge, Division
of Petrology and Volcanology, Smithsonian Institution, Washington, D.C. He has studied volcanoes
throughout the world, with particular attention to
Central America, the Philippines, Papua, New
Guinea, and, most recently, Mount St. Helens in
the state of Washington. He is the author of
numerous articles in the field of volcanology and co-
author of the *The Lunar Rocks*, a study of lunar
volcanic rocks.

Sidney Horenstein is a geologist in the Department
of Invertebrates at the American Museum of Natural
History and a faculty member of the Department of
Geology at City University of New York. He
organized and served as coordinator of the Environmental Information Center of the American
Museum.

CONTENTS

Planet Earth
VOLCANO

TIME
LIFE
BOOKS

This volume is one of a series that examines the
workings of the planet earth, from the geological
wonders of its continents to the marvels of its
atmosphere and its ocean depths.

Cover
Incandescent projectiles of lava shoot from a
subsidiary cone on Mount Etna, Sicily, as a crater
wall collapses, sending a river of lava cascading down
its flank. Etna is one of the world's most active
volcanoes, with more than 150 sizable eruptions
since 1500 B.C., when records were first kept.

The greatest single cataclysm known to have occurred on earth took place nearly 20,000 years ago on the Indonesian island of Sumatra. There the eruption of a volcano blew a 20-by-60-mile depression in the island's center. From it burst a gas-laden cloud of incandescent ash that enveloped the island at speeds of more than 100 miles per hour, eventually settling to form a 10,000-square-mile sheet of volcanic rock, more than 1,000 feet thick in places. Some volcanologists speculate that the ash cloud may have blotted out enough of the sun to help plunge the planet into the last great ice age.

Yet for all its terrible power, the eruption that formed Toba, as this area was named, was not merely a paroxysm of destruction. It was also a monumental act of creation, for volcanoes are among nature's mightiest engines, builders of the land, makers of the sea, producers even of the atmosphere.

The eruptions of volcanoes are the source of the primeval and continuing regeneration of mountains and plains. The ocean floor, science now knows, is the result of millions of years of slow but ceaseless volcanic extrusions emanating from a 30,000-mile-long chain of deep-sea rift valleys.

A volcano's noxious ash and gases are essential to life on earth. The billions of tons of mineral-rich ash that fall to earth after an eruption are transformed in time into the most fertile of soils. Volcanologists calculate that, judging by their present rate of activity, volcanoes could have accounted for nearly a quarter of the oxygen, hydrogen, carbon, chlorine and nitrogen in the biosphere, and may, in fact, have been the primal source for most of the earth's air and water.

The science of volcanology is young, and the secrets of volcanism are well protected. The magma chambers that feed the fiery cones are locked beneath miles of cold crust, and the eruptions themselves are so violent that close study is often impossible.

Yet a comprehensive theory of volcanism is slowly forming and with it a system for predicting and, in small ways, controlling volcanic activity. But none of this diminishes the volcano's fearful majesty. Science, by tracing the volcano to its infernal roots, is only enlarging the scope of its splendor.

A fountain of molten lava erupts from a fissure on Hawaii's Kilauea volcano in May 1969. The blast initiated a five-year series of eruptions that resulted in Mauna Ulu (growing mountain), a volcano 400 feet high and more than a mile across. The eruptions buried 10,000 acres in repeated lava flows.

Lava from Piton de la Fournaise volcano cuts a gash
into the countryside of Réunion island in the Indian
Ocean in April 1977. The crusted black lava, seen
overwhelming the town of Sainte-Rose, crept along at
only several feet per hour, while the red-hot central
channel flowed at one mile or more per hour.

As rocks explode skyward, a river of 1,800° F. lava gushes at 550 feet per second from Mount Tolbachik on the U.S.S.R.'s Kamchatka Peninsula. Soviet scientists accurately predicted the eruption date—July 6, 1975—and when the mountain awoke, instruments were on hand to record the event.

Curtains of steam fill the air and floods of lava pour from the ground at Gjástykki, a "field of fissures" in northeast Iceland. The September 1977 eruptions were part of an age-old process in which the island is slowly being torn apart by volcanic rifts that at the same time rejuvenate the land with fresh lava.

Roiling clouds of steam, gases and pulverized rock
continue to burst from Washington State's Mount St.
Helens hours after its eruption on May 18, 1980.
Three quarters of a cubic mile of rock was lost, leaving
a gaping amphitheater in its stead—and turning a
picture-postcard world into a barren moonscape.

Brilliant ropes of lava snake into the sea from the slope of Italy's Stromboli volcano during one of its more violent outbursts in 1967. Known as the Lighthouse of the Mediterranean, the island cone is unique for the regularity of its mild eruptions, which occur approximately every 20 minutes, shooting into the sky a shower of incandescent ash.

THE AWAKENING OF THE DRAGON

The people of the city of St. Pierre on the French Caribbean island of Martinique had been living in the shadow of their volcano for more than two centuries, and it had never harmed them. By 1902 they had even come to regard it with a certain affection, as though it were a great amiable beast of some sort, a peaceful dragon sleeping away the eons in their backyard.

To be sure, in 1792 the volcano had stirred in its slumber and belched up a cloud of powdery gray ash that had dusted the tropical vegetation for a few miles around, and in 1851 it had done so again. However, these were only minor disturbances in which no one had been killed, injured or even seriously inconvenienced, and by 1902 the incidents had been almost forgotten. There was nothing in the history of the volcano to suggest to the 30,000 people of St. Pierre, known as Pierrotins, that it was capable of killing all but two of them in the space of a few minutes. And there was not the remotest suggestion that this ordinary-looking mass of earth, rock and vegetation would soon mark a dramatic turning point in the infant science of volcanology.

Sometimes the Pierrotins called their volcano by name—Mount Pelée. More often they called it simply "the mountain." Roughly conical in shape, 4,500 feet high, with a base that covered 39 square miles, it dominated the northern end of Martinique and served as an almost theatrical backdrop for the city below it. At the mountain's summit there was a bowl-shaped basin containing a clear lake, the Lac des Palmistes. The Pierrotins were fond of picnicking there. Below the summit there was a second crater, L'Étang Sec, that had once also held a lake but in 1902 had been dry for years. On three sides the crater of L'Étang Sec was shut in by tall cliffs but on the fourth side there was a V-shaped notch like a colossal gun sight. Four miles below this notch lay the city.

The notch was scarcely an unusual thing to be found on the heights of an old volcano, nor was Pelée much different in other regards from numerous mountains in the Caribbean islands. Rain clouds borne on the westering trade winds often clustered around its summit. More than 20 short, swift rivers had their sources there, radiating in all directions and scoring Pelée's jungle-green sides with deep ravines separated by knife-edged ridges. One of the rivers, the Roxelane, ran between steep banks through the heart of the city. Another, the Blanche River, emptied into the sea just north of St. Pierre.

The city was laid out in the shape of a shallow crescent about two miles long and a quarter mile wide, lying between the sea and a long wooded ridge on the landward side that repeated the curve of the shore. The principal avenue, the Rue Victor Hugo, ran the length of the crescent and was intersected by many short streets that began near the water's edge and ended against the ridge.

The rubble-strewn ruins of the main thoroughfare of St. Pierre, Martinique, frame the cloud-capped heights of Mount Pelée, the volcano that destroyed the city just weeks before this photograph was taken in 1902. The eruption shot a superheated cloud of volcanic ash and gases down the ravine visible in the background and through the prosperous Caribbean city, snuffing out 30,000 lives in minutes.

There was no harbor, merely a roadstead, which shelved off so steeply that large ships could anchor within 100 yards of the shore.

The writer Lafcadio Hearn, who lived in St. Pierre for two years, from 1887 to 1889, described it as "the quaintest, queerest, and the prettiest withal, among West Indian cities; all stone-built and stone-flagged, with very narrow streets, wooden or zinc awnings, and peaked roofs of red tile, pierced by gable dormers. Most of the buildings are painted in a clear yellow tone, which contrasts delightfully with the burning blue ribbon of tropical sky above. There is everywhere a loud murmur of running water, pouring through the deep gutters contrived between the paved thoroughfare and the absurd little sidewalks, varying in width from one to three feet. The architecture is quite old; it is seventeenth century."

In view of what happened to St. Pierre, Hearn's phrase "stone-built" is worth repeating. Most of the houses in the city, constructed for coolness in the tropical climate, had strong masonry walls two or three feet thick. There were iron girders in the larger buildings, which included a cathedral, a large theater where actors from France performed every winter, a military hospital, a college and numerous factories, banks, warehouses and rum distilleries.

Hearn found the people of St. Pierre as fascinating as the city. "A population fantastic, astonishing—a population of the Arabian Nights. It is many-colored, but the dominant tint is yellow, a rich, brownish yellow. You are among a people of half-breeds, the finest mixed race of the West Indies. Straight as palms, and supple and tall; these colored women and men impress one powerfully by their dignified carriage and easy elegance of movement."

Among the 30,000 Pierrotins there were about 8,000 white Creoles, who controlled the wealth not only of St. Pierre but of much of Martinique, which stemmed mainly from the export of sugar and rum. The Creoles formed a closely knit society, sophisticated and thoroughly French, and were proud that their city was known as the Paris of the West Indies. In politics they were

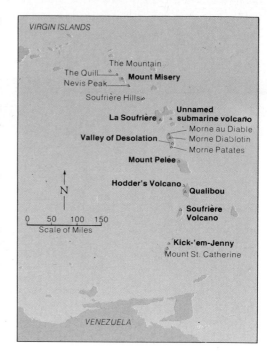

Although Mount Pelée is the best-known of the Caribbean volcanoes, it is merely the centerpiece of the volcanic Lesser Antilles island chain, which stretches in a 450-mile crescent between the Virgin Islands and Venezuela. Nearly all the islands in the chain have active volcanoes: Nine have erupted in modern times (*bold type*); the others, prior to 1500 (*light type*). Two active volcanoes and one dormant cone bear the same generic French name, Soufrière, which means "giving off sulfurous gases."

Its precipitous slopes corrugated by the ravines of more than 20 tropical rivers, Mount Pelée towers dramatically over the northern end of Martinique, rising 4,500 feet above sea level in barely four miles. The mountain itself was covered only with a lush rain forest, but at the turn of the century the fertile soil at its base supported a ring of prosperous sugar plantations, numerous villages and the commercial center of the island, the city of St. Pierre.

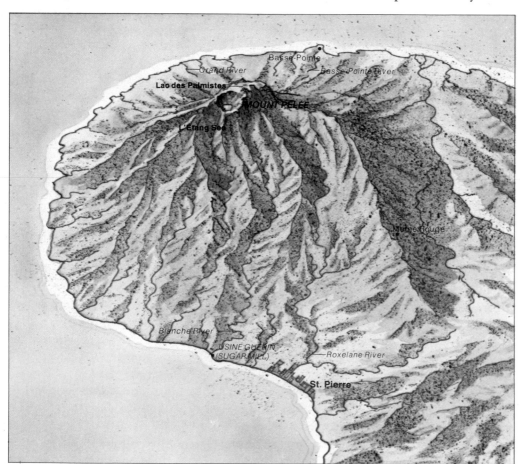

While shipping brokers dicker in the shade of tamarind and mango trees, roustabouts wrestle casks of rum and hogsheads of sugar onto lighters bound for the fleet anchored off La Place Bertin, hub of Martinique's thriving export trade. The tower in this 1887 print served both as a lighthouse for the crowded St. Pierre roadstead and as a semaphore station to announce the sighting of incoming vessels.

conservative, but otherwise so liberal that St. Pierre was also known as one of the lustiest ports in the Caribbean.

These were the people who were annihilated by Mount Pelée. Today, the casual tourist in the Lesser Antilles gives scant thought to them, or to the blast that killed them. He may not realize that no matter where he goes among these islands he will be standing on a volcano; the possibility that he will witness an eruption is remote, but it exists.

The Lesser Antilles, which separate the Caribbean from the Atlantic, form an arc that begins just east of the Virgin Islands and stretches 450 miles south almost to the coast of South America. Included in the arc are St. Kitts, Nevis, Montserrat, Guadeloupe, Dominica, Martinique, St. Lucia, St. Vincent and Grenada. All of the islands have been built up from the floor of the sea by volcanic action, a process that is continuing. A few miles north of Grenada, there is a submarine volcano named Kick-'em-Jenny, which has erupted at least eight times since 1939, on one occasion sending a column of brown smoke 900 feet into the air. In 1962 the probable center of Kick-'em-Jenny's eruption was 762 feet underwater. In 1966 the volcano had risen 132 feet closer to the surface, and when soundings were taken in 1978 it had grown another 105 feet. At its present rate of growth, Kick-'em-Jenny will break the surface and emerge as a volcanic island around the year 2000.

Many of the volcanoes in the Lesser Antilles have long been extinct, their tops beneath the sea and deeply buried under layers of coral debris. But 17 are classified as active, and of these, nine have erupted in historic times, which is to say since the arrival of Columbus. In the 20th Century there have been eruptions at La Soufrière on Guadeloupe, at Hodder's Volcano, a submarine mountain near St. Lucia, at a second Soufrière on St. Vincent—and at Mount Pelée. An American geologist who in 1902 hurried to the region to report on the eruption of Pelée put it thus: "Across the throat of the Caribbean extends a chain of islands, which are really smouldering furnaces, with fires banked up, ever ready to break forth at some unexpected and inopportune moment."

The moment for St. Pierre has been well established. The date was May 8, 1902, and the time was 7:52 a.m., the position in which the hands of a clock on the wall of the military hospital were later found frozen. But the volcano did not suddenly erupt without warning at that minute. It issued a long series of advance notices, each plainer and more ominous than the preceding one.

As early as February an odor of sulfurous gas was noticeable in St. Pierre. It was only a mild whiff and soon passed away. On April 2 puffs of steam were seen issuing from fumaroles—or vents—high on the mountain. On April 23 a slight fall of ash descended on the city and several earth tremors were felt, of no great consequence but strong enough to knock dishes from shelves. On April 25, the crater of L'Étang Sec near the summit opened and Pelée hurled up a huge cloud of ash charged with rock fragments. A similar eruption occurred the following day, covering much of the landscape with gray-white powder.

Nevertheless, the public authorities saw no reason for concern. Indeed, a few of the hardier citizens decided to climb the mountain to see what might be taking place up there. They found that the crater of L'Étang Sec, long dry, now contained a 650-foot-wide, steaming-hot lake. Beside it stood a newly formed volcanic cone, about 30 feet high, from which boiling water cascaded into the lake, while from deep underground came a bubbling, muttering sound.

In the last days of April the volcano continued to spew out clouds of ash, and the fumes grew stronger. Mrs. Thomas Prentiss, wife of the American consul in St. Pierre, wrote to her sister in Massachusetts: "We can see Mount Pelée from the rear windows of our house, and although it is nearly four miles away we can hear the roar. The city is covered with ashes. The smell of sulphur is so strong that horses on the streets stop and snort. Many of the people are obliged to wear wet handkerchiefs over their faces to protect them from strong fumes of sulphur. My husband assures me that there is no immediate danger."

The St. Pierre daily newspaper, *Les Colonies,* gave only small space to the volcano. An election was scheduled for May 11 and it appears that the conservative editor was anxious that the conservative voters of St. Pierre remain in the city to cast their ballots. Whatever the case, on May 2 *Les Colonies* published a reassuring story about a picnic to be held on the mountain: "We remind our readers that the grand excursion organized by the Gymnastic & Shooting Club will take place next Sunday, May 4. If the weather is fine, the excursionists will pass a day they will long keep in pleasant remembrance."

By May 2 the gray-white powder had reached a depth of several inches in rural areas close to the volcano. Some country roads were blocked by ash-laden branches snapping off the trees, and birds were dying. Shortly before midnight on that day, Mount Pelée erupted with a series of frightening detonations that awakened everyone in the city. Rushing into the streets, the Pierrotins saw above the volcano a vast black cloud, darker than the night, filled with bright zigzags of lightning. Mrs. Prentiss, writing again from the consulate, felt "as if we were standing on the brink of Hell. Every few moments electric flames of blinding intensity were traversing the recesses of black and purple clouds and casting a lurid pallor over the darkness that shrouded the world."

On the following day *Les Colonies* began to take more notice of what was going on. "The rain of ashes never ceases," complained the paper. "At about half-past nine the sun shone forth timidly. The passing of carriages is no longer heard in the streets. The wheels are muffled. Puffs of wind sweep the ashes from the roofs and awnings, and blow them into rooms whose windows have been imprudently left open." In the same issue *Les Colonies* announced that "the excursion which had been organized for tomorrow will not take place, the crater being absolutely inaccessible."

While the volcano continued its roaring and trembling, cascades of rain fell on its upper slopes, filling to bursting the banks of the numerous rivers that originated there. Boulders and large trees were swept down the mountainside and out to sea in the torrents, along with the carcasses of asphyxiated cattle and innumerable dead birds, which drifted in clumps on the water.

By now, St. Pierre's cathedral was crowded day and night with men and women who waited for hours to make their confessions. Even *Les Colonies* conceded that "St. Pierre is in a state of agitation. The city is depressed." But there was no mass exodus. As many as 2,000 people did depart eventually, many of them taking refuge in Fort-de-France, Martinique's capital, 12 miles to the southeast. However, an equal number of peasants from the countryside fled into the city, so that the population remained at about 30,000.

One woman set down her feelings in a letter, dated May 4, to relatives in France. "I am awaiting the event tranquilly. My only suffering is from the dust, which penetrates everywhere, even through closed doors and windows. We are all calm. If death awaits us there will be a numerous company to leave the world. Will it be by fire or asphyxia? It will be what God wills."

If many of the humans near the volcano were calm, other creatures were not. According to *Les Colonies,* "In the meadows the animals are restless, bleating, neighing and bellowing despairingly." And at the Usine Guérin, a large sugar mill at the mouth of the Blanche River just north of the city, there occurred a nightmarish invasion by ants and centipedes. Driven from the slopes of Mount Pelée by ashfalls and earth tremors, countless thousands of them swarmed into the mill because it lay in the path of their retreat: *fourmis-fous,* small, yellowish,

A turgid sea of debris-clogged mud chokes the coastal village of Basse-Pointe, victim of a calamitous side effect of Mount Pelée's volcanic fury. Five hours before the eruption that destroyed nearby St. Pierre, a flood of superheated water raged down the mountain, transforming the Basse-Pointe River into a torrential mudflow that swept away everything in its path—trees, boulders and homes.

speckled ants, and *bêtes-à-mille-pattes,* foot long black centipedes. Both species are venomous enough, in large numbers, to kill an adult.

In the yard of the mill, terrified horses screamed as the ants and centipedes climbed up their legs and bit them, while workmen attempted to dislodge the creatures by dousing the horses with buckets of water. Other workmen over-turned barrels of lubricating oil to make a sticky barrier against the invasion. Inside the mill men flailed at the centipedes with stalks of sugar cane, splatter-ing the walls and floor with insect blood, or crushed them beneath burlap sacks. In the nearby villa of the millowner, housemaids killed them with flat-irons and boiling water.

Although a good many millworkers were badly bitten, none died. In one district of St. Pierre, however, there was an invasion of a deadlier sort: Scores of snakes suddenly appeared in the streets. Among the reptiles were fer-de-lances, pit vipers with yellow-brown backs and pink bellies, six feet or more in length, whose bite can be fatal within minutes. As the snakes swarmed through the quarter they killed chickens and pigs, horses and dogs, and attacked men and women who did not speedily get out of their way. Many children were killed and the uproar was so great that the mayor of St. Pierre called out soldiers to deal with the snakes. Rifle fire crackled through the streets for more than an hour, during which at least 100 fer-de-lances were dispatched, but by that time some 50 humans and more than 200 animals had died from their bites.

The date was May 5, three days before the climactic eruption. In the crater of

A rivulet of hot mud meanders through the ravaged landscape of Soufrière volcano on the island of St. Vincent, weeks after it erupted on May 7, 1902. At the time, the people of St. Pierre assumed that Soufrière shared a subterranean reservoir with Mount Pelée on neighboring Martinique. But today scientists believe that, though the same upwelling of magma deep within the earth could have triggered both volcanoes, each had its own reservoir and the Soufrière blast did nothing to blunt Pelée's fury.

L'Étang Sec high on the mountain the steaming lake had grown larger, and at about midday it burst the dam of volcanic ash plugging the notch overlooking St. Pierre. An immense torrent of near-boiling water flooded into the gorge of the Blanche River and swept down toward the coast, four miles away and 3,000 feet below. Moving at terrible speed, it quickly broadened into a mud slide a quarter of a mile wide and 100 feet deep, a brown slurry laden with jungle debris, tree trunks and boulders that weighed as much as 50 tons. In its path was the sugar mill.

There is no record of the number of people who were in the mill. Many of the workmen had quit and gone home after their encounter with the ants and centipedes, but it appears that about 30 were still there. All of them died, buried beneath a mass of hot mud so deep that only the top of the mill's tall chimney remained to mark where they lay.

On the day of the mud slide the Governor of Martinique, Louis Mouttet, received a report from a committee he had commissioned to assess the danger from the volcano. The committeemen were all thoughtful citizens and one of them was a respected professor of natural science at the St. Pierre *lycée,* or high school. They reported that they felt "there is nothing in the activity of Pelée that warrants a departure from St. Pierre," and added: "The relative positions of the craters and valleys opening toward the sea justifies the conclusion that the safety of St. Pierre is completely assured." Thereupon Governor Mouttet and his wife, to emphasize that there was no cause for alarm, made preparations to leave their residence in Fort-de-France and move over to stay in St. Pierre. Troops were also to be stationed on the road from St. Pierre to Fort-de-France, with orders to turn back refugees who were trying to get out of the city.

On May 6, the eruptions seemed to be gathering force. Pelée's thunderous detonations could now be clearly heard on the island of Guadeloupe, 100 miles to the north. The mountain's summit was hidden by thick clouds of steam, and an incessant rain of ash sifted slowly down, covering everything with up to a foot of gray powder. In the nearby forests, leaves on the trees turned brown and fell to earth; on the sugar and coconut plantations, the fields of cane and groves of palms were withered and bowed by the blankets of hot ash. Monsignor Gabriel Parel, Martinique's Vicar General, went with another priest to look at the Blanche River, scene of the catastrophic mud flood the day before. "It was still a roaring torrent," reported Parel, "rolling rocks, tree trunks and smoking mud onward in its crashing course. With its streaming line of smoke, it resembled a locomotive rushing headlong into the sea."

At around 5 p.m., telegraphic communication was suddenly broken between Martinique and the islands of St. Lucia and St. Vincent to the south. Undersea avalanches had snapped the cables. Of the handful of cables leading into Martinique from the outside world, only one remained, connecting the island to Dominica in the north.

On May 7 Pelée awakened St. Pierre at 4 a.m. with a prodigious roaring. Glancing up, the Pierrotins saw two fiery craters glowing like blast furnaces near the summit, and above them a cloud filled with lightning. When daylight came it appeared that the whole Caribbean was strewn with clots of ash, pumice and vegetation swept into the sea by the flooding rivers. The dozen or so ships lying in the roadstead, most of them waiting to take on cargoes of sugar and rum, seemed almost to be moored on dry land.

The captains of the ships—with one exception—seem not to have been greatly alarmed by the menacing appearance of Pelée. The exception was Captain Marino Leboffe of the Italian bark *Orsolina,* whose home port was Naples. Leboffe knew a little about volcanoes, or at any rate about Mount Vesuvius, which he had often observed against the Neapolitan skyline. In midmorning, Leboffe announced that he was taking the *Orsolina* out of St. Pierre. It did not matter to him, he said, that he had loaded aboard only half his cargo of sugar. When the port authorities refused him permission to sail and threatened him with arrest, he ignored them. He was leaving. "I know nothing about Mount Pelée," he said, "but if Vesuvius were looking the way your volcano looks this morning, I'd get out of Naples." Leboffe took the *Orsolina* out, and his ship was far away over the horizon when Pelée exploded next day.

On the afternoon of May 7 word reached St. Pierre that Soufrière volcano on St. Vincent, 90 miles to the south, was in violent eruption. Although they did not know the number of casualties—2,000 people were killed—the Pierrotins were curiously cheered by the news. They supposed that there might be a submarine connection between Soufrière and Pelée, and that an eruption at Soufrière might somehow relieve the pressure beneath their own volcano.

The last issue of *Les Colonies,* dated May 7, devoted much space to Pelée although the largest headline on the first page still dealt with the election scheduled for May 11. There were several men who saw the matter clearly. One was the American consul, Thomas Prentiss, who wrote an extraordinary letter about the crisis. Instead of sending it through diplomatic channels, Prentiss took the remarkable step of addressing it directly to the President of the United States, Theodore Roosevelt. What outraged Prentiss were the soothing editorials in *Les Colonies* and the bland proclamations by city officials that all was well, that St. Pierre had nothing to fear from its increasingly restive volcano. He regarded it as the worst sort of political manipulation, designed to lull the populace into remaining for the elections at all costs. "To abandon the elections would be unthinkable," Prentiss wrote bitterly. "The situation is a nightmare where no one seems able or willing to face the truth."

At about 7:50 a.m. on May 8 Mount Pelée blew up. There were three or four violent explosions in quick succession and then two huge black clouds of volcanic material shot out of the mountain. One went straight up and expanded across the whole sky, blotting out light so completely that in Fort-de-France, people could not see companions only two or three feet away. The other cloud did not rise, but clung to the slopes of the volcano and bore down on St. Pierre, its path directed by the V-shaped notch near the summit.

This rolling, superheated volcanic cloud moved at about 100 miles an hour and within two minutes struck the city with shattering force. The thick walls of even the largest buildings were blown down and scattered into rubble. As it swept over the city the incandescent cloud set the wreckage of St. Pierre ablaze. Huge bonfires of shattered timbers roared up, and on the quays and in the warehouses thousands of barrels of rum exploded, the flaming liquid running through the streets and out into the water of the roadstead.

Of the 30,000 souls in St. Pierre on the morning of May 8, only two men survived. One of them was a young shoemaker named Léon Compère-Léandre, who seems to have owed his life to luck, to robust good health and to the fact that his house was near the edge of the path of the cloud. He recalled that he had been sitting on his doorstep when "I felt a terrible wind blowing, the earth began to tremble, and the sky suddenly became dark. I turned to go into the house, with great difficulty climbed the three or four steps that separated me from my room, and felt my arms and legs burning, also my body.

"I dropped upon a table. At this moment four others sought refuge in my room, crying and writhing with pain, although their garments showed no sign of having been touched by flame. At the end of 10 minutes one of these, the young Delavaud girl, aged about 10 years, fell dead; the others left. I got up and went into another room, where I found the father Delavaud, still clothed and lying on the bed, dead. He was purple and inflated, but the clothing was intact. Crazed and almost overcome, I threw myself on a bed, inert and awaiting death. My senses returned to me in perhaps an hour, when I beheld the roof burning. With sufficient strength left, my legs bleeding and covered with burns, I ran to Fonds-Saint-Denis, six kilometers from St. Pierre."

Léon Compère-Léandre lived in relative obscurity until 1936. The other survivor, Auguste Ciparis, became a minor celebrity. Ciparis, a convicted felon, had been serving his time in a dungeon in the St. Pierre prison. His cell had no window, merely a small grated aperture in the wall above the door. When he was interviewed by an American journalist not long after the catastrophe, Ciparis was in critical condition. His injuries had not yet been treated and, said the reporter, "he had been more frightfully burned, I think, than any man I had ever seen."

Ciparis said that on the morning of May 8 he had been waiting for his breakfast when his cell suddenly became dark, and almost immediately gusts of hot air mixed with ashes came through his door grating and seared him. The

A cloud of lethal gas and incandescent volcanic ash thunders down Mount Pelée on December 16, 1902, in an eruption similar to the one that had destroyed St. Pierre seven months before. The French volcanologist Alfred Lacroix captured this remarkable sequence of photographs over a five-minute period while the glowing cloud, or *nuée ardente,* as he called it, swelled to a height of 13,000 feet during its course down the mountain.

intense heat lasted only a few moments, during which he held his breath. His clothing did not catch fire but his back was severely burned beneath his shirt. There was a container of water in his cell and when he reached for it he was astonished to find it cool enough to drink.

Ciparis remained trapped underground for nearly four days before he was rescued by men who were exploring the ruins above him and heard his cries. He recovered, received a pardon and eventually joined the Barnum and Bailey Circus, with which he toured for several years as "The Prisoner of St. Pierre," telling his story and exhibiting his scars. He died in 1929.

There were other survivors, not in St. Pierre itself but on the ships in the roadstead. On the morning of May 8 the number of vessels had increased to 18, and when the burning cloud swept out across the water it capsized 16 of them and set them afire. Chief Officer Ellery Scott of the Quebec-line steamship *Roraima* wrote an account of his experience that may stand for all.

The *Roraima* had a crew of 47 and carried 21 passengers, several of them children. She was anchored 700 yards offshore when Scott saw the cloud engulf St. Pierre and rush toward the ship. "Then came darkness blacker than night. The *Roraima* rolled and careened far to port, then with a sudden jerk she went to starboard, plunging her lee rail far under water. The masts, smokestack, rigging, all were swept clean off and went by the board. The iron smokestack came off short, and the two steel masts broke off two feet above the deck. The ship took fire in several places simultaneously, and men, women and children were dead in a few seconds."

After the first blast came a rain of ash mixed with water. Scott, who had escaped injury by huddling under a tarpaulin cover, described this ashy shower as "of the consistency of very thin cement. Wherever it fell it formed a coating clinging like glue, so that it coated those who wore no caps, making a complete cement mask right over their heads. The assistant purser had his head so weighted down with the stuff that he seemed to feel giddy and was almost falling. When he asked me to break the casing off his head I was afraid it would scalp him when I took it off. I could feel the heat on my own head very plainly through my tarpaulin covering, and his scalp must have been badly scorched."

Scott searched for the *Roraima's* captain, who was so badly burned that he could not be recognized and had to tell Scott who he was. "Find out how the ship is and what is the condition of our people," said the captain. Scott followed the order, "finding the after end of the ship all on fire and people burned and dying everywhere, and flames breaking out in several places forward." But when he returned to make his report, the captain was gone. "He had either fallen or jumped overboard to relieve his own sufferings, which must have been very terrible."

Scott organized a bucket brigade to fight the fires—the ship's pumps would not work—and found only four crewmen still able-bodied. Several of the others, who had lost the flesh on their hands, tried to carry buckets in the crooks of their elbows. As the fires were brought under control, "gradually we collected the survivors and laid them on the deck forward, all of them crying for water, but many of the unfortunates could not drink at all." Their mouths and throats were badly burned. "When we put the water into their mouths it stayed there and almost choked them, and we had to turn them over to get the water out." Scott broke open the ship's icehouse door and gave them bits of ice to suck.

Several hours after the blast the French cruiser *Suchet,* sent from Fort-de-France, came alongside the *Roraima* and took off the survivors, some of whom died later in hospitals. Only about 20 of the ship's 68 passengers and crew lived through the holocaust, and on the other vessels in the roadstead the proportion of casualties was even higher.

In the aftermath, other witnesses to the calamity came forward with tales of horror—and of fantastic good fortune. On the fatal morning, Fernand Clerc, one of the island's most prominent planters, was in his St. Pierre home with his wife and four children and a number of friends. He had risen early, and by seven was ready to breakfast when he happened to notice the barometer acting crazily. The pointer of the instrument was describing a series of wild swings "with a tendency toward fluttering," Clerc recalled. A premonition seized him, and he ordered his carriages immediately made ready. But only his family fled with him. "My friends thought I was over-timid and refused to leave." As the Clerc family passed down the street, they saw Thomas Prentiss, the American consul, and his wife standing on the consulate balcony. "They waved to me and I returned the salute, calling to them at the same time that they had better accompany me," remembered Clerc. But Prentiss declined and Clerc drove on.

The carriages climbed into the hills, and within 45 minutes Clerc and his family had arrived at one of his country houses three miles above the city. At that point, Pelée erupted before their eyes. "The cloud that had for so many days surmounted Pelée seemed to topple over with a loud noise and tumble into the city," said Clerc. "Behind the smoke came a sheet of flame." The Clerc family watched in fascinated horror as the cloud rolled down the mountain like "a great torrent of black fog, accompanied by a continuous roar of half-blended staccato beats of varying intensity, something like the throbbing, pulsating roar of a Gatling-gun battery going into action."

It then began to grow dark as the clouds from the volcano blotted out the sun and commenced raining hot ash on Clerc's hillside estate. Within 10 minutes the only light was a faint glow from the burning city below. The Stygian gloom was so thick that Clerc could no longer see his family, just a few feet away, and he had to grope for them in the dark. At last, after 20 minutes in this hot, suffocating blackness, a powerful wind began to blow the ashes away. Down in the valley, Clerc could see that his sister's plantation had been blown completely flat. He descended on foot and worked his way into the devastated city. "Tongue or pen can never describe what I saw," he said. "About me everywhere were my relatives and friends burning. I saw I could do no good—all were dead—not one alive. I hastened back and at the first opportunity sent my family to Guadeloupe."

One of the most astonishing escapes from Pelée was that of a young girl, Harviva Da Ifrile, who apparently looked straight into the mouth of a volcanic vent as it yawned open and spewed forth flames just before the main eruption. Even allowing for exaggeration born of terror, it is an incredible story.

Little Harviva—her exact age is unknown—was on her way to services at the cathedral in St. Pierre when her mother sent her on an errand to her aunt, who had a pastry shop halfway up the mountain. The shop was near an ancient crater known as the "Corkscrew," for the tourist trail that wound down to its floor; Harviva's aunt catered to the visitors after their journey into the depths of the mountain. But on this day, when Harviva approached the Corkscrew she felt a hot wind and saw tendrils of smoke coming from the pit. She

Blazing ships, ignited by the cloud of fiery ash from Mount Pelée, founder off St. Pierre in this *Harper's Weekly* illustration published shortly after the tragedy. Of the hundreds of passengers and crew members on board 18 vessels, only a few survived to provide eyewitness accounts of the eruption.

The thriving commerce and civic clutter that marked St. Pierre as one of the principal ports of the Lesser Antilles are evident in the photograph at right, taken in the 1880s. But in 1902, the scene was one of utter devastation *(below)* after Mount Pelée, in the background, hurled a *nuée ardente* down on the city through the notch near its summit.

Tangled girders, pipes and barrel hoops mark the site of a rum distillery, blown to bits by exploding casks of rum. Red-hot particles of ash in the *nuée ardente* ignited the liquor, which ran through the streets, completing the job of incineration.

ran to the top of the path and looked down. "There I saw the bottom of the pit all red, like boiling, with little blue flames coming from it." She watched two guides hurrying a woman up the path as fast as they could run. "Then I saw a puff of blue smoke seem to hit the party and they fell as if killed."

Harviva stared at the "boiling stuff" as it rose in the pit and covered the three bodies on the path. Then she fled screaming down the road to St. Pierre. "Just as I got to the main street I saw this boiling stuff burst from the top of the Corkscrew and run down the side of the hill. It followed the road first, but then as the stream got bigger, it ate up the houses on both sides of the road. Then I saw that a boiling red river was coming from another part of the hill and cutting off the escape of the people who were running from the houses."

Harviva ran to the shore and jumped into her brother's boat, rigged with sail and moored next to a stone wharf. As she did, she saw him some distance up the hill racing toward her. "But he was too late, and I heard him scream as the stream first touched then swallowed him." Somehow, Harviva got the boat out into the water and away from the rolling cloud of superheated ashes and gases. She headed for a grotto along the shore where she and her chums liked to play pirate. "But before I got there I looked back—and the whole side of the mountain which was near the town seemed to open and boil down on the screaming people. I was burned a good deal by the stones and ashes that came flying about the boat, but I got to the cave."

From the safety of her cave, Harviva heard an "awful hiss as the boiling stuff struck the sea, and the cave filled up almost to the top with water." Then, mercifully, she lapsed into unconsciousness and remembered nothing more until the French cruiser *Suchet* plucked her from the ocean drifting two miles at sea in her broken and charred craft.

News of the disaster in Martinique was telegraphed around the world and relief was quick in coming, at least by the standards of the time. President Roosevelt, acting with his customary vigor, immediately gave $200,000 on behalf of the American people—seemingly a small sum, but large compared with the donations of the Kings of England and Italy, who contributed $5,000 each. Roosevelt ordered a fast warship, the cruiser U.S.S. *Dixie,* to be stocked with 1,250 tons of food, medicine and other supplies and sent to Martinique forthwith.

A dramatic circus poster touts the amazing story of Auguste Ciparis (also known as Ludger Sylbaris), one of two survivors in St. Pierre proper. The 25-year old criminal—later pardoned—owed his life, and his subsequent career as a sideshow attraction, to his incarceration in St. Pierre's jail, where he occupied a thick-walled cell (*top*) facing away from the blast.

Roosevelt also made provision for several scientists, who were assigned hammocks in the *Dixie's* cramped quarters, to hurry south to study what had happened in St. Pierre. Among them were Edmund Hovey of the American Museum of Natural History and Thomas Jaggar Jr. of Harvard University, a brilliant geologist who would henceforth devote his life to volcanology. These men were joined in Martinique by Angelo Heilprin, of the Philadelphia Geographical Society, and by other scientists from Europe, including Tempest Anderson and John S. Flett of the Royal Society of London, and most importantly, as it turned out, Alfred Lacroix, from the French Academy of Sciences. As a journalist on the *Dixie* observed, "There can be little doubt that the catastrophe which overwhelmed St. Pierre will be more thoroughly investigated than any other volcanic outburst recorded in history."

That in fact turned out to be the case. In 1902 the study of volcanoes was not a science in itself but only a minor branch of geology. Few scientists would have called themselves volcanologists. Knowledge of the subject was limited, instruments inadequate and the prediction of eruptions largely a matter of guesswork, not a great deal more sophisticated than the thinking of Captain Leboffe when he took the *Orsolina* out of the roadstead of St. Pierre. The incandescent cloud that destroyed the city was so unfamiliar to scientists that they had not even a name for it, much less an understanding of what it was. But the eruption of Pelée, at great human cost, changed matters. It gave such a stimulus to the young science of volcanology that 1902 may be said to be one of the landmark dates in the history of man's effort to grasp the workings of his planet.

The first of the scientists to arrive were the Americans, Jaggar, Hovey and their colleagues on board the cruiser *Dixie;* accompanying them among the journalists was author and lecturer George Kennan, who would write an account of great importance to the investigation of Mount Pelée. The *Dixie* had sailed from New York on May 14, just six days after the catastrophe, and docked in Martinique at daybreak on the 21st.

Had she arrived 48 hours earlier, the study of Mount Pelée would have been advanced enormously. For at 5 p.m. on May 20, Pelée burst forth in a second, stupendous explosion, the awesome, rolling black clouds surpassing even those of May 8. No lives were lost in St. Pierre; there was no one left to die. But the blast flattened most of what remained of the ruined city and buried the wreckage still deeper in ash.

Harvard's Jaggar was astonished by the completeness of the destruction: "Mountain slope and cliff are bare, the verdure of the hillside ends abruptly along a sharp line, and there begins the new volcanic landscape, clean-chiselled, rocky, weird, gray, uniform, without any color, without any motion except steamjets on Pelée's slopes." The area of total devastation comprised roughly eight square miles and was triangular in shape. The tip of the triangle was an immense crater on the mountain slope, below which was a V-shaped fissure, framed by high ridges on either side that fanned down to the sea. This was the notch through which the boiling mud of L'Étang Sec had come thundering down on May 5.

Beyond the triangle of absolute destruction was a second zone of damage spreading over 24 square miles. In this zone, the effects of the rolling black cloud gradually diminished until they ceased altogether, in places as abruptly as if a knife had been drawn across the landscape. The scientists were continually amazed by the sharpness of the line between ravaged and apparently unharmed areas. "In many places the line of demarcation passed through single trees," observed Hovey, "leaving one side scorched and brown, while the other side remained as green as if no eruption had occurred." Hovey ventured the explanation that the overall topography of the area, with its ravines flanked by a series of tall, razor-backed ridges, had contained the descending volcanic cloud—in much the same way a gorge funnels the racing waters of a torrent. In this he was only partially correct.

Moving into St. Pierre itself, the scientists were dumfounded by the force of the black cloud. Not only were buildings leveled, but massive objects had been tossed about as though made of cardboard. At a coast-defense fort several heavy 6-inch cannon were blown entirely off their mounts, and near the cathedral a three-ton statue of the Virgin Mary was hurled 40 feet from its pedestal. Geologist Angelo Heilprin saw "twisted bars of iron, great masses of roof sheeting wrapped like cloth around posts against which they had been flung, and girders looped and festooned as if they had been made of rope."

Various witnesses notwithstanding, there apparently had been no lava flow from the volcano at any time during the eruption. At least if there had been, the scientists found no evidence of it. The death and destruction appeared to be entirely the work of the volcanic cloud, formed of superheated steam and other gases made heavy by billions of particles of incandescent ash and traveling with enough force to carry along boulders and blocks of volcanic material. At the rum distillery, the burned-out tanks, massive containers of quarter-inch boiler plate riveted together, looked to Hovey "as if they had been through a bombardment by artillery, being full of holes which vary in size from mere cracks at the bottom of indentations to great rents, 24, 30 and even 36 inches across."

Sifting through the wreckage and examining the evidence, the scientists concluded that the temperature of the incandescent cloud had been between 1,300° and 1,800° F., enough to soften glass (1,292° F.) but not enough to melt copper (1,981° F.) because copper telephone wires were found intact and not fused together. As it swept through St. Pierre, the cloud had annihilated the people by both blast and heat, doing its work in a few moments. Many of the corpses were torn apart and others dreadfully burned—a reporter who ventured into the still-smoldering city found "an open and comparatively smooth stretch of ground strewn with hundreds of dead bodies. Not a shred of clothing was upon any of them, not a single hair."

But the cloud's effects were erratic. In some locations, as the survivors Compère-Léandre and Ciparis had witnessed, people were left with their clothing strangely intact. The phenomenon suggested to the scientists that in the turbulence of the cloud, there were areas that were momentarily free of incandescent ashes and volcanic particles; the victims had escaped incineration, only to die of the fantastic heat that pervaded everything. This was particularly true of people huddled in buildings, or crouched behind protective walls in the path of the cloud. What the fiery ash could not reach, the heat did.

In some of the houses along the path of this freakish cloud were found families who seemed to have died instantly at their breakfast tables, on which plates, cutlery and glasses were undamaged. In a jewelry shop the heat had been so intense as to fuse hundreds of watch crystals into a lump, but in a kitchen not far away were found still-drinkable, corked bottles of water, and packets of starch in which the granules were untouched.

To the effects of blast and heat, the scientists added another deadly element: asphyxiation. At one point in the studies, Hovey actually entered part of Pelée's L'Étang Sec crater and reported that "the sulphur gases made the atmosphere difficult to breathe, but the most uncomfortable sensation was due to the irritation caused by the fine angular dust getting into the respiratory passages and the eyes. Such a mixture raised to a high temperature and containing a large amount of dust and a considerable percentage of sulphur gases would be almost instantaneously fatal to life."

The prosperity of St. Pierre is reflected in the imposing altar and crystal chandeliers of Mouillage Cathedral *(right)*. But only a shell of the massive stone edifice *(far right)* survived the May 8 eruption; inside, the bodies of worshippers gathered for morning Mass lay beneath tons of rubble and ash.

But what had caused this boiling, poisonous cloud? And why, instead of rising skyward, had it roared down the mountain to engulf St. Pierre? Every investigator had his own theory. Heilprin likened the blast to that of a "giant mortar." He believed that part of the crater floor had blown out and exploded in "free air under a heavily depressing cushion of ascending steam and ash." This overburden of steam and ash, reasoned Heilprin, had forced the blast in a lateral direction, to be channeled down on St. Pierre by the surrounding walls of rock on three sides.

For his part, Jaggar argued that the cloud initially had risen skyward to a very great height and then, "following the law of gravitation, descended with great velocity to the crater, where it encountered matter in ascension, and was deflected in a horizontal direction." This action, continued Jaggar, "was like a blowpipe effect and shot the death-dealing billows of falling hot sand and gravel down the mountain slopes in the direction of St. Pierre."

Both explanations contained an element of truth, but both were off the mark, as the investigators would presently discover. At dusk on July 9, the British researchers Tempest Anderson and John Flett, by a great stroke of luck, became the first scientists to have front-row seats at an eruption apparently virtually identical to the cataclysms of May 8 and 20.

Anderson and Flett were offshore, cruising past St. Pierre in a sailboat (geologist Jaggar was also in Martinique, but he was in Fort-de-France, 12 miles away), when in the gathering darkness they saw a dull red glow suffuse the summit of Pelée. The glow became brighter and brighter until the whole scene was brightly illuminated, and the sailors cried in terror: "The mountain bursts!" The men watched in awe as an immense red-hot "avalanche," as they termed it, swept down the flanks of Pelée and across the ruins of St. Pierre to the sea. "It was dull red with a billowy surface," reported the Britishers. "In it there were larger stones which stood out as streaks of bright red tumbling down and emitting showers of sparks."

Anderson and Flett failed to time the avalanche of volcanic material, but they estimated the duration of its passage down the mountain as no more than a minute. "Undoubtedly the velocity was terrific," they said. "Had any buildings stood in its path they would have been utterly wiped out, and no living creature could have survived that blast."

Now came a second act in the drama. Hardly had the crimson glow of the avalanche faded than a cloud shaped itself against the starlit sky precisely where the avalanche had been. This cloud seemed to result from the impact of the avalanche and to retain some of its momentum; it was as if lighter particles of volcanic material had begun to rise slightly and continue forward as the heavier particles settled to earth. "The cloud was globular, with a bulging surface covered with rounded protuberant masses which swelled and multiplied with terrible energy," reported Anderson and Flett. "It rushed forward over the waters, directly toward us, boiling and changing its form every instant. It did not spread out laterally; neither did it rise into the air but swept on over the sea in surging masses, coruscating with lightning."

When the cloud was about a mile from the scientists, they could see to their vast relief that its advance was slowing. It became paler in color as the ash started to settle into the sea. A short distance before it reached the vessel, the cloud rose from the sea and passed directly over the heads of the men. Stones, some as large as chestnuts, rained down on the boat; then came a shower of smaller, pea-shaped pellets, and finally a downpour of dry, gray ashes. The air smelled faintly of sulfuric acid. As it passed out to sea, the cloud broadened and expanded until it covered the entire sky except for a thin sliver of horizon.

Anderson and Flett had no doubt whatsoever that they had witnessed a counterpart to the blasts of May 8 and 20. And it convinced them that previous explanations were in error. Nothing they saw supported Heilprin's theory of an

How Pelée Helped Win the Canal for Panama

When Mount Pelée exploded in 1902, the American public was preoccupied with an issue of great national importance: a Central American canal connecting the Atlantic and Pacific Oceans. Such a passage was deemed vital to the emerging U.S. Navy and merchant marine because it would obviate the need to voyage 8,000 miles around Cape Horn. In addition, the canal was a high-stakes engineering challenge that symbolized U.S. aspirations as a world power.

The question was: Where to construct the canal? In the 1880s the French, fresh from their engineering triumph in digging the Suez Canal, had tried to cut a waterway through the Colombian territory of Panama—and had failed. After a decade of work that cost 1.4 billion francs (about $287 million) and claimed the lives of 20,000 men, the project was abandoned.

Mindful of the French debacle, governmental commissions and prominent politicians in America recommended a route through neighboring Nicaragua. But a few beleaguered Panama lobbyists fought on. American railroad magnates stood to profit because they already controlled the Panama Railway, while shareholders in the ruined French canal company could recoup by selling its Panamanian assets.

Then came the May eruptions of La Soufrière and Mount Pelée, which suddenly riv-

eruption directed downward by the weight of air above, or Jaggar's idea of a deflected descending column of volcanic ejecta. Rather, what they observed led them to theorize that "the lava which rises in the chimney is charged with steam and gases, which explode as usual. But some of the explosions happen to have just enough force to blow the mass to atoms and lift the greater part of it over the lip of the crater without distributing the whole widely in the air. The mixture of solid particles and gas behaves like a heavy liquid, and before these particles have time to subside, the whole rolls down the mountain under the influence of gravity and consequently gathers speed and momentum as it goes. The heavy solid particles are gradually deposited and the remaining steam and gases, thus relieved of their burden, are free to ascend—as was the case with the black cloud which rose over our heads on July 9th."

Anderson and Flett believed that the sole motive power for the cloud was gravity. "The black cloud did not start to rush down the slopes at once," they said, "but rolled and tumbled, squirted and seethed for quite a perceptible time. Then it began to move with greater and greater speed down the hillside. Faster and faster it came until it struck the sea, when its velocity began to diminish. It was like a toboggan on a snow slide. It was not the blast of a gun: It was the rush of an avalanche. Gravity did the work and supplied the energy."

Later analysis substantiated their belief in the role of gravity in giving the incandescent avalanche most of its direction, speed and momentum. But gravity alone could not fully explain the events on Mount Pelée, and it was left to the Frenchman, Alfred Lacroix, to carry the scientific detective work on Mount Pelée a long step further.

Lacroix and his confreres from the Academy of Sciences had arrived in Martinique on June 23, had completed their investigations by August 1 and had sailed for home. But then on August 30, Pelée had erupted in full force yet again, and this time the volcano claimed another 2,000 victims. As before, the terrible black cloud shot down the mountain and through the ruins of St. Pierre. But now there was a second cloud that found its way to the hillside village of Morne Rouge, four miles northeast of the city. Morne Rouge had been spared by intervening ridges in all the earlier eruptions, and its citizens had seen no reason to flee. Most of them paid with their lives.

At the news, Lacroix hurried back to Martinique and remained there studying Pelée until mid-March of 1903. His final report became a classic in the annals of volcanology.

To begin with, Lacroix gave the black cloud a name appropriate to its incandescent appearance: *nuée ardente,* or "glowing cloud." (Volcanologists now prefer "glowing avalanche" as a slightly more accurate description.) During his investigations, Lacroix came across something that his British and American colleagues had overlooked—or possibly ignored. He observed that the volcanic ejecta from the eruptions—fragments of all sizes from the finest dust to blocks as large as cottages—had not always followed a path downward along the steepest slopes of the mountain. Much of the material had swept down along relatively gentle slopes of only 10 or 12 degrees. Lacroix reasoned that gravity alone could never have imparted the fantastic force that these projectiles attained. Such a trajectory, he concluded, could have resulted only from a fierce lateral blast that had literally shot the material from the mouth of the volcano straight down the slopes of Mount Pelée. In this, his theory was diametrically opposed to that of Anderson and Flett. But in the end, Lacroix was proved right—and with the unknowing assistance of the American geologists and the journalist George Kennan.

During his investigation, Lacroix learned that on May 21, Hovey and several others had observed through Pelée's V-shaped fissure what they believed to be a growing cone of volcanic debris inside the crater. They estimated its height at perhaps 200 to 500 feet, and by May 31 they thought it had grown to 1,440

The parting shot of the great canal debate in the U.S. Congress was this tiny one-centavo Nicaraguan stamp, which attested to the presence of active volcanoes in that country.

eted attention on Nicaragua's own volcanic nature. Advocates of Panama had previously railed about Nicaragua's 12 volcanoes without success; only one volcano was anywhere near the proposed canal, and it was quiescent. Now the lobbyists redoubled their campaign, hammering away at the "terrible object lesson" of Pelée. More heaven-sent evidence of the "volcanic menace" followed in late May, when news reached Washington that a Nicaraguan volcano was erupting.

Three days before the U.S. Senate was scheduled to vote on the route, Philippe Bunau-Varilla, formerly chief engineer of the French canal company and now a prominent lobbyist for Panama, prepared an elegant clincher. He previously had observed, "Young nations like to put on their coats of arms what best characterizes their native soil. What have the Nicaraguans chosen? Volcanoes!" Now, after canvassing every stamp dealer in Washington, he mailed a Nicaraguan postage stamp featuring a smoking volcano to every Senator.

Swayed by this inspired bit of propaganda—and the glowering Caribbean volcanoes—the Senate approved the Panama Canal by eight votes.

feet. The next day, June 1, Angelo Heilprin, accompanied by George Kennan, had become the first geologist to reach the rim of L'Étang Sec and to peer down into the crater at this strange cone.

Reported Kennan: "I was tremendously startled to find myself suddenly on the very brink of a frightful chasm about 75 feet across and hundreds of feet in depth, out of which came a roar like that of a titanic forge with the bellows at work, and a curious crackling sound which suggested the splitting of rocks in intense heat. The wall of the chasm under my feet was absolutely perpendicular and by bending forward a little I could see down 150 or 200 feet. Beyond that point clear vision was lost in a sort of bright, vapory shimmer, like the shimmer at the top of a white-hot blast-furnace. On the other side of the immense fissure was a huge chaotic mass of volcanic debris, piled together in the wildest confusion, and out of it, into the throat of the chasm, projected three or four long, angular toothlike rocks, which had been so calcined as to be almost white. With a powerful glass I had seen these same white rocks from St. Pierre, and I knew, therefore, that if the ascending vapor-column south of us were removed we might look straight out through the chasm at the ruined city beyond it. My impression was that the chasm into which we looked was only one side of a more or less circular pit or bowl, and that the pile of rocks which seemed to form the western wall of the fissure was a central cone of volcanic debris."

By June 27, the cone had risen above the rim of the crater. On July 6, Jaggar reported seeing the cone, whose summit sported a large monolith shaped like a shark's dorsal fin. Anderson and Flett also saw this monolith on July 9, but because of cloud cover that periodically obscured the mountain mistook it for a crag on the crater lip. Analyzing all these reports and observing this strange cone and monolith himself, Lacroix, however, came to an entirely different conclusion than the others. This cone, he argued, was actually a volcanic dome that had built up inside the crater and was plugging the vent like a cork in a bottle. When the pressure inside the dome from the steam-and-gas-charged furnaces below reached a critical point, something had to give. In this instance, said Lacroix, the path of least resistance was through a weak spot in the dome, next to the fissure. It was through this weak spot and fissure that the lethal blasts had escaped, shooting out fanlike as they burst from their prison.

Later geologists positively substantiated Lacroix's findings—at least as they explained the lateral eruptions subsequent to May 8. In fact, analysis of huge volcanic boulders found in St. Pierre showed that most were actual fragments from the cone or dome that had become highly porous in transit as gas was released, thus accounting for their traveling such long distances. But there is still an aura of mystery surrounding Mount Pelée and the initial May 8 eruption. While most volcanologists agree that the lateral blast issued from a dome that was growing in the throat of the volcano, there are no scientific witnesses and no absolute proof. Some scientists suggest that the May 8 blast could have issued laterally from a simple fissure in the side of the volcano—and that the series of domes began to grow thereafter in response to complex geological factors arising from the initial eruption. In any case, thanks to Alfred Lacroix, it was now known that a volcanic plug, or dome, could cap a seething chamber of molten lava, or magma, until the fantastic pressures within blew out the side in an awesome lateral blast of gases and volcanic material. And this phenomenon was known thereafter as a Peléan eruption.

All through the fall of 1902 and for close to a year afterward, there were numerous small eruptions but no further deaths, as Pelée slowly sank back into slumber. However, before it did so, the volcano gave one last demonstration of its incredible power.

The dome's famous dorsal fin, or spine, as it became known in volcanology, was destroyed in the July 9 blast observed by Anderson and Flett. But in mid-

Alfred Lacroix

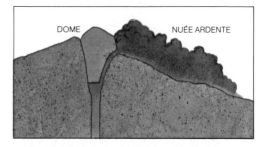

Volcanologist Alfred Lacroix spent a year studying Mount Pelée after the 1902 eruption, then published a landmark treatise on the dynamics of the volcano. He determined that the puzzling mountain-hugging movement of a *nuée ardente* can be caused by a lateral blast of volcanic material. When a dome of solidified lava plugs the vent of a volcanic crater, as shown above, pressure builds up beneath the obstruction until something gives way—in the case of Mount Pelée, a carapace at the dome's side.

An obelisk of hardened lava rises above Mount Pelée in a phenomenon as startling to the scientific world as the deadly *nuées ardentes* that preceded it.

October, Lacroix and others noticed another gigantic shaft of solidified lava rising from the dome in the crater of L'Étang Sec, forced straight up by the pressures deep within the mountain. The spine, soon called the Tower of Pelée, was 350 to 500 feet thick at its base and varicolored, ranging in hue from ruddy brown to purplish, gray and white. At night, the spine glowed with a tracery of red incandescent lines, and frequently a luminous spot could be seen at its tip. As it rose, great blocks of lava continually broke off from the top and went crashing down into the crater. But it rose at such an astonishing rate, often as much as 50 feet a day, that it continued to grow taller. By the end of November, the Tower of Pelée had reached a height of 800 feet, and after seven months it soared 1,020 feet above the crater's mouth. At its maximum height it was twice as tall as the Washington Monument and of an immensity equal in volume to the Great Pyramid of Egypt. No geologist had ever witnessed the emergence of such an object from the earth and few, had it not occurred before their own eyes, would have been prepared to believe it.

The Tower of Pelée was too unstable to endure and by September 1903 it had collapsed into a mass of rubble. But while it stood, a great obelisk, it seemed to represent, in the words of Angelo Heilprin, "nature's monument dedicated to the 30,000 dead who lay in the silent city below." **Ω**

Volcanoes have left their singular imprints everywhere on the face of the earth. Sometimes their handiwork is easily identified; while the memory of a fiery eruption is fresh, there can be no mistaking the cause of the altered shape of the land. Even with the passage of time, obvious features such as craters and cones are easily associated with their sources. But the otherworldly shapes and colors of many volcanic landforms, their origins hidden deep below the surface or lost in antiquity, have inspired explanations couched in myths and legends and in tales of heroic giants and warring gods.

Only with the advent of the science of volcanology has it been understood that volcanic forces have shaped not only a few isolated geologic oddities, but much of the surface of the planet. Successive lava flows during millions of years have built up huge basalt plateaus on every continent. Nearly 200,000 cubic miles of basalt underlie the Paraná basin, which sprawls across southern Brazil, northern Argentina, Paraguay and Uruguay. Although massive, such volcanic remnants are not obvious to the casual observer, and many smaller landforms are much more spectacular because of unique interactions between volcanic materials and their surroundings.

The many varieties of volcanic rock formations have been determined by their composition, the way they were first deposited and the rate at which they cooled. In some places rivers and pools of lava slowly hardened in place; in others, ashes and cinders were welded by their own heat and weight into solid heaps or plains; elsewhere, magma forced its way into the joints and cracks of subsurface rocks and solidified there.

Then began the long wearing away, as wind, ice and water eroded the surrounding rock and the softest parts of the volcanic deposits, leaving mysterious forms. Sometimes rain and groundwater provided the crowning touch, by collecting amid the volcanic debris in pools that provided a cool, sometimes brightly colored contrast to the heat and violence that attended the creation of their surroundings.

Volcanic needles spike into the desert skyline at Assekrem, Algeria, rising 1,000 feet above the surrounding Ahaggar Mountains. The area is dotted with about 100 such extrusions, which were formed six million years ago when extremely viscous lava, forced upward through surface fissures, hardened before it could flow away.

A 10th Century chapel perches atop a volcanic
neck 250 feet above Le Puy, in the Auvergne region of
France. The column was formed when debris from
volcanic explosions hardened in the vent of a volcano
two million years ago, and was later exposed when
the softer rock of the surrounding cone eroded away.

A monumental remnant of an ancient eruption,
Ship Rock towers 1,400 feet above the sediments of a
New Mexico desert. The same molten material
that formed the promontory hardened without
erupting in a fissure that was then far below the
earth's surface, to be exposed eons later by erosion
as the long thin wall, or dike, at left.

Spectacular basalt columns 50 million years old
ring the island of Staffa off the west coast of Scotland.
The surfaces of a slowly cooling and contracting
lava flow cracked like drying mud into patterns of
rings. As the lava hardened, the cracks deepened,
transforming the mass into closely packed columns.

An outcropping of basalt columns called the Giant's Causeway stretches 600 feet seaward from the coast of County Antrim, Northern Ireland. Local legend describes it as the start of a bridge on which giants could cross the North Channel to Scotland without wetting their feet. The columns, formed in the period of volcanic activity that shaped the cliffs of Staffa, are mostly six-sided, up to 20 feet in height, and average 18 inches in diameter.

Named by early prospectors and explorers in awe of its seemingly supernatural regularity, the Devils Postpile rises at the base of the jagged peaks of California's Sierra Nevada. Glaciers scoured the top of the 900,000-year-old volcanic formation and quarried away one of its sides to reveal the 60-foot columns. Subsequent erosion contributed to the litter of rock fragments below the cliff.

The cinder cone of Sunset Crater, daubed with a palette of colors, rises 1,000 feet above the Arizona desert. Lava fragments thrown into the air during an eruption in 1065 fell back to heap up around the volcano's central vent, leaving a crater a quarter mile in diameter and 400 feet deep. Sulfur and iron in the cinders are among the substances that cause the yellows, oranges and reds that give the cone its name.

Chapter 2

ASSEMBLING PIECES OF THE PUZZLE

As Martinique's Mount Pelée so tragically demonstrated, a great volcanic eruption is the most awesomely spectacular of nature's destructive phenomena. In a matter of minutes, a fiery mountain's cataclysmic power can transform a tranquil landscape into a seething crucible of incandescent ash and bubbling lava. In a single day, the explosive forces within can burst forth to tear the crown off a towering peak or devour a large island in the sea. And a volcano's smothering blankets of ash can blot out plant and animal life across hundreds—and in rare cases even thousands—of square miles. Indeed, in historic times a volcano on the Mediterranean island of Thera quite likely was responsible for the sudden demise of a mighty civilization, a culture perhaps as large and admirable as that of Classical Athens.

Yet volcanoes have a less sinister side. If their raging fires are the perfect embodiment of nature's chaotic unpredictability, they are also vital to the maintenance of a stable, life-giving environment on earth. Scientists suspect that the earth's atmosphere and its oceans were gradually boiled out of the planet's primordial mass over the course of billions of years. Volcanoes, the primary vents through the crust to the inner earth, are believed to be crucial to this continuing process. In fact, recent research has shown that the elements that make up the earth's atmospheric air and water are generally found in the same proportion in the vapor released by volcanoes.

Even the voluminous blankets of ash that smother the land surrounding an erupting volcano eventually play a beneficent role. Their glassy, sterile particles break down to release vital nutrients such as potassium and phosphorus, and soils of unparalleled fertility are born on landscapes of devastation. Below the soil, much of the earth's hard rock crust is formed from lava exuded from ancient volcanoes. Most astonishing of all are the silent volcanoes extending for tens of thousands of miles beneath the sea, which ceaselessly churn out millions of tons of new crust each day to form a vast, slowly moving patchwork of continents and sea floors.

There are more than 600 active volcanoes in the world today, most of them strung together in arcing necklaces of fire along the boundaries between moving sections of crust known as tectonic plates. The area around Indonesia, which lies on such a boundary, has more than 100 active volcanoes, and the coastal range at the juncture of the North American continent and the Pacific Plate is one of the most active volcanic areas of the world, with more than a dozen volcanoes that have erupted in historic time.

Yet many mountain ranges that were at one time explosively volcanic are now subdued in dormancy. The remnants of volcanoes in New England or in

On the verge of a discovery destined to change the course of geology, James Hutton and an assistant examine a vein of basalt tucked between layers of sandstone near Edinburgh, Scotland, in 1785. Hutton determined that such veins were of igneous, or volcanic, origin rather than the product of sea-floor sedimentation, as was then generally believed.

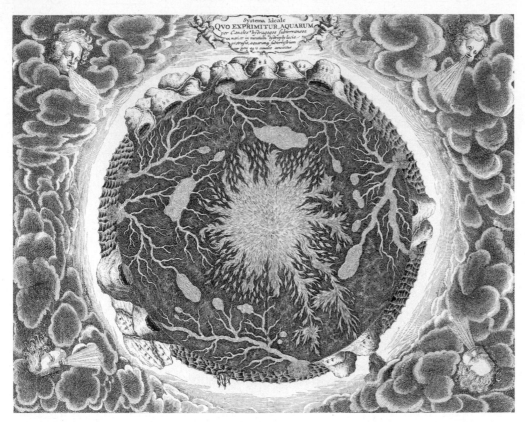

In a 17th Century engraving by Jesuit Athanasius Kircher, a fiery core feeds volcanoes and heats a rootlike network of ocean-fed waterways that provide thermal springs on the earth's surface. In his book *Mundus subterraneus (The Subterranean World)*, Kircher explained these as physical manifestations of large-scale natural forces but, like his contemporaries, he kept within the bounds of Biblical doctrine.

South Africa—where precious diamonds are frozen in the ancient lavas—indicate that these areas were once shaken and blasted by volcanic outbursts. For centuries, people have inhabited volcanic landscapes largely unaware that the verdant mountains were once fountains of fire, or that their crops flourished in fertile soil laid down by broad ashfalls from ancient eruptions. Although the philosophers and natural historians of Greece and Rome guessed that volcanic activity was responsible for many of the earth's surface features, this insight was lost during the long millennium that separated the Fall of Rome from the dawn of modern science.

When, toward the end of that dark period, an interest in the origins of the earth reemerged, it took the form of the almost universal belief that the shape and composition of the earth's surface were a consequence of the Great Deluge recounted in the Book of Genesis. Or if not that, then surely these features were the product of a primordial sea that according to the Bible engulfed the earth on the second day of Creation. These hypotheses had much to recommend them; not only did they account for such paradoxes as the fossil remains of fishes found in the Alps hundreds of miles from the sea, but they were in comfortable harmony with the teachings of the powerful churchmen of the day.

Sedimentary rocks—layered rocks formed from the hardened accumulation of loose sediment such as sand, silt and organic matter—fitted neatly into this picture. But volcanoes were a persistent puzzle that seemed to defy the Biblical account. One of the more imaginative efforts to reconcile the two was made by a Frenchman named Benoît de Maillet, who, reversing the letters of his last name for a title, wrote *Telliamed* in 1716. He argued that volcanoes were the result of the combustion of "oil and fat of animals and fishes concentrated in certain places" in the sediments laid down during the Flood. Eventually, Maillet dolefully predicted, the entire globe would be consumed in a great spattering ball of fire.

At about the same time, an Italian scholar, Antonio-Lazzaro Moro, wrote a treatise suggesting that all the land mass above the ocean's floor was flung from the mouths of a number of titanic volcanoes in the universal sea. Remarkably,

Moro was able to shepherd this daring theory past the scrutinizing eyes of religious scholars, but at a price. So many concessions to the Biblical story were made along the way that what remained was of dubious scientific value: To explain the origin of volcanic fires, for example, Moro could say only, "It pleased the Creator."

The doctrine of the primordial sea remained safely intact well into the 18th Century. To be sure, the Mediterranean volcanoes, notably Mount Etna, in Sicily, and Mount Vesuvius, looming over the Bay of Naples, continued to provide spectacular evidence of volcanism in action. But in the blinkered view of the leading theorists, volcanoes and the matter they ejected were freakish, local phenomena that had no important place in the overall scheme of things. Or so it seemed until 1751, when an inquisitive Frenchman on a springtime vacation jaunt to south-central France made the first of a staggering series of discoveries about the earth's fiery past.

Jean-Étienne Guettard was the grandson of a village apothecary in rural France. Long childhood rambles into the countryside in search of the plants and herbs necessary for the druggist's trade had earned him an intimate knowledge of natural history. He had been fascinated on his expeditions to observe that the distribution of plants coincided with the occurrence of certain minerals in the soil. Spurred by his love of learning, he trained as a medical doctor, but his consuming interests remained in the natural sciences and he soon joined the entourage of the Duke of Orléans as curator of the Duke's extensive natural history collection.

Before Guettard's time, great scientists had devoted themselves to concocting broad generalizations about nature. Because of the scarcity of authentic observations of how nature actually worked, few of these theories could be proved. Aristotle had taught that theory must stem from observed fact, but even his own scientific tenets—such as his assertion that volcanoes in the earth were analogous to the spasms of disease in the human body—teetered for centuries atop the flimsiest of supporting evidence. Guettard was among the first scientists to be satisfied with only those conclusions that could be supported by his observations. He had made numerous field trips throughout France identifying the rocks he found at the surface and eventually compiled one of the world's first geological maps.

But his most noteworthy contribution was made on his 1751 trip—which started out as more of a leisurely ramble than a scientific investigation. Accompanied by a friend, a lawyer named Chrétien-Guillaume de Lamoignon de Malesherbes, Guettard was journeying southward to soak in the salubrious hot-spring baths of Vichy. After that, the companions planned to visit the famous Puy de Dôme, one of a number of *puys,* or peaks, that rose from the gentle Auvergne countryside, some in gentle hillocks, others at precipitous angles resembling loaves of French bread on end.

As they passed through the town of Moulins, near Vichy, Malesherbes called Guettard's attention to a curious black stone that was used as a milepost along the road. Guettard, who had seen specimens of rock from Mounts Vesuvius and Etna, immediately recognized this stone as a chunk of volcanic lava. Traveling on, the two friends came upon building after building constructed from the same material. It was not possible that so much rock could have been transported to France from Vesuvius—the nearest known volcano. All of a sudden, it struck Guettard that there must at one time have been active volcanoes in southern France.

Upon inquiring, Guettard was told that the black building stones had come from the quarries at the village of Volvic, south of Vichy. "Volvic!" exclaimed Guettard, in another flash of understanding; the village's name must have been a contraction of the Latin phrase *volcani vicus,* meaning "volcanic village."

Guettard and Malesherbes went to Vichy for a few days of relaxation, but the idea of the volcanic village continued to intrigue them, particularly when they noticed that the pump house at the Vichy baths was built of the same black rock. Leaving Vichy, they proceeded to the Puy de Dôme area in Auvergne— excitement mounting with each step. At Rion, about 25 miles southwest of Vichy, they saw that every building in the town was made of black stone, and learned that Volvic was just four miles away.

Without further delay, the two pressed on to Volvic and went straight to the quarry. There Guettard's hunch was confirmed. He identified the outcrop from which the black building stones had been cut as a solidified river of lava that had flowed from higher ground, probably the high granite ridge he could see a short distance from the quarry.

Behind the ridge rose a hill with the symmetrical sides and truncated crown of the typical volcanic cone. Underfoot, as the two men ascended the hill, Guettard noticed red and black pumice among the blocks of rugged, spongy lava fragments that he knew were unique to volcanoes. In the light of his previous observations of the ubiquitous black lava, the geology of the surrounding landscape took on a startling clarity. At the crest of the hill, he could trace the crumbling vestiges of the lip of a long-dead volcano arcing away to either side. In front of him the smooth, bowl-shaped center of the ancient crater lay silent and carpeted with grass, upon which cattle grazed placidly. Behind him, low, winding ridges and hillocks overgrown with vegetation and cross-cut by gullies and stream beds marked the paths of what he recognized as ancient lava flows.

Returning to the quarry, Guettard examined the lava where it had been laid open by the rock cutters. The cross section exposed sheets of lava inclining gently away from the crater, each separated from the next by a layer of clay, sand or loam. Guettard conjectured that the sheets of lava had been generated by separate volcanic episodes and that the intervening layers of sediment had accumulated between eruptions.

When they reached Clermont-Ferrand, the largest town in the area, Guettard and Malesherbes procured the services of an amateur naturalist who agreed to serve as a guide. The three men made their way up the steep escarpment of Puy de Dôme, and from the 1,600-foot-high vantage point, they could see that the surrounding countryside was dotted with the cone-shaped hills that are characteristic of a volcanic landscape. The naturalist, who had spent years studying the local terrain, was astounded that he had never realized its true nature.

What Guettard was discovering had in fact been known centuries before, but had been lost to history during the Dark Ages. The Romans, who had inhabited the region 1,700 years earlier, had surely known of the volcanoes—they had given the quarry town its name. And before the Romans came, inhabitants of the area were undoubtedly aware of the fiery nature of their mountains. Modern carbon-14 dating of the vestiges of oak trees caught in the lava indicates that the most recent eruption in Auvergne occurred about 6,000 years ago—at the height of Europe's middle Stone Age culture.

But Guettard and Malesherbes knew none of this. They had only the evidence before their eyes. On May 10, 1752, Guettard delivered a paper to the French Academy of Sciences in which he stunned that august body with his assertion that the very heart of France had once been an area of active volcanoes. His argument was unassailable and his paper, entitled "Memoir on Certain Mountains in France That Have Once Been Volcanoes," marked the start of serious scientific study of the role of volcanoes in the mechanics of the planet.

Guettard's paper spawned one of the two great schools of geologic thought that vied for ascendancy for more than 50 years at the end of the 18th Century and the beginning of the 19th. Their divergence centered on the origins of

The 4,806-foot peak of Puy de Dôme dominates a chain of 50 extinct volcanoes in France's Auvergne region. The volcanic origins of these peaks were known to the Roman conquerors of ancient Gaul, familiar with the volcanoes of their homeland. But the character of the mountains was overlooked by subsequent observers until Jean-Étienne Guettard identified them as volcanic in 1751.

granite and basalt, the materials that make up much of the earth's crust. The vulcanists—Guettard's direct heirs—believed that such rocks were formed in a molten state in the earth's superheated interior. Guettard's discovery in Auvergne was a first step in the development of their theory.

The neptunists, who took their name from the Roman sea deity, continued to believe that all earth features had been formed under a vast ocean that had covered the entire planet eons ago. Basalt and granite were no exceptions; these rocks, they insisted, were formed by chemical precipitation, a process in which solids form in liquids much like the scale that builds up on the bottom of a well-used teakettle.

On one thing, however, both sides were in agreement: Sedimentary rocks, the shales and sandstones that occurred in vast regular layers, or strata—and that sometimes bore the imprints of primitive sea creatures—were laid down in the ocean.

The neptunists enjoyed a great numerical advantage as the debate commenced. For one thing, their theory could be more easily reconciled with the Biblical account of Creation. For another, the vulcanists' case, resting as it did on Guettard's discovery in the Auvergne Mountains, was severely limited for years by a crucial flaw in his analysis of the region. While he had established unequivocally the volcanic origin of the black lava that he had found in the area, Guettard saw no connection between the lava and a multitude of other

51

rock formations, found throughout the European continent, that he and his fellow geologists knew as basalt.

Eventually, lava would be classified as a basalt, and all basalts would be recognized as volcanic in origin. Thus vulcanism would triumph, and the volcano's elemental role in shaping the earth's crust would be everywhere understood. But victory would have to await the work of younger men in years to come, for Guettard was content to accept the assumption of the neptunists that basalts were sedimentary in formation.

His error was not surprising. Basalt was often found among rocks that were unquestionably sedimentary, in locations where any trace of an ancient volcano had long since vanished. Although it was uniformly fine-grained, basalt appeared in many different shapes and in widely varied colors, ranging from yellowish through brown and green to black—all of which led Guettard to agree that basalts were far different from the lava of Auvergne.

The classic example of his confusion, which lasted virtually to the end of his life, was the debate over a bewildering geological formation found at the western edge of the Auvergne *puy* region. There loomed a hillside composed of millions of tightly packed hexagonal stone slabs, each about a foot across, stacked one atop the other in columns hundreds of feet high. For centuries the people of Auvergne, while standing in awe of the seemingly supernatural uniformity of La Roche Tuilière, meaning "the tile rock," had nevertheless put the stones to practical use as paving and roofing tiles.

In Guettard's day, scientific explanations for the tile rock ranged from the bizarre to the plausible; one was that the rocks were the petrified remains of a bamboo forest; another saw each tile as an individual crystal formed by the same process that produced gemstones; but the consensus was that they somehow had been formed as sediment.

That is what Guettard adamantly believed, even in the face of powerful arguments from his own disciples as the years went on that the tile rock was volcanic in origin. Guettard's insistence was based on the fact that it was a graygreen rock, not black like the lava of Auvergne. Moreover, it was far from any vestige of a volcanic cone or crater, and its astonishing configuration set it even further apart from typical lava flows. "How is it possible," Guettard asked in a letter to a fellow naturalist, "that if these columns were formed in the violent fires of a volcano, the granite they rest on has remained intact and was not fused with them?"

The question was a good one. It was not until years after Guettard's initial investigation of the Auvergne Mountains that geologists came to understand that the columnar basalts, as the tile rocks are called today, were lava flows that in this case had intruded into cold granite formations perhaps millions of years older. Both basalt and granite are igneous rocks—solidified from molten or partly molten material—but the molten basalt loses its heat too quickly to melt the granite, so that the contact between the two remains clearly defined. In fact, it is precisely the cool surface of the granite that begins the process of columnar jointing.

As it cools, the lava contracts, but its own tensile strength is not sufficient to allow the extremities of so large a body—sometimes acres in area—to shrink toward one central point. Instead, as the lava cools, thousands of localized centers of contraction develop, and the surface of the flow cracks and divides into the strikingly uniform pattern of hexagonal plates. These cracks extend down through the entire thickness of the lava to form thousands of tall, tightly packed columns. At right angles to these pillars, horizontal cracks, also caused by cooling, slice the basalt into individual tiles.

Guettard's mistaken interpretation of the complex nature of the tile rock, and his more fundamental error of insisting that basalt was sedimentary in nature, made his general theory of volcanism increasingly hard to defend. In his

One of nature's geological wonders, an escarpment of remarkably uniform columns was exposed by erosion at La Roche Tuilière in the Auvergne Mountains of France. Mineralogists were unable to determine the origin of these columns until Nicholas Desmarest in 1771 published geological proof that they were formed during the cooling of a lava flow from a prehistoric volcano.

Nicholas Desmarest's map of the Auvergne Mountains shows many extinct volcanoes in close proximity to one another. It was in studying the remnants of these volcanoes, which last erupted some 6,000 years ago, that 18th Century French geologists confirmed that central France was a volcanic area.

waning years he suffered miserably from an acute case of narcolepsy, a disease that causes uncontrollable lapses into deep sleep. Nonetheless, he regularly attended the sessions of the Academy of Sciences until he became too ill to get about. He died in 1785, shortly after the igneous origin of basalt was proved to him by a fellow Frenchman whose discovery, like Guettard's own, would face a decades-long battle for acceptance.

Nicholas Desmarest was a quiet, unassuming bureaucrat who took up geology merely as a hobby. But he developed such a passion for the science that friends, only half in jest, said he would have smashed open the most beautiful sculpture just to examine the marble. His field trips were made on foot, with a packet of cheese for food, and a bedroll so he could spend the night at the spot where he had finished his day's investigations.

For Desmarest, the geology of Auvergne was a vast and intricate jigsaw puzzle. While Guettard had understood the secret of the region in a sudden burst of understanding, Desmarest's contribution was more typical of the geologist's discipline. By the painstaking assemblage of many observations, he was able to reconstruct the exact shape of the lava flows from the long-gone infernos and describe how the dark, sprawling ridges of basalt had been brought to the surface.

Then Desmarest went one step further. By comparing the rocks of Auvergne, which he now knew were indisputably volcanic in origin, with similar rocks from elsewhere in Europe, he was able to pinpoint other regions that had once been the scene of volcanic activity but that showed no discernible traces of cones or lava flows.

Gradually in the 1770s a picture was taking shape of a continent dappled with ancient volcanoes. But unfortunately for Desmarest and the vulcanists, one of the key formations happened to be the Scheibenberg, a basaltic peak in the Ore Mountains of Germany. And the Scheibenberg was a favorite haunt of Professor Abraham Gottlob Werner, Inspector of Collections at the nearby Freiberg School of Mines.

In the entire history of geology, perhaps no man has so overwhelmed the minds of his fellow scientists. Werner's spellbinding classes in what he called "geognosy"—meaning knowledge of the earth—attracted students from all over Europe. Under his hand, the Freiberg School of Mines grew from a regional trade school into a major center of philosophy and science. And for nearly 30 years at the end of the 18th Century, Werner managed to override the inspired insights of Guettard and Desmarest by sheer force of personality.

The lecture was Werner's medium. He scorned the pen, published few papers and never answered his mail. In fact, his invitation to join the French Academy of Sciences as a distinguished foreign member lay unopened for years because he feared that if he read it he would have to respond in writing. But behind the lectern, he was messianic. And the voluminous notes taken by his students during his lectures were copied and passed on to students at other universities.

This "Pope of Science," as Werner was later called, would scatter a few rocks before him on a table and then mesmerize his listeners with his theories about the rocks' origin, history, effects on civilization and philosophical significance. There was no place in Werner's cosmology for volcanoes; like other neptunists, he believed that virtually all the rocks of the earth's crust had solidified from a primordial sea—the "universal solvent," as he called it. He went to great lengths to demonstrate how each different kind of rock had been deposited in layers reaching around the globe one on top of another, to be broken up and heaped into mountainous piles by a second deluge.

Volcanoes, Werner proclaimed, were very recent and superficial phenomena—merely underground veins of coal that had caught fire and burned their way to the surface. Basalt, pumice, obsidian and, for that matter, all types of rock were of aqueous origin; even lava was just aqueous rock melted by the burning coal. He believed that volcanoes were unworthy of serious geological inquiry.

Werner's intellectual empire eventually came to grief, and by a stroke of geological justice, it foundered on rocks of basalt. The same dark stone that had confused Guettard and fascinated Desmarest occurred in abundance in the environs of Freiberg. Most accessible of all were the basalts of the Scheibenberg peak, where Werner would pause on field trips to expound on their aqueous origin. Indeed, in 1788 in one of his few scientific papers, he used the outcropping at the Scheibenberg—layers of basalt lying atop a layer of sandstone—to demonstrate that basalt everywhere in the world must be younger than sandstone. "All basalt was formed as an aqueous deposit in a comparatively recent formation," he wrote. "All basalt originally belonged to one widely extended and very thick layer, which has since been disrupted, with only fragments of the original layer remaining."

Although Werner seldom traveled far from Freiberg, his students did, and among them were some of the keenest young scientific minds in Europe, who ardently wished to prove his theories. "We may say of him," commented the French geologist Baron Georges Cuvier some years later, "that nature everywhere found itself interrogated in his name." Nature, however, felt no obliga-

A Glossary of Volcanic Rocks

At first glance, the rocks ejected by volcanoes are remarkable chiefly for their curious, infinitely varied appearance. But when classified by shape, size and texture, they reveal much about past volcanic eruptions.

The sheets of rock formed by lava flows are the easiest to classify because they take on the appearance of the flows themselves. The two principal types bear Hawaiian names. Pahoehoe lava is hot, fluid and fast-moving; when it cools it hardens into a relatively smooth surface. Aa lava, cooler and more viscous, forms a rough, blocky crust. Aptly named pillow lava occurs when water suddenly chills molten pahoehoe lava, dividing it into sacklike segments.

The rocks blown violently from a volcano, called ejecta, usually are classified by size. Particles smaller than two millimeters across ($^1/_{10}$ inch) are called ash, while peb-

Pahoehoe Lava

Aa Lava

Pillow Lava

Ash

Lapilli

bles and cobbles less than 64 millimeters in diameter (about 2½ inches) are called lapilli, from the Latin for "little stones."

Larger rocks are divided into two categories: Angular chunks of old rock or hardened lava, which are ejected as solids, are called blocks; rounded rocks, ejected as molten, plastic-skinned blobs, are called bombs.

Volcanic ejecta of all sizes are also classed by texture. Pumice, a rock that floats on water, contains millions of bubbles created by expanding gases. In coarser cinder, bubbles are larger and usually interconnected.

Because the thick beds deposited by an explosion contain an amalgam of ejecta, they have yet another set of labels. The most common is tuff, a compacted mixture of ash and small lapilli. A volcano's history often is clearly visible in the tuff bands deposited by successive eruptions.

Blocks

Bombs

Pumice

Cinder

Tuff

tion to tailor its phenomena to the good professor's theories, and before long his sharp-eyed students noticed discrepancies. And once again the Auvergne region of France, with its demonstrably volcanic basalts, became an arena for geologic conflict.

In 1803, Werner's prize student, a young French geologist named Jean Francois D'Aubuisson de Voisins, spent weeks in Auvergne studying the basalt formations surrounding the *puys*. Like Desmarest before him, he tracked the lava flows from the ancient volcanoes' mouths down into the valleys, and repeatedly found them to be composed of basalt. "The facts which I saw," wrote D'Aubuisson, "spoke too plainly to be mistaken; the truth revealed itself too clearly before my eyes. There can be no question that basalts of volcanic origin occur in Auvergne."

Within 10 years of D'Aubuisson's recantation, two of Werner's most famous protégés broke with their former master. Primarily as a result of field trips to Auvergne, the great German geologist Leopold von Buch and the intrepid explorer Alexander von Humboldt adopted Desmarest's theory of the volcanic origins of the area's basalts, thus creating a sizable breach in the ranks of the neptunist forces. But the French vulcanists, while understanding that volcanoes were a vital force in shaping the earth's crust, could offer no adequate explanation of how volcanoes worked or why they occurred. Consequently, neptunism staggered on; Werner's flawed theory of the earth had enormous force because it presented a complete explanation of the formation of all the observable rocks and minerals of the earth's surface. The vulcanists had enough verifiable facts to know that neptunism was ridiculous, but they had no comprehensive theory of their own.

Actually, an ingenious theory of the earth that could comfortably accommodate what the vulcanists now knew about Auvergne and about basalt had been developed in 1785. It was so well constructed that when it finally became generally known, it provided the basic framework for modern geology.

In the spring of 1802, the British philosopher and natural scientist John Playfair published a book summarizing the geological observations of a friend of his, a Scotsman named James Hutton. Hutton had died five years earlier, after a lifetime of puzzling over the craggy skerries and cairns of his native Scotland. He had published his researches, but they had gone largely unnoticed because of the obscurity of the journal in which he chose to print them and the unfortunate prolixity of his writing. Playfair rearranged Hutton's work into a more logical order and transformed his cumbersome sentences into lucid prose. The result, *Illustrations of the Huttonian Theory of the Earth,* lifted Hutton's work from obscurity to the status of a scientific landmark.

On a field trip in 1785 into the heart of Scotland's dank Grampian Mountains near the Tilt River, Hutton had discovered red granite penetrating the limestone beds. Hutton was so enraptured that his companions at first thought he had discovered gold. But, to Hutton, the sight, and what it signified, were even more precious.

Werner had said that the rocks of the earth's crust had been laid down one after another, beginning with granite, the oldest layer. According to Werner, limestone was one of the more recently formed rocks. But Hutton was now finding evidence to the contrary; he was looking at a formation of granite that had punched through and dislocated the limestone. He realized that the granite must be the younger rock; molten granite had been forced up through the limestone beds.

Hutton knew that no source of heat on the earth's surface was capable of melting so much rock. He speculated that within the earth there might be a "fluid mass, melted, but unchanged by the action of heat." By unchanged, he meant that the ingredients of igneous rocks like granite and basalt were present

Scotsman James Hutton, called the founder of modern geology because he was the first to understand the earth as an ever-changing dynamic system, sits at a table cluttered with rock samples in this 1780 portrait by Scottish artist Sir Henry Raeburn. Hutton was famous for collecting carefully documented field evidence to support his theories. "His study is so full of fossils & chemical apparatus of various kinds," wrote a visitor to Hutton's Edinburgh home, "that there is hardly room to sit down."

in the solution. Prudently, he stopped there and returned to what he could see at the surface.

Hutton constructed a dramatic and comprehensive counterproposal to the neptunists' concept of the primordial sea and its static deposits. The earth, he wrote, was a complicated, dynamic system, whose enormous interior heat kept its surface in a constant state of agitation. In the meantime, the forces of erosion were breaking down old rocks into sand and pebbles, which eventually formed sandstones and conglomerates. And organic matter such as shells, bones and leaves sank each year into the soil and accumulated at the bottom of the sea, to become rocks like limestone and coal. As these beds of sedimentary rocks sank beneath the continuing accumulation of sediments, heat and pressure gradually transformed them into denser, more highly crystalline rocks like marble and schist.

As the process continued, the forces of heat and pressure became so great that these metamorphosed rocks partially melted and mixed with the already molten substances of the earth's interior. Where the overlying strata cracked, this fluid moved up to harden into igneous rocks like granite and basalt, frequently in the form of dikes, such as the red granite that Hutton had found in the Grampian Mountains.

On its journey upward, the molten material, whenever it could, would also fan out horizontally between layers of sediment and cool in broad underground

Arthur's Seat, a 325-million-year-old volcanic plug, looms 822 feet over Edinburgh, Scotland, in this 1774 etching. So named because King Arthur supposedly oversaw the defeat of the Picts from its height, the formation served geologist James Hutton as a natural laboratory in which he found evidence that led him to conclude that basaltic rock is formed from molten materials from the earth's interior.

sheets of igneous rock called sills. Then, over the course of millions of years, surface erosion would wear away the overlying strata, exposing the sills and dikes and breaking them down into sand and grit. Thus the cycle began again.

But there was one important exception. Sometimes the rising material would punch its way through to the earth's surface and spew columns of molten rock into the atmosphere. Here, for the first time, was a theory that gave to volcanoes an integral and plausible role in the building of the earth's crust. "A volcano is not made on purpose to frighten superstitious people into a fit of piety and devotion," Hutton wrote, but "should be considered a spiracle to the subterranean furnace."

Hutton saw the volcano as a kind of release valve for the pressure pent up in the inner earth. Scientists today would disagree with this particular point, but in its broad strokes, Hutton's theory still stands. The earth's crust is alive with movement, albeit imperceptibly slow, and its processes of breaking down and building up are all intricately related in a vast, dynamic system.

Hutton's theorizing, however, stopped at what happened in the earth itself. Not even his brilliant work could have prepared the world for the devastating atmospheric effects of a titanic eruption that roared to life in 1815 halfway around the world from Hutton's scrubby Scottish hills.

During the evening of April 5, 1815, sounds resembling cannon fire coming across the water caused Sir Stamford Raffles, the Lieutenant Governor of Java, to dispatch two boats from Batavia—now Jakarta—to search the Java Sea for what he thought might be a vessel in distress. Just to be on the safe side, he marched a detachment of troops into the city in case the noises were from an attack by rebels on one of the nearby British outposts. That same day, about 900 miles to the east, at Macassar on the island of Celebes, the captain of the East India Company's armed cruiser *Benares* heard what sounded like a heavy artillery barrage, with intermittent volleys of rifle shots. Swiftly taking aboard a detachment of troops, he sailed south into the Flores Sea looking for pirates.

None of the patrols found the source of the disturbances, and soon returned to their bases. That was just as well. For if they had, there was nothing they, nor all the troops and ships in the world, could have done about it. The noises, as they would learn, came from the distant island of Sumbawa, 200 miles south of Macassar and 750 miles from Batavia. The volcanic mountain of Tambora, which had lain somnolent beneath a lush cloak of jungle vegetation throughout recorded history, was in the process of destroying itself.

When the fantastic paroxysms tapered off a week later, Tambora's 13,000-foot eminence would be reduced by a third; 10,000 people on Sumbawa and the surrounding islands would be dead, with another 82,000 soon to die in the ensuing famine and disease; and halfway around the world the following year farmers would experience bitter summer weather such as had never been known in living memory. But the extent of this fantastic event was not even imagined in Batavia on April 6, the day after the ships were dispatched.

That morning a light sprinkling of ashes began to fall over the city, and there was no longer any doubt about what had caused the noises. A volcano had erupted, although, judging from the volume of the sounds, most Batavians thought that it had occurred nearby. In the afternoon, the air was quite still. An unusual, pervasive feeling of pressure caused people to fear that an earthquake was about to strike. But their alarm subsided when nothing happened for the next five days other than the continued light ashfall. Then on the evening of the 10th and continuing through the next day, a series of tremendous explosions rocked the entire 2,500-mile-long island chain.

At Gresik on the Java coast, 300 miles from the eruption, one of Raffles' correspondents awoke on the morning of the 12th from what seemed like an unusually long night's sleep. Although it was still dark, he discovered by holding his watch up to a lamp that it was 8:30 a.m.—two and a half hours after sunrise. At nine there was still no daylight. By 10 o'clock, he later wrote Raffles, there was "a faint glimmer of light overhead," and an hour later the birds began chirruping as if at the break of day. Amid the sound of distant explosions, the correspondent sat down to a candlelight breakfast.

Other reports soon pinpointed the scene of the cataclysm as Tambora. On April 18, Raffles sent a shipload of rice to relieve the starving islanders. When the vessel arrived at Sumbawa, its commander, Lieutenant Owen Phillips, found a scene of utter devastation. The mountain of Tambora, which had once been a majestic landmark visible for miles out at sea, was now flattened into a broad plateau, and much of the island was covered by a two-foot-thick coating of ash and mud. Phillips reported that the sea around the island was jammed with thousands of uprooted trees and huge floating islands of pumice—a light, brittle, sponge-textured volcanic rock that trapped so much gas in its vesicles that it remained afloat. Many of the 127,000 people who had survived the blast were racked by a virulent cholera that had broken out after the eruption. Thousands had already died and the rest straggled about despondently in the knee-deep ash, willing to trade their most valued possessions for a few ounces of rice. Corpses lay strewn along the roads, and the villages were deserted by their inhabitants, who had fled into the interior looking for the few remaining heads of palm and stalks of plantain to eat.

From the testimony of a local raja, Phillips pieced together this vivid description of what had happened: "About seven, P.M. on the 10th of April, three distinct columns of flame burst forth, near the top of Tambora mountain, all of them apparently within the verge of the crater; and after ascending separately to a very great height, their tops united in the air in a troubled, confused manner. In a short time the whole mountain appeared like a body of liquid fire extending itself in every direction."

The mountain continued to rage with unabated fury, reported Phillips, but after an hour of terror, it was concealed from view by a thick curtain of falling ash. "Stones at this time fell very thick at Saugar," a town about 25 miles away from the eruption, wrote Phillips, who went on to say that "some of them were as large as two fists, but generally not larger than walnuts." Around 10 p.m., continued Phillips, "a violent whirlwind ensued, which blew down nearly every house in the village of Saugar. In the part of Saugar adjoining Tambora, the whirlwind's effects were much more violent, tearing up by the roots the largest trees, and carrying them into the air, together

A Remarkable Geological Partnership

In 1968 near Edinburgh, Scotland, a descendant of John Clerk, the artist who illustrated James Hutton's historic 18th Century geology text, *Theory of the Earth*, discovered among the family papers a folio of 70 drawings that had been misplaced nearly two centuries before.

Clerk had prepared the drawings from on-the-spot sketches of rocks and landscapes in southern Scotland during a series of field trips that he and Hutton made together between 1785 and 1788. The trips were among the most momentous geological excursions of all time because Hutton observed many features— meticulously portrayed in Clerk's drawings—that helped him formulate the subsequently accepted basic principles of geology.

No one knows the precise roles that the two men played in the creation of the drawings, but it is clear that the geologist and the artist formed a remarkable scientific partnership. Besides being a skilled artist, Clerk was an accomplished geologist in his own right, "whose pencil," wrote John Playfair, Hutton's biographer and friend to both men, "is not less valuable in the sciences than in the arts." Clerk could produce an accurate sketch in just 10 minutes, and took pains to preserve the strata and rock detail in his watercolors by varnishing many of them.

Clerk's rendering of the irregular layering of rock along the banks of the River Jed (*bottom right*) appeared as an engraving in Volume 1 of *Theory of the Earth*. Most of the other drawings—including the strata in Edinburgh (*top right*) and the map of Glen Tilt (*middle*), where Hutton's discovery of granite veins amid older rock formations convinced him that granite is an igneous rock—were intended for a follow-up volume that Hutton was writing at the time of his death in 1797.

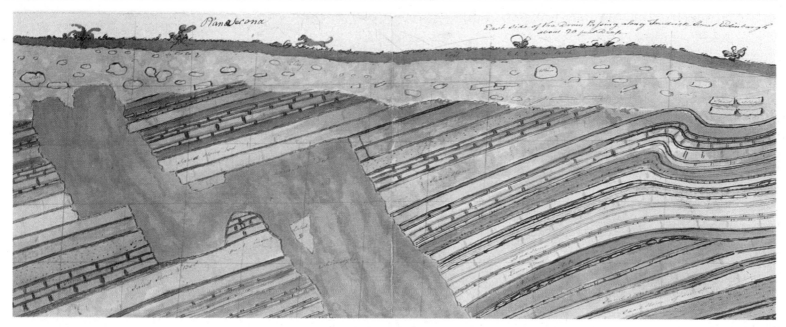

Beds of different rock types, including sandstone, schist and limestone, are invaded by a dike of basaltic rock, known as whinstone in Scotland, in this detail of strata lying along a section of the Frederick Street sewer in Edinburgh. The grid squares represent spacings of about one yard and the topsoil is recorded as being six to eight inches thick.

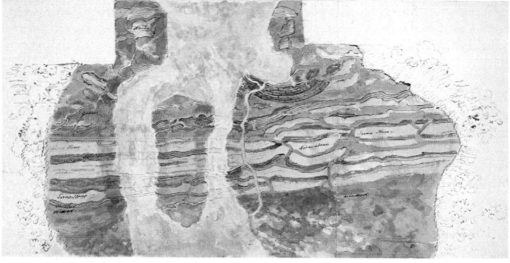

Veins of rust-colored granite traversing older fragments of limestone, schist and mixed rock can be seen on this geologic map of the Tilt River and Glen. James Hutton was overjoyed to locate such a junction of schist and granite; it proved, he wrote, that "granite had been made to flow, in a state of fusion, among the broken and dislocated strata."

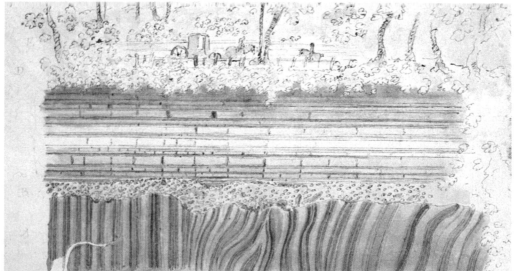

A bed of pudding stone, a pebbly sedimentary rock, lies sandwiched between a layer of upright schist and linear beds of sandstone in this watercolor of an unconformity, or irregular layering of rock, along the River Jed south of Jedburgh. Hutton was the first geologist to recognize that the pudding stone was formed by erosion of flaky, crystalline schist.

with men, houses, cattle and whatever else came within its influence."

The lieutenant reported that "the sea rose nearly twelve feet higher than it had ever been known to be before, and completely spoiled the only small spots of ricelands in Saugar, sweeping away houses and everything within its reach."

Tambora continued to rumble and burn for three months before finally falling silent. Its loudest detonations had been heard more than 1,000 miles away, and it had cast a blanket of ash over an area of more than one million square miles. The eruption had caused severe earthquakes on islands hundreds of miles distant from Sumbawa, and for four years thereafter, ships in the Java Sea would have to dodge the floating islands of pumice. But the most widely felt effect of the eruption came when people all around the world noticed that something odd had happened to the weather.

Geologists now calculate that Tambora blew an estimated 36 cubic miles, or 1.7 million tons, of debris into the sky. Most of it fell to earth in the vicinity of Sumbawa within a few hours. The remainder, however, was pulverized into a talclike dust light enough to remain suspended in the atmosphere. The dust was carried high into the stratosphere, where it began circling the earth, reflecting incoming sunlight back into space and robbing the earth of some of its heat. It also acted like a giant filter, causing spectacular orange sunsets. At first, no one much minded the days ending with such flamboyance—in fact, it has been suggested that the phenomenon inspired the murky lighting in paintings by the famed British artist J. M. W. Turner.

But the haze that lingered for many months after the eruption may have affected more than the sunsets. Cities as far distant from Tambora as Geneva, Switzerland, and New Haven, Connecticut, which had been experiencing somewhat cooler than normal weather since 1812, reported even lower temperatures during the summer of 1815, and the next year set records that in both cases still stand. In France, where people were already short of food as a result of the Napoleonic Wars, the summer's crops were so scanty that grain cars on the way to market had to be guarded against bands of starving citizens. By the end of the year people were subsisting on whatever plants were still growing or animals still living—including their pets.

People fared considerably better in New England. Although the summer weather there was just as severe as in France, the New Englanders were not afflicted by war as well. Nonetheless, Chauncey Jerome, a 26-year-old clockmaker's apprentice in Plymouth, Connecticut, remembered finding clothes his wife had set outside his house to dry on the night of June 10 frozen the next day. On the 4th of July, 1816, he watched some men pitching quoits at noonday, and they were all wearing overcoats. New Englanders wryly called the year "Eighteen hundred and froze to death."

It snowed in June throughout New England, and a killing frost on August 21 destroyed most gardens from Maine to Connecticut. Samuel Latham Mitchill, a professor of natural history at Columbia College, in New York City, noted in his journal that he had to pay four dollars for half a barrel of buckwheat meal, when the usual price was about half that. In Boscawen, New Hampshire, Enoch Little confided to his diary at harvesttime in September: "Frosts killed almost all the corn in New England and not half of it is fit to roast. On frosty ground, the orchards were barren; the prospects as to fodder are most alarming."

The cause of the year without summer went undetected for years. No one seemed to suspect that Tambora was a major factor. Some experts blamed the cold weather on sunspots; others thought that a large collection of icebergs in the North Atlantic was responsible. Had Benjamin Franklin still been alive, he might have solved the puzzle, for in 1784 he had attributed the unusually cold winter to "a dry fog" that was caused by eruptions in 1783 of Mounts Asama in Japan and Laki in Iceland. But his analysis went unremembered—or unheed-

ORIGINAL CONE

The awesome effect of the 1815 eruption of Tambora on the island of Sumbawa in the East Indies—the most powerful eruption in recorded history—can be seen in this drawing of the volcano before and after the blast. Tambora's majestic 13,000-foot cone (*dotted line*) was flattened into a 9,300-foot plateau as an estimated 36 cubic miles of debris blew into the sky. Ejecta from this eruption caused temperatures around the world to drop almost 2° F. below normal for an entire year.

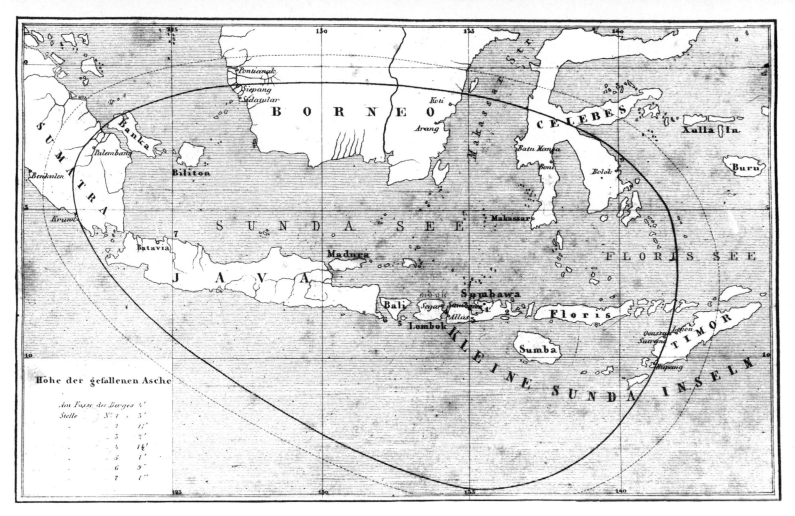

The area of ashfall from the 1815 eruption of Tambora is shown on this map by Swiss scientist Heinrich Zollinger, who mounted an expedition to the region in 1847. The solid line circumscribes the area of ashfall that was observed by Zollinger and covers one million square miles from southern Sumatra to Timor; the dotted line represents the scientist's estimate of the total extent of ashfall.

ed. In fact, one theorist suggested bitterly that the widespread use of Franklin's lightning rods had upset a natural flow of warming electricity from the earth's core and had brought on the frosty weather.

Though no geologist was able to study Tambora while it erupted, reports of its magnitude, eruptive force and the range of its ashfall added amazing scope to the growing picture of volcanism's effects on the earth. The mills of science ground slowly in those days, and it was not until 1847, three decades later, that the first purely scientific expedition went to Sumbawa to study Tambora.

Led by a Swiss botanist, Heinrich Zollinger, the scientists ascended the eastern side of the still-smoking mountain, their feet now and then breaking through the thin surface crust into a warm layer of powdery sulfur. Zollinger had estimated that the old peak—now completely altered—had stood nearly 13,000 feet high. When he reached what he felt was the highest point on the new crater rim, he paused to kindle a fire under a pan of water. The water began to boil at 195.5° F. Making a quick calculation, based on the fact that the boiling point of water declines with altitude, Zollinger concluded that the mountain's highest point was now only about 9,000 feet above sea level.

Before him, where there had once been a mighty peak, there was now a three-mile-wide crater with a sickly yellow-green lake in one corner of it. The great eruption had caused a substantial mountain virtually to disappear. But while 19th Century geologists by now had gained a remarkably sophisticated picture of volcanism's broad significance, they were still ignorant of just how the individual volcano worked.

Standing on what remained of the volcano, Zollinger could only react in amazement to his discovery. Decades would pass before an explanation for what exactly happened at Tambora was forthcoming. Ω

INSIDE THE INFERNO: HOW VOLCANOES WORK

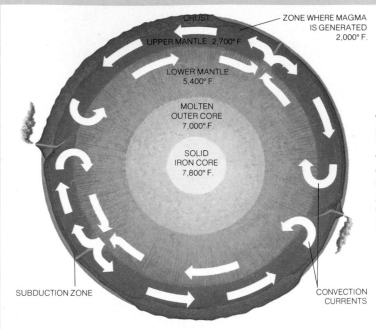

CRUST

UPPER MANTLE 2,700° F.

ZONE WHERE MAGMA IS GENERATED 2,000° F.

LOWER MANTLE 5,400° F.

MOLTEN OUTER CORE 7,000° F.

SOLID IRON CORE 7,800° F.

SUBDUCTION ZONE

CONVECTION CURRENTS

This schematic drawing shows heat distribution inside the earth. The innermost layers may reach 7,800 ° F., but their heat plays little part in volcanism because intervening rock is a very poor conductor. The heat to generate magma comes largely from decaying radioactive elements in the plastic upper mantle. Arrows reveal convection currents, the conveyor belts within the mantle that propel tectonic plates on the surface.

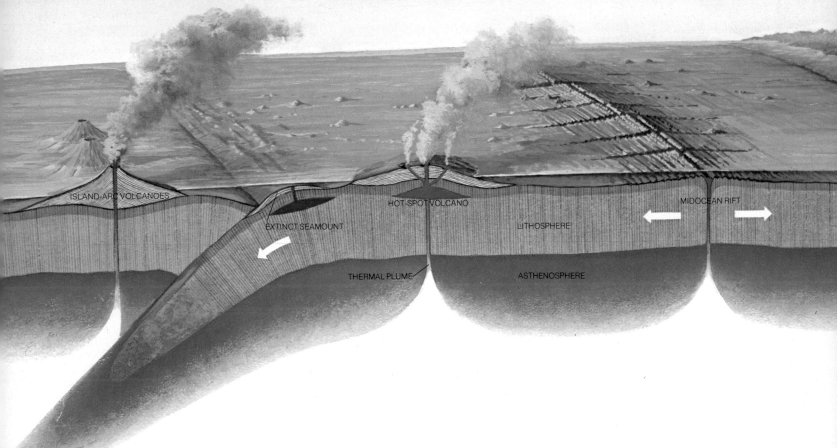

ISLAND-ARC VOLCANOES

EXTINCT SEAMOUNT

HOT-SPOT VOLCANO

LITHOSPHERE

MIDOCEAN RIFT

THERMAL PLUME

ASTHENOSPHERE

Beneath island-arc volcano chains such as the Aleutians, the Antilles or the Indonesian archipelago, two plates are colliding in midocean. As the thinner, denser plate dives under its neighbor into the hot mantle, a part of the plate, which has a relatively low melting point, may turn to volcanic magma.

Within a plate, hot-spot volcanoes such as the Hawaiian Islands are formed by an anomalous rising plume of superheated material deep within the mantle. As a plate slides across the stationary hot spot, the plume creates a volcanic chain with extinct peaks at one end and active volcanoes at the other.

As two plates separate along a midocean rift, such as the mid-Atlantic Ridge or the East Pacific Rise, magma periodically wells up through a submarine fissure system thousands of miles long. The new crust created by such eruptions replaces the crust destroyed by subduction at the outer plate margins.

For most of the 20th Century, the central mystery of volcanoes has not so much concerned the behavior of the mountains themselves—their chemistry and plumbing (*following pages*) has long been the subject of study—but rather their roots deep within the earth. The first glimmerings of understanding finally emerged in the 1960s from the theory of plate tectonics, which revolutionized so many geological disciplines.

According to this theory, the earth's outer layer, the lithosphere, is an ever-changing mosaic of huge, rigid plates, which float on an asthenosphere of hot, plastic rock. Thermal convection currents in the asthenosphere drive the plates a few inches a year, creating a crazy quilt of collisions, side-by-side slippage and outright separation.

Volcanoes are concentrated on two such boundaries: subduction zones and rifts. In areas of subduction, one plate grinds beneath another, melting parts of both and sending magma spurting to the surface. At rifts, where convection pulls plates apart, the upwelling magma extends their edges. These two forces always balance: As subduction destroys a plate at one edge, rift volcanism rebuilds the opposite side.

This elegantly symmetrical model accounts for most volcanoes, but its omissions are equally fascinating. Midplate hot-spot volcanoes apparently are fueled by a deep thermal plume, perhaps generated by decaying radioactive isotopes. And volcanic cataclysms such as flood basalts and ash flows (*pages 70-71*) seem only indirectly related to plate tectonics.

Even today, writes one volcanologist, "the questions of where magma comes from and how it is generated are the most speculative in all of volcanology." Plate tectonics provides only some of the answers.

OCEANIC PLATE

SUBDUCTION ZONE

CONTINENTAL PLATE

FLOOD BASALT

CONTINENTAL RIFT VALLEY

When an ocean plate dives beneath a thicker, lighter continental plate, it produces a coastal range of volcanic mountains, such as the Cascades or the Andes. These mountain ranges are set back 100 miles or more from the subduction trench, directly above a magma source at least 60 miles down.

Inland flood basalts, such as India's Deccan Plateau or the Columbia River Plateau in the United States, are one of the great enigmas in plate tectonic theory. Their magma periodically spurts to the earth's surface through hundred-mile-long swarms of fissures, flooding vast geological regions.

Rift-valley volcanoes, such as those found along the East African rift system, are the precursors of midocean rifts. As a continental plate is pulled in two, the unsupported crustal blocks at the joint drop and magma rises through the resulting fractures, building volcanoes along the valley floor.

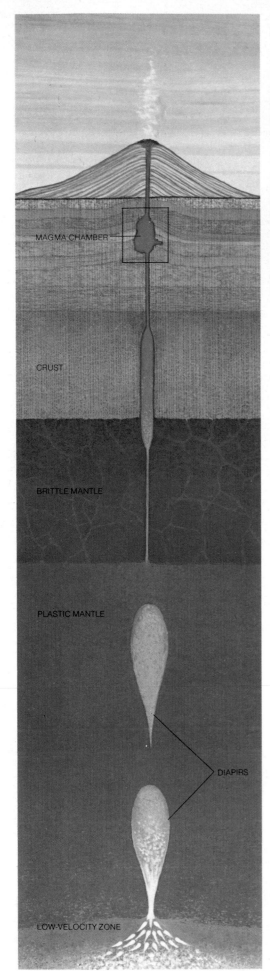

MAGMA CHAMBER

CRUST

BRITTLE MANTLE

PLASTIC MANTLE

DIAPIRS

LOW-VELOCITY ZONE

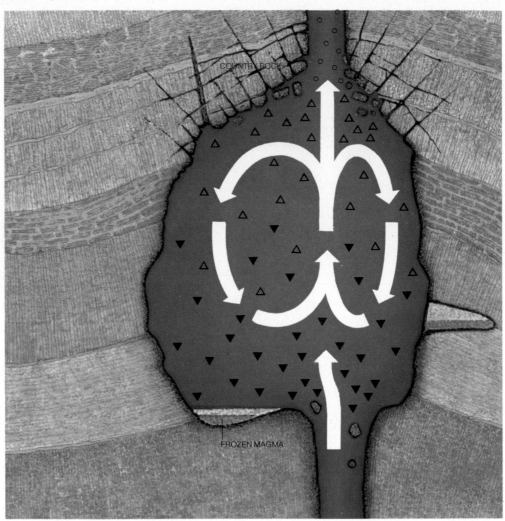

COUNTRY ROCK

FROZEN MAGMA

A magma chamber is in effect a chemical mixing bowl stirred by convection currents *(arrows)*. Some of the red-hot magma crystallizes against the cold surrounding rocks, but in the process many of these so-called country rocks are melted into the magma. Heavy, hard-to-melt minerals *(solid triangles)* gradually settle and crystallize at the bottom of the chamber, while lighter ones *(open triangles)*—quartz, for example—rise to the top. In the low-pressure region at the top of the chamber, water suspended in the magmatic solution rises and begins to form bubbles—a prelude to eruption.

According to one respected model, when magma is generated deep within the earth, the comparatively light, buoyant liquid gradually aggregates into huge tadpole-shaped diapirs, which periodically float upward through the denser, plastic mantle— accounting for the episodic behavior of most volcanoes. Where the plastic region changes to brittle mantle and then crust, the diapirs wedge their way up through fractures to a magma chamber a few miles below the surface of the earth.

64

A Soda-Pop Model of Volcanic Eruptions

Although the exact mechanisms that generate magma within the earth remain a mystery, the theoretical requirements are well known. Rock melting can be precipitated by three factors: increasing temperature, decreasing pressure or the addition of a constituent that lowers the melting point.

These factors combine to generate magma in a low-velocity zone, so named because it slows seismic waves. The zone ordinarily lies 60 to 200 miles beneath the surface, but it is much shallower near midocean ridges, continental rifts and perhaps subduction trenches. Rock in this zone is very close to its melting point (it actually contains microscopic pockets of magma), and any of the three factors can cause extensive melting.

The theory of plate tectonics provides all three. Sedimentary rock from a subducting plate, which has a relatively low melting point, partially melts in the hotter mantle; the plate also carries down water, lowering the melting point of mantle rock; and it pushes up some mantle rock, thus reducing the overlying pressure. At oceanic or continental rifts, convection currents heat underlying rock and carry it upward.

The violence of an eruption will depend on the rising magma's content of two components: silica and water. The concentration of silica determines the viscosity of molten rock; water in the magmatic solution provides the explosive potential of steam. In a magma chamber near the surface, the magma can be further enriched by water and silica melted from the surrounding rock, called country rock, and by groundwater.

In principle, the eruption (below) resembles nothing so much as the opening of a bottle of soda pop, with superheated steam bubbles in place of carbonation bubbles. In a sealed bottle the gas is held invisibly in solution by overlying pressure; when the bottle is opened, bubbles of expanding gas ordinarily float to the surface quietly and steadily, as they do in a quiet volcanic eruption.

But if the liquid is under great pressure, it becomes supersaturated with gas; when the bottle is uncorked, liquid foams out. In a volcanic explosion, the pressure on viscous, water-charged magma is so great that the bubbles expand explosively.

Water content (*circles*) and silica content (*squares*) together decide magma's eruptive potential. A low-water, low-silica mixture (*upper left*) yields a quiet eruption of runny lava. In a low-silica, high-water mixture (*upper right*), expanding steam bubbles surge up freely through the runny lava, shooting fire fountains hundreds of feet into the air. A low-water, high-silica mixture (*lower left*) extrudes pasty lava, slowly building a huge dome. But in a high-water, high-silica magma (*lower right*), viscosity prevents steam from bubbling to the surface; when the overlying pressure suddenly decreases, the trapped gas simply explodes.

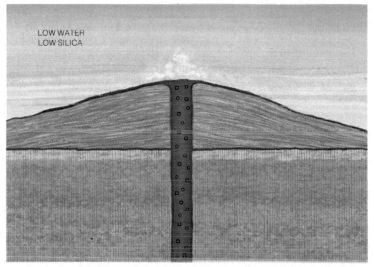

LOW WATER
LOW SILICA

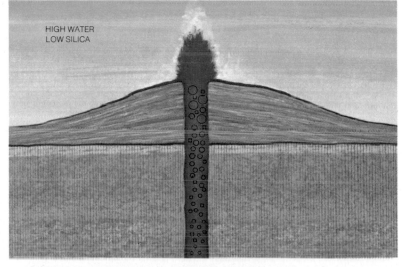

HIGH WATER
LOW SILICA

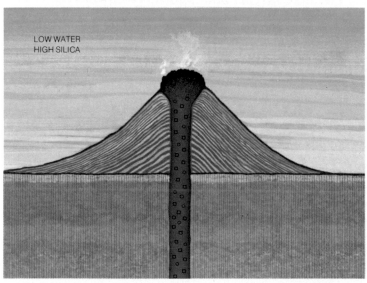

LOW WATER
HIGH SILICA

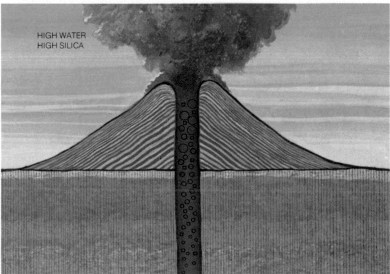

HIGH WATER
HIGH SILICA

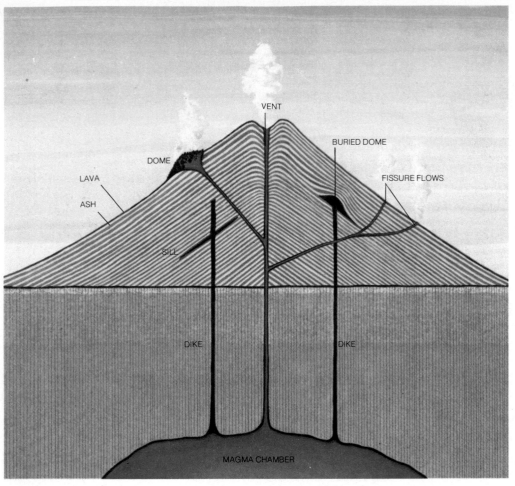

VENT

BURIED DOME

DOME

FISSURE FLOWS

LAVA

ASH

SILL

DIKE

DIKE

MAGMA CHAMBER

A composite cone, the basic structure of virtually all subduction volcanoes, is built from alternating layers of lava and of ash and cinders. The cone generally is reinforced by sheets of hardened lava, called sills, and by riblike vertical dikes. The central crater often is enlarged by inward collapse, as magma that previously supported the crater's walls recedes into the vent. Magma that extends sideways through a volcano's flanks gives birth to parasitic craters, crinkly domes and fissure flows of lava.

A Spectrum of Eruptive Types

Volcanoes do not fit neatly into discrete categories. Almost any volcano can erupt in many ways, and nearly all eruptions in fact consist of several different phenomena.

Long-term volcanic patterns are slightly more predictable. Many volcanoes tend to discharge liquid lava in their youth and erupt explosively as they age. Within one eruptive episode, violence generally declines after the initial eruption. But even these guidelines are eminently fallible. Thus, the eruptive types shown here and on the following pages illustrate principles rather than the great complexity of actual eruptions.

Once a volcano is primed with magma, the nature of an eruption depends on gas and silica content and also on obstructions in the vent. When the conduit is clear—as in most Hawaiian volcanoes, for example— gas-rich magma percolates upward and begins to form bubbles, or vesiculate, when the overlying pressure can no longer hold the gas in solution. The expanding bubbles push the entire magma column up, starting a more or less gentle, effusive eruption.

Conversely, when the vent is sealed by a dome or an accumulation of debris, great pressure builds beneath this obstruction. As the cap nears its bursting point, the final explosion may be triggered by the tiniest change—sometimes even the slight strain of earth tides from the gravitational fields of the moon and sun.

Any eruption's character also is influenced by the geometry of the vent—especially its length. If magma erupts through a cap deep inside a volcano, the long vent shoots gases skyward at supersonic speeds. By contrast, an eruption near the top of the vent would expand horizontally and vertically, at a correspondingly lower speed.

Once an eruption begins, it apparently continues by a sort of chain reaction. The initial discharge exerts back pressure that momentarily holds gas within the underlying magma column in solution. But as this pressure eases, successive surges of magma expand and vesiculate, spewing out more and more ejecta. The rate of eruption may actually increase as rapidly rising magma heats the vent and scours it out.

The pace slackens only when the volcano taps deeper levels in the magma chamber, where gas content usually decreases and viscosity increases. The eruption can finally end in three ways: The magma column itself can recede into the earth; overlying rock can pinch the vent shut when the column's pressure falls; or viscous magma can plug the vent with a pasty dome.

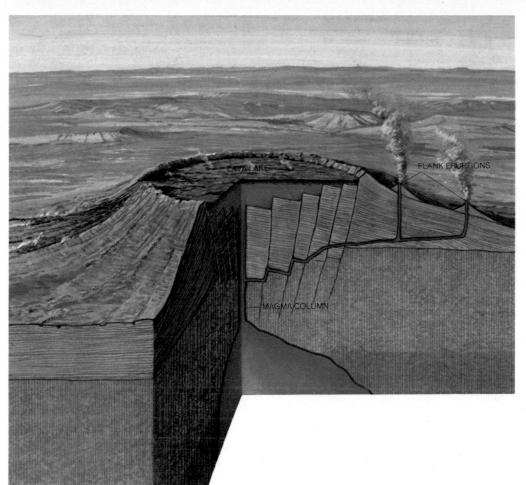

EFFUSIVE ERUPTION

Extremely hot, low-silica magma generated within the mantle erupts in runny lava flows, shown here on a Hawaiian volcano. A classic Hawaiian eruption begins at the summit; later the bulging magma chamber, pressurized by summit subsidence and the magma column's weight, sends lava gushing through mile-long fissures on the volcano's flanks.

LAVA LAKE

FLANK ERUPTIONS

MAGMA COLUMN

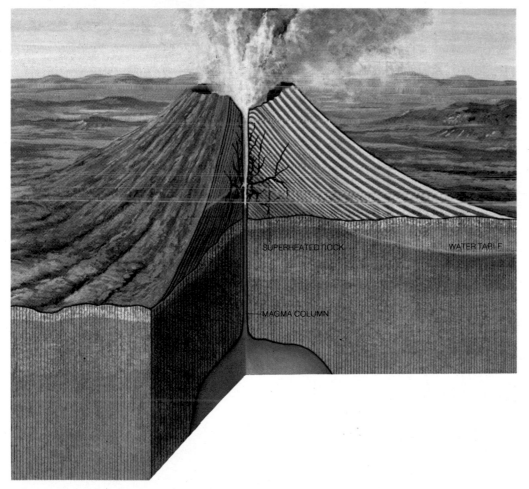

STEAM EXPLOSION

At the onset of many eruptive sequences, a rising column of magma heats and cracks rock close to the underground water table, generating steam that eventually builds up sufficient pressure to break through to the surface of the earth. Such explosions commonly blow old rock out of a clogged vent or a flank crater. The eruption often continues for several hours, as thermal shock fractures the superheated rock, progressively exposing more surface area and generating yet more steam.

SUPERHEATED ROCK

WATER TABLE

MAGMA COLUMN

SUBMARINE ERUPTION

Near the surface, undersea volcanoes always erupt violently; their magma explodes when it touches water, spewing out black rooster-tail clouds of steam and ash, and sometimes creating rafts of floating pumice. If the fragile, gently sloping cone emerges above sea level, lava flows may armor the cone with a rock carapace; otherwise waves soon wash the infant island back into the ocean deep. Below 1,000 feet, a submarine volcano (*inset*) is imperceptible from the surface; underwater pressure keeps volcanic gas and steam in solution, while pillows of lava roll down the volcano's sides.

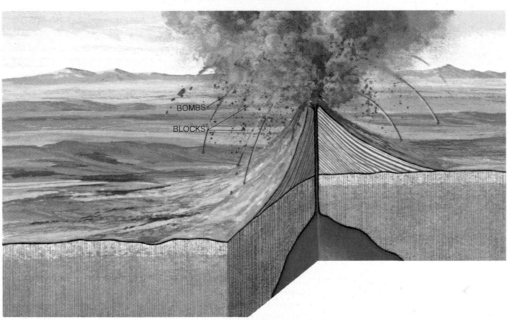

STROMBOLIAN TYPE

When magma is viscous, the trapped gases tend to escape spasmodically, showering the mountainside with ejecta—molten, plastic-skinned bombs and angular, glowing blocks. The timing and power of such eruptions vary considerably: The volcano on the Italian island of Stromboli placidly spits out sizzling bombs every few minutes, with muffled thumps that do not disturb nearby villagers. But neighboring Vulcano remains quiescent for decades before its more viscous magma explodes, hurling huge igneous blocks a mile or more.

PLINIAN EXPLOSION

When extremely gas-rich, viscous magma explodes deep inside a volcano, the vent serves as a gun barrel; a tremendous blast shoots straight up at nearly twice the speed of sound, creating a vertical column of ash as much as 20 miles high. Such explosions, named for the 79 A.D. eruption of Mount Vesuvius that killed Roman naturalist Pliny the Elder, shred the magma to microscopic particles $1/250$ inch in diameter, burying the region downwind beneath yards of dusty, drifting ash.

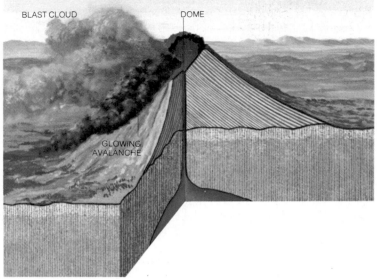

GLOWING AVALANCHE

When viscous, gas-rich magma erupts under fairly low pressure, a dense, incandescent cloud of superheated ash and pumice, suspended in trapped air and their own escaping gases, falls back to earth before it can cool and literally rolls downhill in a fiery, turbulent avalanche (often called a *nuée ardente*, French for "glowing cloud"). Such avalanches occur both by themselves and in the later stages of another, more violent eruption. If the cloud erupts vertically (*left*), the speed of the avalanche is determined by gravity and rarely exceeds 100 miles per hour; in a lateral blast (*above*) the initial velocity may reach 300 miles per hour.

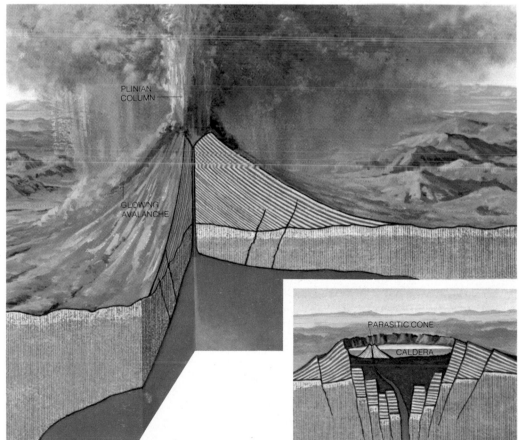

PAROXYSMAL EXPLOSION

As viscous, high-pressure magma explodes from a large, shallow reservoir—at Krakatoa in Indonesia or Santorini in Greece, for example—it may span the spectrum of volcanism for days on end: A Plinian ash column shoots miles into the stratosphere, glowing avalanches sweep downward, and tens of cubic miles of airborne ejecta bury the countryside. After such eruptions, the entire volcano often collapses piecemeal into its empty magma chamber (*inset*); the resulting caldera, a basin many miles across and perhaps a mile deep, may be filled by the ocean or by a lake like Oregon's Crater Lake.

Cataclysms That Reshape Whole Continents

Although violent outbursts like the ones at Pelée and Tambora are regarded with fear and awe, even these calamities are eclipsed by two little-known types of volcanism.

As recently as six million years ago—a brief interval by geological standards—volcanic flood basalts rent the earth's crust with fissure swarms hundreds of miles long, repeatedly burying the Columbia River Plateau in the Pacific Northwest beneath a molten pond 100 feet deep. And in New Zealand about two million years ago, volcanic ash flows—seething froths of ash and pumice—buried whole mountains beneath a steaming blanket 70 miles in diameter.

Though such cataclysms shaped parts of every continent, understanding of them is meager; they are not readily explained by plate tectonics and scientists have not witnessed actual eruptions. But the evidence of ancient volcanic deposits is sobering.

Flood basalts apparently are generated atop the upper mantle. When tension opens fissures in the crust, the fluid magma spurts directly to the surface. The sheer volume of an eruption dwarfs all other volcanic activity: A week-long flow can release 360 cubic miles of lava, 10 times the volume of Washington's 14,400-foot Mount Rainier.

Like flood basalts, major ash flows usually are unrelated to volcanic peaks—though small ones are common components of ordinary summit eruptions. Major flows occur when a line or ring of fissures develops over a reservoir of silicic magma and the magma shoots to the surface, depositing up to 250 cubic miles of sandy ash in vast beds hundreds of feet deep. The result is a veritable moonscape—which is why U.S. astronauts trained at an Alaska ash flow, the Valley of Ten Thousand Smokes.

Both ash flows and flood basalts are rare geological events, but to volcanologists they remain an abiding concern. "Even though there have been no historic eruptions comparable to those before recorded human history," a standard textbook notes, "sooner or later they must recur."

FLOOD BASALT

Extremely fluid magma suddenly spurts to the surface through a line of hundreds of offset dikes, each one as much as 15 miles long and 50 feet wide. The lava from such individual fissures, about five cubic miles per day, is so hot and runny that it speeds down the slightest slope at nearly 10 miles an hour, creating a lava sheet as much as 100 miles wide. Over the millennia, such eruptions can create a 300,000-square-mile lava plateau nearly a mile thick.

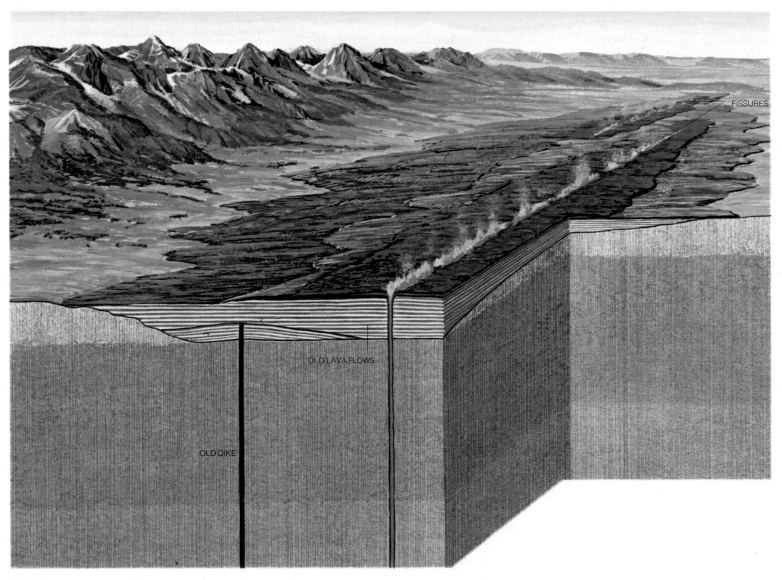

FISSURES

OLD LAVA FLOWS

OLD DIKE

CINDER CONES

RING FRACTURES

ASH FLOW

MAGMA CHAMBER

ASH FLOW

Barely a mile beneath the earth's surface, a huge
magma reservoir gradually undermines and domes
the crust. When the roof of the reservoir breaks,
magma immediately erupts in a tremendous
Plinian explosion, which creates a ring of fractures.
The expanding gases drive a turbulent, ground-
hugging froth of pumice and ash out from the ring
fracture, obliterating the entire landscape; the roof
subsequently collapses to form a caldera.

Chapter 3

THE RISE OF MODERN VOLCANOLOGY

James Hutton and the 18th Century French geologists who founded the science of volcanology envisioned the volcano as a vent in the earth connecting its vast subterranean causes with its manifold surface effects. Through their wide-ranging field trips, arduous observations and inspired deductions, they managed to lift the veils of mystery from many of the volcano's manifestations and sketched, in skeletal form, a global system of crustal formation in which the volcano played a role that was not only spectacular, but fundamental.

Yet for all the solutions that they had found, numerous mysteries remained to bedevil them and to forestall a widely acceptable explanation of the workings of an ever-changing earth. As the 18th Century ended, fitting together the many pieces of the colossal puzzle awaited the invention of sophisticated instruments that were capable of peering deep within the earth. Even more important, the investigators themselves had to break through a rigid mind-set before they could take the next step forward.

The preeminent expert of the time, James Hutton, held up to ridicule the idea that anything could be learned about volcanoes in the laboratory. Yet the most elusive mystery of volcanism was the nature of the molten material far below ground that was increasingly becoming recognized as the source of much of the earth's surface. There was, of course, no way to examine this material in its fiery caldrons, and few of the early investigators had even managed to observe it in the form of lava during a volcanic eruption. To a scientist, then, the only alternative was to attempt the simulation in the laboratory of conditions that he could not observe elsewhere.

Hutton, alas, thought this profitless. In his *Theory of the Earth,* he warned against "superficial" men who "think they know those regions of the earth which can never be seen, and who judge the great operations of the mineral kingdom from having kindled a fire and looked into the bottom of a little crucible." Even as he wrote, one of his closest colleagues was setting up an experiment in a "little crucible" that would accomplish one of the most dramatic advances in the history of volcanology.

Sir James Hall, a Scotsman of wealth and leisure, had immersed himself in the investigation of volcanic processes at an early age. He was no doubt influenced by the fact that his father had been a close friend of Hutton's, and the youth probably listened in fascination to their discussions. Hall avidly pursued studies in chemistry and geology, investigated the volcanoes of Italy, Sicily and the Lipari Islands, and became an advocate of the new chemical theories of his friend, the French chemist Antoine Lavoisier. The scientific community was in

A U.S. Geological Survey drilling rig bores into the crust of a lava lake created by the eruption of Kilauea Iki in Hawaii. Beginning in the 1800s, studies of the chemical and physical properties of lava—and the subterranean material from which it originated—yielded a progressively larger picture of the role of volcanoes in shaping the earth's crust.

an uproar over Lavoisier's suggestion that all elements could exist in solid, liquid or gaseous states—and his discovery of oxygen and its role in combustion and other chemical reactions.

After inheriting Dunglass, the family's great estate located among the craggy cliffs of East Lothian, near Edinburgh, Hall set up a well-equipped laboratory. And there, beginning in 1789 he committed himself, despite Hutton's contempt for such experimentation, to testing some of the great man's theories.

A 1776 scientific paper relating a curious incident at the Leith glassworks not far from Dunglass had prompted Hall to begin his experiments. An enormous lump of raw green glass—made by heating a mixture of beach sand and a few other materials—had inadvertently been cooled at an extremely slow rate by the glassmakers. To their astonishment, during the cooling process it somehow lost all the properties of glass and was transformed into a white, opaque rock composed of large crystals. When a piece of this rock was re-melted and cooled rapidly, it again became a lump of translucent green glass. The shrewd laird of Dunglass was enthralled.

Hutton had said that all rock was part of a process that began and ended in a molten state far below the surface. One of the strongest objections to his theory was based on the argument that since rocks lost their crystal structures when melted, such obviously crystalline rocks as granite and basalt could not possibly ever have been molten. Hutton himself had been at a loss for an explanation of this seeming contradiction.

Hall now suspected that a difference in the rate of cooling might produce two entirely different kinds of rock from the same molten material. To test his hunch, he gathered samples of whinstone—the local name for basalt—and melted them at a nearby iron foundry. When he cooled them rapidly they turned into glass. But when he cooled them slowly over a period of several hours, he was delighted to discover that they returned to a rocky substance very similar to their original state. In later experiments Hall was able to control the size of the crystals formed by varying the rate of cooling; the slower the melt was cooled, the larger the crystals that were formed. He had discovered, in the laboratory that Hutton so disdained, a basic axiom of geology that would have broad ramifications for volcanologists.

Hall went on to put another important postulate of the Huttonian theory to the test in his crucible. Hutton had argued that rock like limestone and marble was formed deep inside the earth by the combination of great heat and pressure acting upon the residue of sea shells deposited on the ocean floor. This process was a cornerstone of Hutton's theory of a cycle of rock formation, but when limestone was heated experimentally, it simply broke down into its chemical components of calcium oxide and carbon dioxide. Hall reasoned that if Hutton was right, it must be the great pressure of the overlying earth that held the two substances together throughout the molten stage and allowed them to form new rock.

To test this hypothesis, Hall conducted an exhaustive series of experiments. His basic procedure was to place some ordinary chalk—chemically identical to limestone, only much softer—inside a gun barrel whose open end was sealed with a plug. He lowered the gun barrel into a furnace and with a complex mechanical apparatus applied 900 pounds of weight to the plug—enough to duplicate inside the gun barrel the pressure that would be found 3,000 feet below sea level. Hall then fired the furnace until the gun barrel reached a temperature of around 1,800° F. The astounding result: a chunk of white marble.

Under pressure, the carbon dioxide and calcium oxide had remained bonded to make a new and vastly harder rock that could not possibly be formed under any amount of heat at sea-level pressure. Thus, Hall had demonstrated in the laboratory that a variety of rocks and minerals might be formed from the same

With this crude apparatus, 18th Century geologist Sir James Hall proved that heat and pressure could effect a metamorphosis of rock from one state to another. Hall subjected a tube-shaped container filled with chalk to 1,800° F. temperatures generated by a furnace *(bottom left)* and to heavy weight, the pressure of which could be varied by adding counterweights to a bucket *(right)* at the end of a control arm. Eventually, he succeeded in transforming the crumbly chalk into marble.

material by changing three purely mechanical factors: the amount of pressure, the temperature and the rate of cooling *(page 85)*.

Thanks to Hall, Hutton's theory of a dynamic earth, in which a subterranean heat source operated in conjunction with the steady erosive forces of the atmosphere to form most of the rocks of the earth's crust, had not only survived the century, but had been expanded and qualified. With increasing detail, scientists were developing the concept of a moving crust laced with seams and pockets of molten rock that hardened under different circumstances into different forms. These rocks in turn sank into the regions of great heat and became molten again. The process was cyclical, orderly and without end.

But volcanoes at first glance exhibited none of these characteristics. On the contrary, they were unpredictable, chaotic and demonstrably transitory. The next major step in incorporating the frightful paroxysms of the volcano into the vast harmony of Hutton's global system came a quarter of a century after Hall's experiments. And it was taken by a man who, like Hall, sought his answers in the nature of earth's molten interior.

George Julius Poulett Scrope was the picture of an English gentleman, a graduate of Harrow, Oxford and Cambridge and a member of the British Parliament. Although of retiring personality on social occasions, he was a fervent espouser of causes and authored numerous tracts on social problems and politics, earning the nickname of Pamphlet Scrope. But his real passion was volcanoes—and why not? While traveling in Europe as a young man, Scrope had witnessed a series of minor eruptions at Vesuvius and had later visited Etna in Sicily and Stromboli in the Lipari Islands. In 1825 he published his first book, entitled *Considerations on Volcanoes,* in which he outlined the revolutionary conclusion that "the main agent in all these stupendous phenomena consists unquestionably in the expansive forces of some elastic aëriform fluid"—in short, gas—"struggling to escape from the interior of a subterranean body of lava."

Scrope went on to make extensive contributions to the science of geology,

A mighty column of dense ash billows from Krakatoa, located in the straits of Java, shortly before its extraordinary eruption in 1883. The gigantic blast, which resulted in the deaths of more than 36,000 people, thrust the world into the era of modern volcanology: Scores of scientists spent years studying the eruption's every aspect.

but his identification of gas as a key driving force of volcanic eruptions was his greatest triumph. And of all the gases that might be emitted during eruptions, Scrope had little doubt that ordinary water vapor was the most important. On many occasions he had observed clouds of steam billowing from lava during an eruption. His theory was that deep within the earth great quantities of water in its liquid state were held in solution in the molten rock. This water-rich molten material—for which Hall borrowed a term from chemistry, "magma," meaning a pasty substance—pressed up against the overlying strata, rising slowly toward the surface through fractures and crevices. As it rose, the pressure upon it diminished and the water separated from the magma as vapor.

Every physics student understood that water expanded when it was transformed into vapor, and the tightly packed subsurface strata could provide scant room for this inexorable expansion. An enormous tension resulted and the magma, with its escort of expanding water vapor, rose to the surface and erupted into the atmosphere.

It was the first systematic explanation of how volcanoes erupt. Other scientists ignored it at first, but Scrope, undaunted, continued his investigations as his Parliamentary duties permitted and waited for the world to catch up. Even-

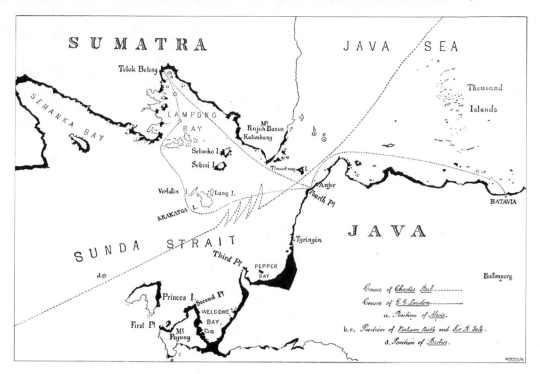

Dark areas on this 19th Century chart mark the coastal regions of Sumatra and Java that were submerged by enormous seismic sea waves generated during the paroxysmal eruption of Krakatoa. The position and course of ships that observed the cataclysm also appear on the chart.

tually it did, and when he died in 1876 few of his colleagues cared to argue with Scrope's basic premises.

Although an accurate, if simplified, explanation of how volcanoes worked had now been achieved, no scientist had yet had the chance to test the theory against direct observations of an eruption. Nor had scientists been able to apply their increasingly sophisticated analytical methods to an active volcano. But in August of 1883 the opportunity arrived with a vengeance.

For three months the people of Batavia had been intrigued by a series of minor rumblings and puffs of ash from a tiny, mountainous island in the Sunda Strait, the channel between Java and Sumatra that linked the Indian Ocean and the Java Sea. At 1 o'clock on the afternoon of August 26 their interest was transformed into awe as the island—known as Krakatoa—began to explode in one of the most stupendous eruptions of all time. Explosion followed upon explosion in ever-increasing intensity. Within one hour a black cloud 17 miles high loomed over the Sunda Strait. At 5 p.m. the first of a series of seismic sea waves, presumably caused by undersea earthquakes accompanying the eruption, battered the coasts of Java and Sumatra. All through the night the deafening explosions continued. "The ear-drums of over half my crew have been shattered," wrote the captain of a British vessel 25 miles from the island.

Another British captain, W. J. Watson of the *Charles Bal,* logged the details of a nightmarish journey past Krakatoa that night. Amid a hail of hot pumice stones, his terrified crew labored to shovel overboard the accumulations of ash, wafted by choking sulfurous winds, that blanketed the vessel deep enough to threaten its stability. Meanwhile, as bolts of lightning leaped back and forth between the island and the sky, an eerie glow enveloped the ship's yardarms and pinkish flames flickered in the rigging. The phenomenon was known as St. Elmo's fire, and would later be explained as the result of an atmosphere supercharged with static electricity.

Shortly before 10 o'clock on the morning of the 27th, a strange stillness fell over the area. For a moment the tortured sailors and islanders thought that their ordeal was over, but, in fact, everything up to that point had been merely a prelude to what was to follow. At two minutes after ten, as if some awful mechanism deep inside the volcano had snapped, the entire island of Krakatoa blew up. In one titanic explosion, a column of rock and fire blasted up into the sky, rising out of sight through the ash-laden atmosphere to a height estimated to have been 50 miles. In a few seconds, the bulk of the 2,600-foot-high mountain was obliterated.

At the same time, a seismic sea wave many times larger than the earlier ones rushed outward from the island and minutes later slammed into the surrounding shores with horrifying effect. At Merak, near the northwestern tip of Java, the height of this black wall of water reached 130 feet. The wave curled over the town, dropped with a thunderous clap and, when it receded, left nothing to indicate that man had ever made his home there. More monstrous waves followed, nine in all. When the waters finally quieted, 36,000 residents of the coastal towns had been annihilated.

The next day the skies began to clear over Krakatoa, and Captain T. H. Lindeman of the steamer *Gouverneur-Generaal Loudon* sailed in close to the Java coast on his way to Batavia. "Everywhere the same gray and gloomy color prevailed," he reported. "The villages and trees had disappeared; we could not even see any ruins, for the waves had demolished and swallowed up the inhabitants, their homes and their plantations. This was truly a scene of the Last Judgment."

Three weeks after the great explosion, the Dutch government appointed a committee led by R. D. M. Verbeek, a mining engineer and geologist, to investigate the causes of the eruption. On October 15, the committee landed on the still-smoldering remnants of the island to begin the task of measurement and interpretation. While his cartographer mapped the new coastlines, the shattered island formations and the changed contours of the ocean floor, Verbeek collected samples of ejecta—the ash and pumice that had been hurled from the volcano. When he analyzed the material later in his home laboratory, he found that the ejecta was not composed of the old rock that had formed the peak of the now-vanished volcano as had been supposed, but was newly solidified magma from deep within the earth.

Verbeek's finding posed a thorny question: If the old cone had not been blasted into the air, then what had happened to it? In addition, and just as mystifying, the soundings taken of the surrounding seabed indicated that there had been only minor earthquake disturbances at the time of the volcanic eruption—nothing large enough to account for the generation of the massive killer waves.

What must have happened, Verbeek reasoned, was that when Krakatoa erupted through the old cone it ejected the contents of an enormous shallow magma chamber that had underlain the volcano. With the immense reservoir empty, the remaining geological structures could no longer support the weight of the volcano and the entire cone had collapsed into the cavity vacated by the magma. Thus the missing mountain now lay submerged under the waters of the Sunda Strait and a bowl-like depression, known as a caldera, was all that was left.

The collapse of so gigantic a portion of the earth, Verbeek thought, must have been responsible for the repercussions in the surrounding water. Crewmen aboard ships near the island had reported a sudden current tugging them toward the volcano shortly after the great blast and just before the horrendous wave. Verbeek speculated that the first movement may have been the result of water pouring in to take the place of the ejected magma. In that case the chamber might have been partially full of sea water when the island collapsed and the falling rock might have suddenly squeezed the water back out into the sea, spawning the mammoth wave. Verbeek was careful not to go too far out on this theoretical limb, and offered his explanation only as a possibility.

With a basic knowledge of earth structures, a rudimentary laboratory for chemical analysis and a faculty for simple logic—albeit on rather a grand

Dust particles from the eruption of Krakatoa color the upper atmosphere in these crayon sketches by a contemporary artist of an English sunset and its afterglow. The dust, which reflected light, drifted around the globe for months, and contributed significantly to knowledge of atmospheric circulation.

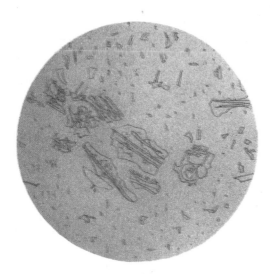

Under a microscope, the ash particles ejected by Krakatoa are visible as irregular pieces of glassy lava. Volcanologists learned that the particles, resembling bubble fragments, did in fact result from the explosion of frothy, gas-saturated magma.

scale—geologist Verbeek had reconstructed the chronology of a cataclysm and found order at the heart of chaos. He had learned his lessons from the island itself—but Krakatoa had more knowledge to impart to avid scientists around the world.

In the year following the eruption the British Royal Society's Krakatoa Committee collected hundreds of journals, notebooks, logs and memoirs from around the globe recounting unusual phenomena encountered in the months after Krakatoa's eruption. The committee carefully reviewed the correspondence and eventually published a 500-page report detailing for the first time the effect of a major eruption on the rest of the world. Some aspects of the eruption were investigated in exhaustive detail by subgroups within the committee. One of the groups, led by the eminent physicist Rollo Russell, concentrated on the ash particles ejected into the atmosphere. From reports sent to the committee by observers, Russell tracked the path of the ash cloud across the face of the planet and determined that it had circled the globe in two weeks—and then had gone on to make a second complete circuit. After that it spread out to the north and south and gradually dissipated.

Samples of Krakatoa's ash uncontaminated by surface dust had been collected from the deck of the British trading vessel *Arabella,* which had been 1,000 miles to the west of the volcano when the cloud had passed overhead. Russell weighed the particles, measured them, studied their shape and analyzed their chemical composition, and he was able to confirm what volcanologists had suspected for a long time: Volcanic ash is not really ash at all. Under a laboratory microscope the particles from Krakatoa turned out to be tiny irregular bits of glassy lava. Each one was slightly concave, as if it had been broken from a minute glass bubble.

The committee's explanation, based on Russell's analysis and on earlier studies undertaken by other scientists, was that some of the magma in the throat of the volcano had been riddled with bubbles of gas. When the volcano erupted, this gas-laden magma hardened in the form of "glass foam" made up of millions of bubbles that were blown apart by the force of the explosion or by the sudden change in pressure as they rose in the atmosphere. The Krakatoa Committee determined that, once airborne, heavier particles such as pumice fell to earth first, but tons upon tons of the smaller glass fragments continued to float in the stratosphere for months, causing the sun and the moon to appear bluish or green all over the world.

Decades later scientists would suggest that a far greater portion of the ash particles than had been thought settled out of the atmosphere in the first month following the eruption, and that the long-lasting atmospheric effects were the result of a chemical reaction that took place at great altitude between atmospheric ozone and sulfur dioxide in the ash. Nevertheless, Russell's analysis of the ash and its interference with the light entering the earth's atmosphere was essentially correct.

Contrary to James Hutton's expectations, the laboratory had yielded a bountiful harvest. The studies of Krakatoa inundated the practitioners of volcanology with volumes of information about the mechanics of volcanoes. Furthermore, the colossal impact of Krakatoa entranced a world that was already in the grip of the scientific fervor of the 19th Century, and weighed the scales heavily on the side of those who saw the volcano as a pervasive element in a global system. Now the science of volcanology needed investigators who were familiar with the new theories and methods and who could apply them in the field to the analysis of new eruptions.

Of the men who advanced volcanology into the 20th Century, none was more unrelenting, perspicacious or heroic in his efforts than a frail, soft-spoken American named Frank Alvord Perret. As a 16-year-old studying physics at the

Brooklyn Polytechnic Institute, Perret had been transfixed by the sight of the sun "burnished like a copper ball" by the eruption of Krakatoa half a world away. It was an intense but momentary fascination, and Perret's interest in volcanoes remained dormant as he pursued his studies in physics and engineering with brilliant results. He was impatient for a practical application of what he had learned, however, and left without graduating to take a job in Thomas Edison's East Side laboratory.

Perret proved to be as exceptional a technician as he had been a student, and he soon became Edison's personal assistant. But not long after, the still-restless Perret struck out on his own and started a small firm in Springfield, Massachusetts, the Elektron Manufacturing Company. He developed and marketed an efficient low-speed electric motor for powering elevators, which quickly swept the market. By 1900, at the age of 33, Perret had achieved stunning success in both business and technology. But he did not have long to enjoy it.

Soon after, Perret suffered a totally incapacitating nervous breakdown. It took him several years to recover, and while he was convalescing he read of the devastating eruption of Mount Pelée. Like many others, Perret stood in awe of the volcano's capricious and mysterious eminence, but like only a very few he wondered if he might penetrate its mystery and make sense of its apparent capriciousness. He decided, then and there, to make the study of volcanoes his life's work.

With no experience or training in geology, let alone volcanology, Frank Perret offered his services without pay to Raffaele Vittorio Matteucci, director of an observatory on Italy's Mount Vesuvius. In 1904, Perret began learning about volcanoes with the same intensity he had applied to his earlier studies, inventions and business career. When Vesuvius erupted in 1906, Perret's keen observations and natural scientific ability made his report on the event a classic of volcanology. And its language revealed his reverence for the subject of his studies: "No words can describe the majesty of its unfolding, the utter absence of anything resembling effort, and the all-sufficient power to perform the allotted task and to do it majestically. Each rapid impulse was the crest of something deep and powerful and uniform which bore it, and the unhurried modulation of its rhythmic beats sets this eruption in rank of things which are mighty, grave and great."

Perret went on to study Kilauea in the Hawaiian Islands and Sakurajima in Japan, and to visit countless other volcanoes around the world. He never married or kept a home other than the tents, shacks and makeshift observatories that he threw up on the slaggy slopes of active volcanoes. Shortly after the start of any major eruption, other volcanologists could expect to see him arrive, an erect little figure with a shock of prematurely white hair and a carefully clipped Vandyke beard. After mannerly greetings, Perret would set to work on the volcano with fervent abandon, dashing from fumarole to lava flow to install his crude monitoring devices and record his observations. When his strength gave out, as it frequently did, he would hire porters to carry him about the mountain on their backs.

His experience with Edison and his background in electronics enabled him to design and construct his own instruments. His favorite invention was a simple contact microphone—a slightly modified receiver from an ordinary telephone, mounted in an old Sterno can that was then rigged inside an empty gasoline can and buried six feet deep in the side of the volcano. Copper wires were run from the can to Perret's station and any movement of the earth—even the slight vibration of footsteps in the vicinity of the can—could be monitored at the receiving end of the wires. He also devised a thermometer for taking the temperature of lava, a gas detector and a seismometer to measure the shudderings of the volcano.

In 1929, news that Mount Pelée on Martinique was threatening again

The Volcano That Grew in a Mexican Cornfield

When he went out to till his cornfield on February 20, 1943, Mexican farmer Dionisio Pulido was startled to discover that an 80-foot-long crack had opened in the land during the night. As Pulido and his family looked on in awe, ash and red-hot stones spewed from the fissure. The Pulidos were witnessing a remarkable geologic event— the birth of a volcano.

Pulido raced to the nearby village of Paricutín to report the strange happenings. Soon, scores of geologists were swarming around the site in southwestern Mexico. The volcano, which came to be known as Paricutín, grew with astonishing speed. It was 33 feet high by the next morning and 550 feet high by the end of the first week. The volcano topped 1,000 feet within a year, as vast quantities of ash covered the countryside for 20 miles around. It then rose more slowly to an eventual height of 1,353 feet, while exuding enormous quantities of lava.

Abruptly, nine years and 12 days after its dramatic birth, Paricutín fell silent. Dionisio Pulido had lost his cornfield, and 4,500 people in two villages had lost their homes, but science had gained rare insight into the growth of a volcano.

A church steeple marks the site of the village of San Juan Parangaricutiro, a victim of the eruption of Paricutín, which puffs ash five miles away. The 4,000 residents were safely evacuated as the lava flow advanced through the streets in June 1944.

Like a typical cinder cone volcano, Paricutín grew rapidly, as shown in the diagram at left, and died young. In its nine active years, the volcano erupted some 3.6 billion metric tons of ejecta and lava.

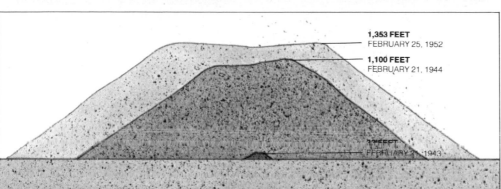

1,353 FEET
FEBRUARY 25, 1952

1,100 FEET
FEBRUARY 21, 1944

FEBRUARY 21, 1943

brought Perret to the island in a matter of days. He found the citizens of the island frantic at the thought of a reappearance of *nuées ardentes* like those that had obliterated the town of St. Pierre and punished the island in 1902. Plans were being made to abandon the island and move the entire population to French Guiana. Perret asked for a week to examine the mountain.

He plotted a curve of the volcano's eruptive cycle, and decided that it had passed its most dangerous stage. It would harm no one, he announced, and the lava flows and *nuées ardentes* that were still to come would follow the old, mostly uninhabited, path to the sea—through the ruins of St. Pierre. His report was immediately printed across the front page of the Fort-de-France newspaper, to the immense relief of the island's residents.

Although volcanologists of later years would learn that any volcano might suddenly defy the most accurately assembled forecast, Perret's reading of Mount Pelée's temperament proved to be right. The dome expanded threateningly and occasional *nuées* seethed from the mountain's crown and rushed down the slopes. But the mountain did not blow up, and the *nuées* passed harmlessly into the sea along well-worn paths, never coming close to any inhabited areas. With the exception, that is, of Perret's field station.

Grateful for his reassurance, the citizens of Martinique built Perret a one-room wood-frame observatory on a spur of the mountain close to the route that the glowing avalanches took on their way to the sea. Perret was enchanted with his perch: "Lighted at night by the crater glow, within touch of the avalanche course, this spot afforded opportunity for that close-range investigation of volcanism which I deemed indispensable." Other geologists visited him there, and the multimillionaire American financier Vincent Astor once climbed to the station with a party of guests from his yacht to render his respects to the famed volcanologist.

On the night of April 15, 1930, Perret was paid a much less cordial visit. Throughout the day, he had been observing the slow growth in the volcano's dome of a towering spine of rock similar to the one that had appeared in 1902. "Just at the close of the swiftly passing tropical twilight," he recalled, "in the dead calm between day and night winds, an unusual sound brought me to my cabin door." The great obelisk had snapped off at the base, leaving a rent in the dome. Through this scar suddenly sprang the smoking black ash of a *nuée ardente*. And at the same moment, another *nuée* began to rise from a smaller crater just to the east of Perret's camp. Both avalanches rushed down the slopes directly toward him.

"My first thought was of instant flight," he recalled, but after a moment's reflection he realized that his best chance was to stay where he was and hope that he was high enough on the ridge so that the main thrusts of the *nuées* would miss him. In mortal danger of being either incinerated or suffocated as the cloud passed, Perret hastily chinked the cracks around his doors and windows and braced for the onslaught. "I recall a sense of utter isolation; awe in the face of overwhelming forces of nature so indifferent to my feeble self."

Even in such peril, Perret could not resist cracking the rear door of the station to peer out. An awesome spectacle confronted him: "Two pillars of cloud a thousand feet in height, apparently gaining in speed every instant and headed straight for my shelter. As I darted within, the blast was upon me—not a terrific shock as the reader might think, but swirling gusts of ash-laden wind, bringing a pall of darkness that might indeed be felt. The dusty air entering every crevice of the shack was hot but not scorching. I felt the gases burning and parching my throat and then came a feeling of weakness." Just in time for him, the *nuées* passed, roaring by on either side, and Perret hung a lighted lantern in the doorway of the station to show the police in St. Pierre that he was alive and unhurt.

He later said that his only regret was in not having a vacuum tube handy to collect samples of the gases as the clouds passed. His subsequent paper on Mount Pelée offered a rich trove of observations of the nature of glowing avalanches. Nothing about volcanoes fascinated Perret more than the *nuée ardente*. It was the embodiment of volcanism at its most amazing and most terrible. Unlike lava or airborne ejecta, which were pushed from below by the force of expanding gas, the *nuées,* he thought, bore within themselves a substantial part of their means of propulsion. Perret believed—and most volcanologists today agree—that much of the explosive gas of a *nuée* was held in suspension in the magma; as the bubbling mixture rose out of the throat of the volcano and began flowing down the side of the cone, the gases were released, causing the bubbles to expand. The whole, in Perret's words, was "lifted by its own bootstraps" and was propelled both by the force of gravity and the expansive forces of the gas within it.

By the time of his death in 1940, Perret's contributions to volcanology had brought him many honors: Among other things, he had been made a knight of the French Legion of Honor and a knight of the Italian Crown. But the tribute that probably would have delighted him above all others was posthumous. The islanders of Martinique declared him an honorary citizen and erected a statue of him in the rebuilt city of St. Pierre.

American volcanologist Frank A. Perret listens through a microphone of his own invention to subterranean rumblings of a volcano near Pozzuoli, Italy, in the early 1900s. By using such equipment, Perret was able to detect changes in the pitch of the sounds within volcanoes, which, as he correctly deduced, frequently foretold an eruption.

Science, said the French mathematician Jules Henri Poincaré, is built up with facts, as a house is with stones. Perret, by dint of his indefatigable volcano watching, gathered more facts and observations relating to volcanoes than any other scientist of his day. But the second half of Poincaré's aphorism asserts that a collection of facts is no more a science than a heap of stones is a house. Facts and observations demand theories, systems and designs to give them coherence.

As the 20th Century reached its midpoint, advocates of the existing theories of volcanism were increasingly hard-pressed to explain what Perret and his colleagues had observed. For while Perret had documented significant similarities that fit the accepted theoretical system, he had also found important differences that posed ever more serious challenges to the old way of thinking.

Perret himself studied volcanoes in Hawaii and found them to be essentially different from his more familiar haunts of Vesuvius and Mount Pelée; the Hawaiian eruptions were far gentler, their lava flows more copious. And he undoubtedly knew something of the even more singular behavior of volcanoes in Iceland.

Iceland showed geologists an entirely different face of volcanism. Its 40,000-square-mile land mass—composed almost completely of black basalt tufted here and there with subarctic pastures and scrub conifers—was lacerated with large, generally parallel fissures, as if the island had somehow been slashed by a great earth-cleaving knife. Many of the Icelandic volcanoes erupted, not from the usual mountaintop, but from a newly created, or sometimes an existing, fissure. Although they were at a loss to explain it, geologists had been aware of the nature of Iceland's volcanoes ever since the dramatic eruption of Mount Laki in 1783.

Early in June of that year a series of fissures 15 miles long had suddenly yawned open near the southern coast of Iceland. After some initial explosive overtures accompanied by voluminous ash clouds, basaltic lava had begun to flood from the rifts and had continued to flow all summer long in a series of spasmodic eruptions from new fissures that opened up in the same area. By August an area of 226 square miles had been paved over by new rock. Mount Laki's eruption had ended in February of 1784, but by then the atmosphere around the island had been darkened by a bluish sulfuric haze that poisoned crops and killed more than half the livestock on the island. Worse yet, the haze was so blinding that the ordinarily intrepid Icelandic fishermen had found it impossible to put to sea. One fifth of the island's 49,000 people died of famine that winter.

Volcanologists in the first half of the 20th Century were collecting evidence of many other nonexplosive floods of lava. One such flood 100 million years ago had created the 200,000-square-mile Deccan Plateau of northwestern India; another around 25 million years ago had left the 88,000-square-mile Columbia River Plateau in the northwestern United States. A spectacular fissure eruption of Hekla volcano in Iceland during 1947 provided an opportunity for concentrated research and made it impossible for the theorists to evade any longer the resulting question: Why did the Icelandic volcanoes behave so differently from the Mediterranean, and the Mediterranean from the Hawaiian? They found the key to the answer in viscosity.

Viscosity may be defined as the internal friction of a fluid. Highly viscous fluids, like tar, have great internal friction that causes them to flow very slowly. Less viscous fluids, like water, flow easily because the individual particles within them move past one another with very little friction. The most abundant component of magma was silica. Geologists knew that more than 50 per cent of the mass of the earth's crust is composed of silica—it is the basic building block of most rock and all magma. And continuing research into magma chemistry yielded the conclusion that the amount of silica in magma generally determined its viscosity: The higher the silica content, the thicker the magma.

When silica made up 70 per cent or more of the mixture, the resulting magma was thick and pasty in consistency; because the rock that formed from it contained large amounts of feldspar and silica, it was called felsic magma. When magma contained no more than 50 per cent silica, it was less viscous and more watery in character; it was called mafic magma for the magnesium and iron, or ferrous, content of the minerals formed from it. Viscosity could also be affected by changes in temperature, or by the presence in the magma of gases or solid objects, such as fragments broken from surrounding rock or large crystals.

This understanding of the varying viscosity of magma led in turn to an explanation of why some volcanoes, notably the Hawaiian and the older Mediterranean examples, blew enormous quantities of gas into the air without exploding in the cataclysmic convulsions of a Krakatoa or a Mount Pelée. Some, like Stromboli in the Lipari Islands, bubbled and sputtered. Others, like Kilauea in Hawaii, just gushed sheets of lava. What these relatively innocent volcanoes had in common was their magma—it was of the low-silica, mafic type. Its viscosity was so light that when the volatile gases separated out of the magma, they were able to rise through it at a steady rate and bubble off into the atmosphere.

On the other hand, explosive volcanoes such as Vesuvius, Tambora, Krakatoa and Mount Pelée shared the characteristic of high-silica, felsic magma, which acted altogether differently. As this ponderous, viscous magma reached the surface, it tended to block the vent of the volcano. It solidified at a much higher temperature than the mafic magma, so that it sometimes formed a scab, or what geologists call a dome, over the mouth of the crater. All of this worked to trap the gas below the surface, allowing it to build up pressure so stupendous that the sides of the mountain would actually swell. Inevitably, at some point the dome burst open and magma—in solid, liquid and semisolid form—mixed with old rock and voluminous quantities of the pent-up gas was blasted into the air.

But even with their new comprehension of the workings of the different types of volcanoes, the scientists could not explain the pattern of worldwide distribution of volcanoes. Of the 600 active volcanoes they had identified, almost all were explosive and existed in narrow belts; one belt, known as the Ring of Fire, described a rough circle around the perimeter of the Pacific Ocean; another stretched across the northern Mediterranean, through Asia Minor and into the Himalayas. And while volcanologists could detail the ways in which the Icelandic and Hawaiian volcanoes were radically different from their eruptive sisters, they could not explain why these two isolated areas exhibited such disparate processes.

The answers came with breathtaking suddenness in the middle of the 1960s. They were the product of a titanic controversy within the scientific community in the tradition of the neptunist-vulcanist dispute of the 18th Century. And when the dust finally settled after a few years, an enlarged framework emerged within which the mysteries of volcanology and all the earth sciences were illuminated as they never had been before; the new view of earth was called the theory of plate tectonics.

The theory described a global system much like the one envisioned by Hutton, but with refinements and enlargements that embraced the discrepancies the older theory had been unable to explain. According to the theory of plate tectonics, the earth's crust was broken into seven major plates, some of which carried continents and all of which were in motion. Their boundaries stretched across the face of the planet in great jagged sweeps like the cracks in the shell of a frozen egg. Their motion was varied, so that in places the plates were grinding past each other, in other sections they were moving away from each other, and in still others they were crunching together. Where they collided, one plate

A Vast Variety of Rock from Nature's Forge

Igneous rocks—named from the Latin word *ignis,* which means "fire"—consist of various combinations of minerals brewed deep within the earth as superheated magma that later solidifies into a rigid mass. There are two main types of igneous rocks: volcanic, which reach the surface of the earth through eruption; and plutonic, after Pluto, the Roman god of the underworld, which are cooled beneath the earth's surface in dikes and sills, and in huge formations known as batholiths.

An almost infinite variety of textures and mineral compositions are found within the two categories of igneous rocks. The rich diversity is caused by variations in the chemical content of magma, the inclusion of older formations that are melted and absorbed by the upwelling molten rock, and differences in the rate of cooling. When magma is rapidly cooled, it forms crystals that are small; slower cooling results in larger, coarser crystals.

Peridotite is the plutonic rock formed deepest within the earth; it cools very slowly and, in consequence, is dark, extremely coarse-grained and lumpy. Because it never reaches the surface in a molten state, peridotite has no volcanic counterpart, but many other rocks appear in both plutonic and volcanic forms.

Basalt and gabbro, for example, are both derived from essentially the same magma; but the volcanic basalt crystallizes faster and hence has a finer texture than its plutonic twin, gabbro. Similarly, andesite, a volcanic rock, is finer-grained than plutonic diorite—though both come from magma consisting of 60 per cent silica. And granite, the root rock beneath many volcanoes whose magma chambers were filled with silica-rich, highly viscous magma, is a rougher, more grainy stone than smooth-surfaced rhyolite, which is the erupted lava cooled from the same magma.

Occasionally, magma with the same composition as rhyolite solidifies so quickly that crystals do not have time to form. The result is obsidian, a beautiful, shiny black volcanic glass that has been treasured for centuries as an item of jewelry.

PLUTONIC IGNEOUS ROCKS

PERIDOTITE

GABBRO

DIORITE

GRANITE

VOLCANIC IGNEOUS ROCKS

BASALT

ANDESITE

RHYOLITE

OBSIDIAN

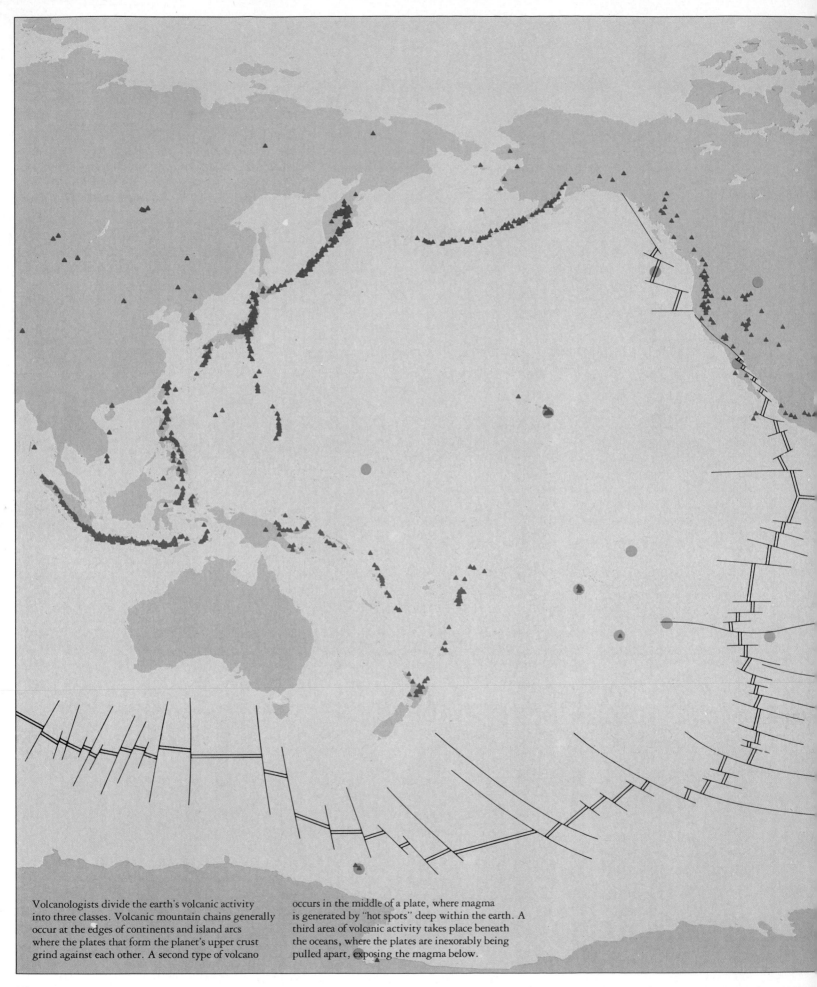

Volcanologists divide the earth's volcanic activity into three classes. Volcanic mountain chains generally occur at the edges of continents and island arcs where the plates that form the planet's upper crust grind against each other. A second type of volcano occurs in the middle of a plate, where magma is generated by "hot spots" deep within the earth. A third area of volcanic activity takes place beneath the oceans, where the plates are inexorably being pulled apart, exposing the magma below.

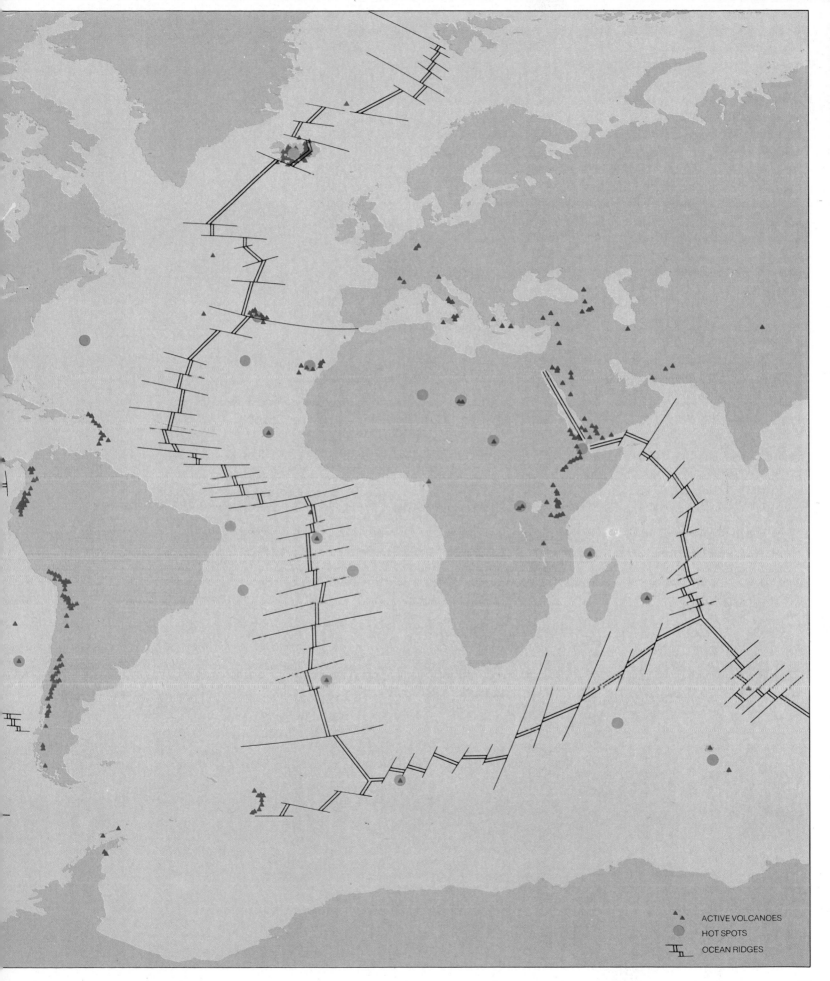

ACTIVE VOLCANOES

HOT SPOTS

OCEAN RIDGES

usually plunged under the other into the molten depths of the earth in an area called a subduction zone.

A map of the subduction zones postulated by the theory of plate tectonics, compared with a map of the world's explosive volcanoes, told the story; they coincided. Apparently the sinking 60-to-100-mile-thick slabs of crust melted as they moved into successively hotter parts of the upper mantle. The magma generated in the process found its way to the surface to form volcanic belts near the subduction zone.

Plate tectonics even provided a basis for explaining the anomaly of Hawaiian volcanoes, which erupted in their mild fashion far from any subduction zone or, for that matter, from any plate boundary. Volcanologists soon postulated a blowtorch-like "hot spot" of molten material boring upward from a fixed position far below the Pacific Plate; as the plate inched northwestward across the hot spot, the volcanoes that formed the Hawaiian Islands blistered upward one after the other in a straight, northwest-southeast line, with the youngest, still-active volcanic islands to the southeast.

But if, as plate tectonics assumed, many of the crustal sections were being massively subducted and consumed, where were they being formed? The answer to that question was on the one hand a critical piece of evidence that clinched the argument on behalf of plate tectonics, and was on the other hand one of the most astounding revelations of the nature of volcanism in the history of science.

Explosive volcanoes have been man's age-old antagonists. Throughout history, they have darkened his skies, buried his cities and energized his mythologies. He, in turn, has mined their mineral riches and defiantly grazed his livestock on their trembling slopes. But in mapping the floors of the world's oceans in the 1950s, scientists realized that these great exploding mountains were only the visible part of the earth's volcanic activity.

Deep beneath the seas, oceanographers found an astounding 40,000-mile-

An ash-laden steam cloud rises from the newborn island of Surtsey, formed near Iceland in 1963 by volcanic eruptions originating on the seabed. For three years the Surtsey eruptions provided spectacular evidence of the prodigious volcanic activity along the 12,000-mile mid-Atlantic rift zone, where two tectonic plates are slowly separating.

long system of midocean ridges, split down their length by volcanic fissures, marking the boundaries of tectonic plates that were moving away from each other. The strange behavior of Iceland's volcanoes was comprehensible as soon as it was understood that here was one of the few places on earth where a midocean ridge could be observed at the surface. Basaltic magma gushed periodically from these long rents in the earth, but the process of eruption was for the most part quiet and steady, like cement being injected into a form. In fact, geologists soon believed that this gray, uniform basaltic magma was, indeed, a kind of global cement that was rising to the surface along the rift zones in enormous quantities to fill in what would otherwise be a widening gap between the parting tectonic plates.

Given the antagonistic properties of fire and water, it would seem likely that when these fissure volcanoes opened up deep beneath the sea, violent disturbances would follow. But that was not the case.

Nowhere is the magnificent and harmonious design of planet earth more evident than at the meeting of raw, red-hot magma and cool, pellucid sea water along the fissures of the midocean rifts. As the hot lava flows from the fissures, the pressure of the surrounding sea is so great that the volatile gases in the magma, which otherwise could cause it to explode in a holocaust of steam and rock, are held in solution. The magma begins to solidify immediately upon contact with the water and breaks off in millions of ingot-like blocks, known as pillow lavas, which pile up alongside the fissures. These are the paving stones of the ocean floor. They slowly migrate across the face of the earth, gradually becoming covered with sediment until, millions of years later, they are finally pulled down again into the earth's internal furnace by the process of subduction. Yet all the while behind them new paving stones are being minted along the rifts in a process—the very genesis of the face of the earth—that goes on ceaselessly in the hushed volcanic factory of the deep sea. Ω

89

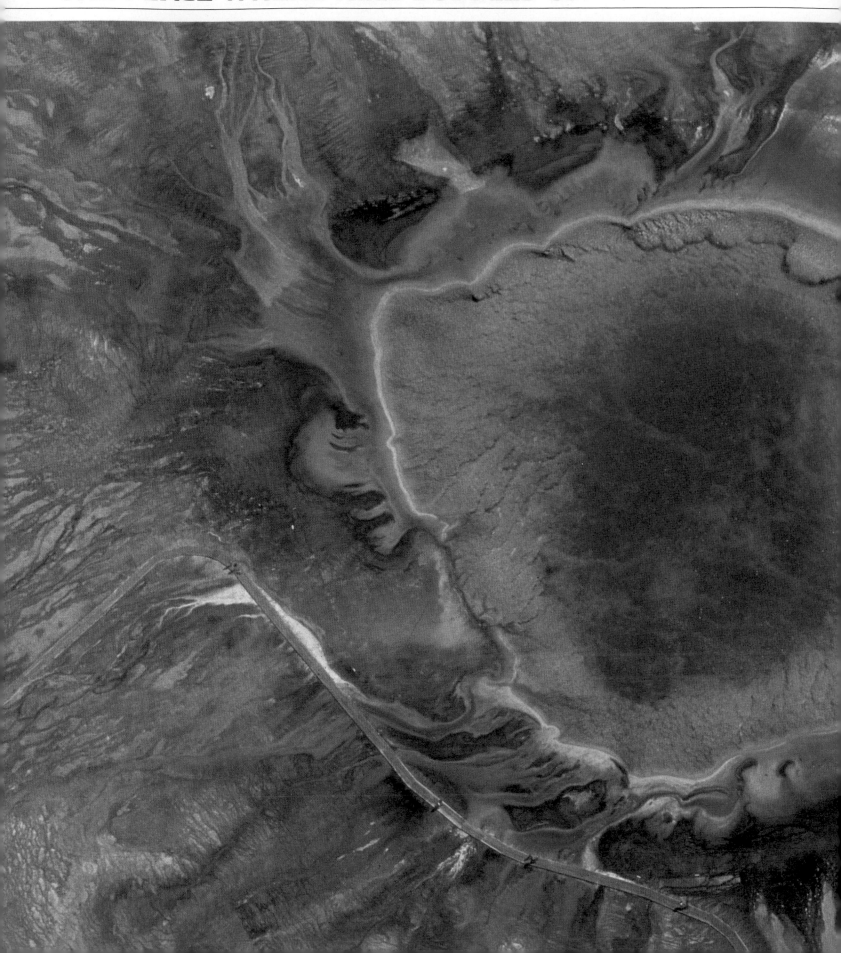

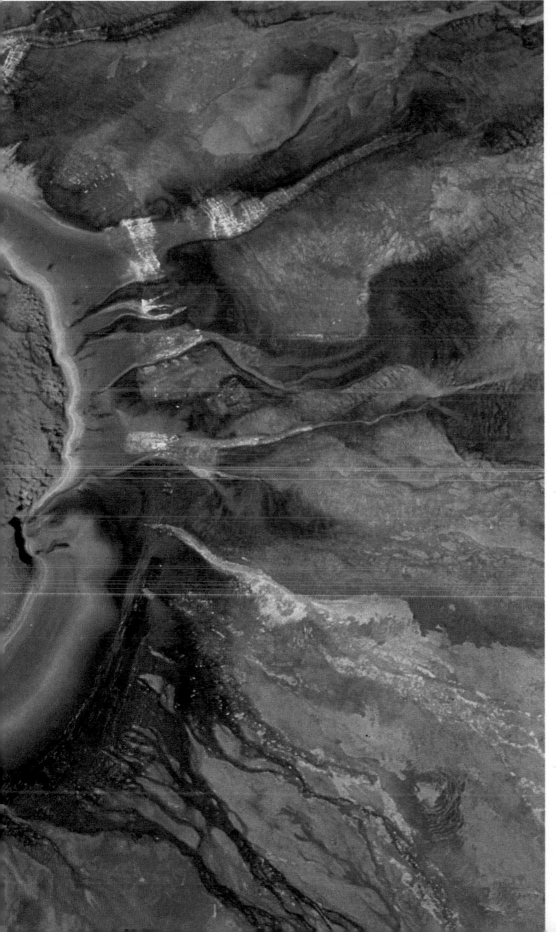

The fur trappers of the early 19th Century who told of finding "the place where hell bubbles up" high in the Rocky Mountains were dismissed as garrulous spinners of tall tales. But their stories of thunderous geysers and craters of scalding mud were soon confirmed by explorers of the Yellowstone plateau. Within a few years the region was attracting visitors from around the world; few remained unawed by its steaming landscape, alive with manifestations of the subterranean meeting of water and volcanic fire.

Although Yellowstone has the greatest concentration of such hydrothermal features, they occur worldwide, and often provide more than spectacular scenery. Unique patterns of plant and animal life arise around hot waters that bubble up year round, even when the surrounding land is blanketed with snow. Human societies, once beset by superstitions about the water's origins, now seek it out. Its many applications range from generating electricity to medical uses of its heat and mineral content.

Nowhere is hydrothermal activity a more common part of daily life than in Iceland, where hundreds of geysers and hot springs well up among the myriad lava flows that have shaped the island. Iceland's earliest settlers in the Ninth Century soon found ways to use their volcanic legacy; laundries were built around hot springs and hot water was used to irrigate the land, protecting crops growing near the Arctic Circle against the frequent summer frosts.

More recently, water has been channeled through insulated pipes to cities, where it heats thousands of homes and warms greenhouses year round. And the technology for generating electricity with hydrothermal steam *(pages 96-97)* holds great promise for a country entirely devoid of fossil fuels.

Like Japan's mineral baths and the spas of Europe, Iceland's hundreds of hydrothermal swimming pools are popular for their soothing warmth. Here the contrast between the beneficial waters and their dangerous source is sharply drawn, as bathers enjoy the products of the same caldron that often overflows in rivers of molten rock, destroying their settlements and ravaging their land.

Blue water wells up from the volcanic depths in the center of Yellowstone's Grand Prismatic Spring, shading through a panoply of colors in the cooler shallows. Different types of algae, each thriving at a different temperature, range from blue-green near the hot center to red-brown in the runoff channels around the edge of the 369-foot-wide pool.

A Giant Boiler in the Ground

FUMAROLE

MUD POT

GEYSER

HOT SPRING

STEAM

COOL WATER

SUPERHEATED WATER

GROUNDWATER

POROUS ROCK

HEATED ROCK

MAGMA CHAMBER

The system that creates geysers and hot springs operates like a giant boiler in the earth, fired by magma, that turns rain into pressurized hot water. Rain water trickles down from the surface through fractures to a layer of porous rock, where it collects like liquid in a sponge. Heat from a magma chamber, usually two or three miles deeper, reaches the permeable layer through the intervening rock by conduction.

Under pressure from the weight of water and rock above it, the water in the permeable layer may reach temperatures of 500 ° F. without boiling. This superheated water is lighter than the cool water that is entering the system and rises back toward the surface, where it may take any of a variety of forms, depending upon the circumstances of its upward journey.

A small stream rising through an unobstructed aperture begins to boil as the pressure drops, and it appears on the surface as a jet of steam from a fumarole. Superheated water that mixes with cool groundwater on the way up does not boil, but surfaces as a hot spring. And some hot springs, choked with mud broken down from the surrounding rock by acid volcanic gases dissolved in the water, become mud pots.

A geyser is the result of a more complex series of events. It begins when superheated water rises into pockets of groundwater that are under enough pressure to prevent boiling. The temperature of the mixing waters rises until a small amount of water boils despite the pressure. The resultant steam, with a volume hundreds of times that of the water from which it was formed, pushes up and out of the pocket, taking some of the water with it and reducing the pressure.

More superheated water then flashes to steam and blasts the remaining groundwater out of the earth in an eruption that may continue for up to several hours. As the eruption subsides, the channel begins to refill with groundwater from above and superheated water from below, and the eruptive cycle begins anew.

A steam-powered spectacle on a regular schedule, Old Faithful geyser spouts 130 feet high in Yellowstone National Park, Wyoming. After gushing steam and hot water for two to five minutes, the geyser is quiet for about 70 minutes.

Subterranean steam splashes mud from a mud pot near Rotorua, New Zealand. The mud is composed of tiny particles etched from the surrounding rock and suspended in hot water. Drying mud from continuous overflows builds a cone around the pot.

A wisp of steam indicates the scalding heat of a spring at Rotorua, New Zealand. Minerals dissolved in the hot water have been deposited on the pool's edge to create a raised lip spotted with green algae.

A foamy cascade of solid rock called travertine covers a hillside at Pamukkale, Turkey. Dissolved by superheated water passing through underground limestone, the rock is redeposited at the surface when the water cools. Impurities in the normally white mineral account for its range of colors.

The Benevolent Waters of Beppu

Eager children find a hot lunch easy to come by in Beppu, where the temperature of roadside springs is high enough to cook an egg. Tourists at many of the city's hotels reduce expenses by cooking their own meals in the ubiquitous spring waters.

The hot springs scattered throughout the volcanic islands of Japan have long been a source of pleasure to both the Japanese and their visitors. The country has a tradition of communal bathing, derived from ancient Buddhist cleansing rituals, that has survived the introduction of hot-water plumbing into private homes. Nearly every town has a public bath, and wherever hot springs rise there are inns or pools where visitors may soak away their cares.

Nowhere in Japan are the waters more important than in Beppu, a city of 146,000 located on the Inland Sea about 500 miles southwest of Tokyo. Beppu's 4,000 hot springs, which attract 12 million tourists each year from Japan and abroad, are the source of the city's livelihood. The springs have been flowing since 867 A.D., when the hydrothermal field 800 feet below Beppu was formed by an eruption of the now-dormant volcano Mount Tsurumi, which looms 4,500 feet above the city.

Beppu's myriad springs have been adapted to a great many uses. The more than 850 lodgings that accommodate the flood of tourists range from traditional inns with small wooden tubs to first-class hotels with huge tiled baths. A zoo uses the waters to heat its animal houses, and tropical plants and flowers thrive in acres of hydrothermally heated greenhouses. Not all of the waters, however, are devoted to serving the tourists. A modern hospital uses the hot mineral springs in rehabilitation programs that attract arthritis and rheumatism patients from all over Japan.

Ever-present vapors wafting over Beppu's roofs mark the springs that bring 10 million gallons of water to the surface daily. In her baskets a woman carries a load of washing from a hot-spring laundry.

Iron oxides impart a crimson color to the scalding waters, and a grim history provides the name of one of Beppu's most famous hot springs—"Bloody-Pond Hell." The springs were at one time the site of frequent suicides, but nowadays sturdy fences keep visitors well away from the hottest areas.

Buddhist statues watch over bathers at Beppu's Jungle Bath, the world's largest hot-spring bath. The 1.6 acres of shallow, interconnected pools wind among plants that thrive in the hot, humid atmosphere.

Electricity Drawn from the Heat of the Earth

The poet Dante fancied that the fumaroles of Tuscany marked the entrance to his Inferno. More worldly attitudes prevailed six centuries later, in 1904, when steam from the fumaroles was piped to a steam engine. A generator turned by the engine produced the world's first geothermal power—electricity drawn from the heat of the earth.

The potential for geothermal power is enormous. It would take 2,000 times the world's supply of coal to produce the heat that exists in the upper six miles of the earth's crust. But most of that heat is stored in dry rock and is difficult to utilize. The first geothermal power plants were therefore built in active hydrothermal areas—New Zealand, Iceland, Japan—where ground-

water and magma provided supplies of superheated water and steam.

The rapidly developing technology, however, is opening many previously inaccessible geothermal fields, so that the potential for exploitation of this relatively clean and nearly inexhaustible energy resource is virtually worldwide in scope.

The world's largest geothermal facility is The Geysers, which sprawls across 15 square miles in California's Mayacamas Mountains, 90 miles north of San Francisco. Opened with a single generating plant in 1960, the project grew in 20 years to include more than 200 steam wells and 15 generating plants with a capacity of 910,000 kilowatts, enough electricity for a city of one million.

Steam rises from the wells and cooling towers of the geothermal generating system in The Geysers' steam field in northern California. Waters from this field once attracted health seekers to a spa nearby.

At The Geysers' geothermal plants, pressurized steam from the earth is piped from drilled wells to a centrifugal separator, where water droplets and debris are removed. The steam is directed against the blades of a turbine, where it drives an electrical generator. The spent steam turns to water, which is pumped to towers where some evaporates. The rest is used to cool generating equipment before being pumped back into the ground. Drilling goes on continuously in the search for more steam.

DRILL RIG

COOLING TOWER

GENERATOR

TURBINE

SEPARATOR

STEAM WELL

PERMEABLE LAYER

ZONE OF INTENSE HEAT

MAGMA CHAMBER

Chapter 4

SHADOWS OVER THE CRADLE OF MAN

By any measure of geologic time, Mount Vesuvius is but an infant among earth features, and as a volcano it is unremarkable in a number of respects. The mountain is scarcely 17,000 years old and stands only 4,200 feet above Italy's Bay of Naples. And yet this relatively minor mountain is the most celebrated of volcanoes. It has been intimately involved with mankind for at least 3,000 years and is surrounded by the largest population—two million people—ever to dwell in the immediate vicinity of an active crater. No other volcano has played so definitive a role in history, or has so dramatized the perils and benefactions that are visited upon those who choose to live along the flanks of an eruptive peak.

Vesuvius is unique in yet another respect. It has failed to prompt the sort of legends, myths and taboos that are a part of the folklore of many other volcanoes. Indeed, Mount Vesuvius was so quiescent during most of the years before it buried Pompeii and Herculaneum in 79 A.D. (and apparently for centuries after that event) that it seems to have been largely ignored by the deities of Greece and Rome and, again, by chroniclers of superstition during the Dark Ages. It did not achieve a full measure of world fame, in fact, until archeologists began uncovering its magnificently preserved lost cities during the 18th and 19th Centuries. Then, when it found renewed life in the same period, geologists began using it as a gigantic laboratory for advancing the young science of volcanology.

Mount Vesuvius, of course, was not the only volcano to cast its shadow over the Mediterranean cradle of civilization. An entire string of active island counterparts—Stromboli, Ischia, Vulcano, Vulcanello, Santorini and Etna—have been intruding on successive Mediterranean civilizations for as long as man can remember. The Phoenicians, the Minoans, the Mycenaeans, the Egyptians and, eventually, the rising peoples of Greece and Rome contributed to the lore of volcanoes as they strove to placate, to understand and, at times, to save themselves from these fire-breathing cones upthrust so inexplicably in their warm blue seas.

More than 150 times in the course of recorded history, one or another of the area's volcanoes has erupted, causing great alarm and inflicting much loss of life and property. But no Mediterranean volcano has exploded with such ferocity or created havoc over so wide an area as did Santorini, which comprised the bulk of the island of Thera in the Aegean Sea when it erupted around 1450 B.C. Scientists agree that it must have been among the most destructive natural catastrophes in the history of the planet.

The present island of Thera, which lies 125 miles from the southern tip of

Looming over Naples, Mount Vesuvius continues to vent billowing clouds of ash weeks after a major eruption in 1944. The volcano has roared to life more than 50 times since 79 A.D., when it buried Pompeii, but after each outburst farmers returned to its slopes to work its mineral-rich soil.

Greece, is a ragged crescent embracing four smaller islands. All are residual fragments of Thera as it existed before the volcano blew away much of the material of its cone and then collapsed into its own crater, forming the deep central harbor, or caldera, that separates the remnants today. Volcanologists calculate that 32 square miles of Santorini disappeared into the air or fell into the sea; they speculate that its thunder traveled to Scandinavia, Asia and Africa, that its shock waves knocked down buildings in Crete and other Aegean islands up to 100 miles distant, and that vast, choking clouds of its ash blacked out sunlight over the entire Mediterranean basin for several days. Santorini generated a succession of enormous sea waves that by some estimates reached a height of 300 feet as they smashed harbors and swept inland across the coasts of Crete and the Peloponnesian Peninsula of Greece. These educated hypotheses have prompted scientists to wonder whether the great eruption may not have been responsible for the sudden and mysterious end of the centuries-old Minoan civilization in Crete (page 102).

History provides no clue as to the forces that the Minoans, the Mycenaeans and other early peoples of the Mediterranean may have held responsible for volcanoes. But the Greeks and Romans did not hesitate to explain eruptions, although they were not always in agreement as to the cause. The Greek poet Pindar felt that the "terrible fiery flood" from Mount Etna was caused by the writhings of "that dragon thing, Typhon" (a hundred-headed monster with glowing eyes and a terrible voice), after it was "bound fast" beneath the mountain by Zeus. But volcanoes were more generally believed to be the chimneys of enormous subterranean forges stoked, in the cases of Vulcano and Etna, by the god of fire, who was known as Hephaestus to the Greeks and as Vulcan to the Romans.

This sooty deity kept busy hammering out armament for his peers, including the shield of Achilles, the arrows of Apollo and Diana, and the breastplate of Hercules. The Romans gave Vulcano—which the Greeks called Hiera—an enduring place in many languages when they renamed it for Vulcan.

However, both Romans and Greeks paid more attention to Etna, which was snow-capped, almost 11,000 feet high, visible at great distances, and thus capable of making Vulcano seem like an inconsequential little pile of cinders. Classical writers and poets described Etna at length, and some of them were original enough to scoff at those who attributed eruptions to the whims of gods and monsters. Lucretius, a Roman poet and philosopher, argued that Mount Etna was hollow and filled with "wind and air," which "forces itself on high" after being heated by "raging about" and then "flings out stones of prodigious weight and rolls on smoke of pitchy blackness."

Sicilians of far later eras remained immune to such efforts at rational thought: They believed for centuries that the crater of Mount Etna was literally the mouth of hell. And well they might, for the volcano continued to erupt with dismaying frequency, sending torrents of lava down its slopes to devour their villages. But this did not dissuade sturdy and enterprising mountaineers in the 18th and 19th Centuries from conducting venturesome tourists to the very brink of the fiery maw.

The ascent, usually accomplished on muleback, involved considerable discomfort—not merely because the pilgrim passed from subtropical to subarctic weather but because when he sought food and lodging on the way he found himself at the mercy of stony-faced locals. "After many enquiries," wrote George Rodwell, an English academic, in 1878, "we were directed to the only inn the town of Aderno could boast. A horrible old Sicilian woman now appeared and showed us, with great incivility, the only room the inmates were willing to place at our disposal. It had not been swept for weeks and as for food they had neither bread, meat, wine, macaroni, fruit or butter; neither did they offer to procure anything."

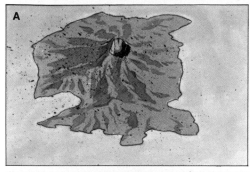

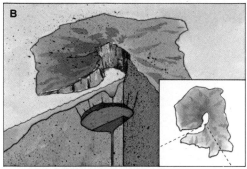

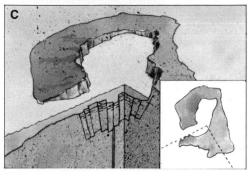

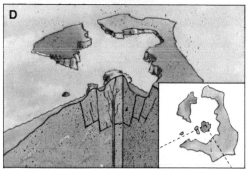

The eruption of Santorini volcano on the Aegean island of Thera is reconstructed in this series of drawings. Before the eruption (A), Thera's dominant feature was the mile-high volcano, which exploded in a paroxysmal eruption, ejecting 15 cubic miles of debris into the atmosphere. Once its magma chamber was depleted (B), Santorini collapsed into the sea, forming a vast crater, or caldera (C). Portions of the rim above sea level, enlarged by later lava flows (D), today form the Santorini Islands.

But if the slopes of Etna were inhabited by a dour, obdurate and insular people, Vesuvius—beginning long before the day of imperial Rome—attracted an increasingly varied population and nourished an increasingly hedonistic way of life. The district's earliest known inhabitants, a people who called themselves the Oscans, were primitive cattle herders. But the tenor of life began changing with the arrival of traders and settlers from Greece around 800 B.C. The Greeks were delighted with the soft climate, safe anchorages and verdant countryside they found along the Bay of Naples at the foot of Vesuvius. The dormant volcano was roughly 6,000 feet high and capped by a broad, flat plain fringed with vegetation. Forests abounding with game grew almost to the summit, and the soil around the mountain, thanks to ancient deposits of mineral-rich ash, was amazingly fertile. In these benign environs, apples, pears, figs, cherries, melons, almonds and pomegranates prospered. It was possible to grow two or three crops of wheat, barley and millet annually, and vegetables and grapes flourished everywhere.

The newcomers got along well with the local people and established trading posts along the shore. Villages and then towns and cities sprang up near the site of present-day Naples—at Herculaneum, along the shore at the foot of the mountain, and at Pompeii, which was built on heights formed of old lava above the navigable River Sarno. As the centuries went by, the towns became centers of Greek religion, drama, architecture and art. Wealth attracted raiders from the north, and a wave of mountain-bred Samnites managed, late in the Fifth Century B.C., to conquer all the settlements around the bay. But the new rulers, too, were seduced by Greek culture and the comforts of life on the welcoming flanks of Vesuvius.

After the conquest by Rome in 88 B.C., Latin became the language of southern Italy and Pompeii became a jewel in the imperial crown, with its own council and big new public buildings—including ornate baths, a Temple of Jupiter and a forum. The city prospered commercially from the bounty of Vesuvius' orchards and vineyards, and in addition became unique as a resort. The mountain was undeniably magnificent and the climate salubrious, the heat of the day relieved by cool breezes blowing in from the sea. Gaius Quinctius Balbus, an immensely wealthy Roman speculator, erected an amphitheater capable of accommodating 16,000 spectators—the entire population of the city plus visitors—and instituted gladiatorial games. Other rich Romans built luxurious villas and hired artists to decorate their homes with lavish frescoes and graceful statuary.

This idyllic state of affairs was twice interrupted in the 150 years before Vesuvius roused itself from its millennium of slumber. The Thracian slave and gladiator Spartacus escaped from his barracks with 70 companions in 73 B.C. and sought refuge on the summit of Vesuvius from troops under Clodius Glabrus, who was attempting to bring him to heel. Glabrus believed the quarry trapped. But Spartacus and his men lowered themselves down precipitous slopes on wild grapevines and surprised and routed their Roman pursuers—after which Spartacus raised an army of rebellious slaves and held much of southern Italy for two years before finally succumbing to Roman numbers.

The second interruption of Pompeian peace and prosperity occurred 133 years later, in 62 A.D., and was directly attributable, though no one dreamed it at the time, to the forces stirring below the majestic mountain overlooking the bay. A violent earthquake rumbled through the area, causing enormous damage in both Herculaneum and Pompeii. Most public buildings and many private homes were completely demolished. Both the Roman Senate and the Emperor Nero agreed, however, to aid in tasks of reconstruction—not only to rebuild two towns dear to so many men of imperial influence but also to erase architectural evidence of the Greek and Oscan past.

During the next 17 years, new temples, grandiose baths, houses, taverns and

Unlocking the Riddles of Atlantis

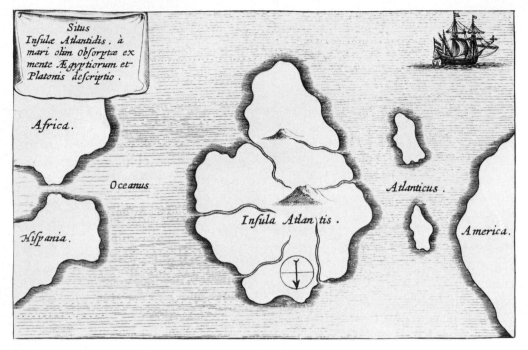

A 17th Century German print depicts a continent-sized Atlantis situated in the Atlantic Ocean midway between Africa and North America (the drawing places north at the bottom of the picture). Despite frequent speculations that Plato's legendary island was located in the Atlantic before its destruction, geologic evidence shows that no such land mass has been submerged there in historic times.

An enduring legend originating with the Egyptians and recorded by the Greek philosopher Plato 2,400 years ago tells of a mighty island empire, known as Atlantis, shattered by "one grievous day and night" of earthquakes and flood. Recent archeological discoveries have indicated that Atlantis may have been found, buried beneath the ash of an awesome volcanic eruption.

According to Plato's account, Atlantis was a lofty civilization whose people were "famous throughout all Europe and Asia both for their bodily beauty and for the perfection of their moral excellence." Atlantis' location and the nature of the calamity that sent it beneath an unnamed sea have remained tantalizing mysteries for centuries.

Plato's description of the island's location was unclear and led students of the story to place Atlantis in the mid-Atlantic, the North Sea, or off the coast of Tunisia, Spain or France—all sites eventually disqualified for one reason or another. But in 1956 a Greek seismologist, Angelos Galanopoulos, proposed that Atlantis was located north of Crete on what was the island of Thera, which was ravaged about 1450 B.C. by an extraordinary volcanic eruption.

The volcano on Thera expelled prodigious quantities of ash and spawned a tsunami that some geologists think may have been the basis of Biblical accounts of a plague of darkness in Egypt and even Moses' parting of the Red Sea. After its blast, the volcano collapsed, carrying almost all of the island into the sea. Under the thick pumice crust that covered what little was left of Thera, archeologists have recently found pottery and pieces of wood from the 15th Century B.C. Ongoing excavations have confirmed that a royal city of the Minoan civilization existed on the island and was destroyed by the volcano. Moreover, at about that time the entire Minoan empire centered on Crete abruptly declined, perhaps the victim of the devastation spread through the Aegean by the cataclysm on Thera.

Aside from the artifacts, Galanopoulos offered a fascinating bit of mathematical speculation in support of his contention that Thera was Atlantis. Plato had described the dimensions of an Atlantean plain as 340 by 230 miles, an area larger than all of Greece. And he placed the time of its destruction at 9,000 years before the rise of Athens—an impossibly early date for such an advanced civilization. Since the legend had come from the Egyptians, Galanopoulos suspected a translation error. He found that dividing Plato's dimensions by 10 yielded an area the size of Thera. Similarly, if 9,000 years was read as 900, the annihilation of Atlantis as related by Plato coincided almost precisely with the time of Thera's eruption.

theaters rose in Pompeii and Herculaneum where there had been only rubble. The tremors of 62 A.D. had been largely forgotten when the earth began shaking again in mid-August of the year 79. No one understood that Vesuvius had begun awakening from its slumber during the first great quake and was now warning of impending doom. But no one was long left in doubt.

A violent new quake shook the countryside at the foot of the mountain on the morning of August 24. There followed, amid the sound of falling masonry, an earsplitting clap of thunder. The summit of Vesuvius, the redoubt of Spartacus, now split open and gleamed with incandescent ash that climbed skyward in a huge, seething cloud. The cloud burst upward with unbelievable speed, its depths lit by incessant flashes of lightning as it spread, churning, into the clear blue sky. Pompeians, hurrying into the streets, were bombarded by showers of stones and fragments of pumice and finally, as a tomblike darkness fell, by a blizzard of fine ash. Herculaneum, nine miles up the shore to the northwest, was subject to a more monstrous phenomenon: A river of mud composed of bits of white, gray and green pumice began to engulf the town.

A fleet of oar-powered war galleys commanded by a Roman officer, Gaius Plinius Secundus, was based at Misenum on the westernmost point of the Bay of Naples when the eruption began. The commander, who was also a famous scholar better known to history as Pliny the Elder, took his fleet across the bay to observe the mountain's behavior at closer quarters and to rescue as many unfortunates as he could. He was eventually asphyxiated by a smothering blanket of ash and gases after going ashore to the south of Pompeii, and his death prompted the only firsthand accounts of the catastrophe—two letters in which his nephew, Pliny the Younger, described his uncle's death for the Roman historian Tacitus and set down his own recollections of the eruption. These constituted the first known account of a volcanic eruption, and were later invaluable to volcanologists and other scientists studying the events of that fateful day.

The nephew, then a youth of 17, had stayed at Misenum with his mother when his famous kinsman set off across the bay. Drawing on reports from survivors of the ill-fated expedition, he related that Pliny the Elder was unable to land near the mountain, for "ashes were already falling hotter and thicker, followed by bits of pumice and blackened stones, charred and cracked by the flames, and the shore was blocked by debris from the mountain." Hordes of terrified citizens left Herculaneum for Naples, five miles to the northwest, and fled Pompeii for the town of Stabiae, four miles to the southwest—some with pillows held to their heads for protection against stones. Similar scenes were reenacted as the ash-choked darkness fell on Misenum, too, and on Stabiae, where the elder Pliny finally managed to get ashore.

The commander decided to remain in the town overnight in order to reassure the frightened citizens. "He gave orders to be carried to the bathroom," wrote Pliny the Younger. "After his bath he lay down and dined. Meanwhile, on Mount Vesuvius broad sheets of fire and leaping flames blazed at several points, their bright glare emphasized by the darkness of the night. My uncle tried to allay the fears of his companions by repeatedly declaring that these were nothing but bonfires left by peasants in their terror, or else empty houses on fire in the districts they had abandoned. Then he went to rest."

While their savior slept, wrote the younger Pliny, "the buildings were shaking as if they were being torn from their foundations," and those who ventured outside found themselves bombarded with falling pumice stones. His frantic companions roused the commander at dawn—or what should have been dawn, since "they were still in darkness, blacker and denser than any night, which they relieved by lighting torches and various kinds of lamp. My uncle decided to go down to the shore and investigate on the spot the possibility of any escape by sea, but he found the waves still wild and dangerous."

At this point, the aging officer seems to have been overcome. "A sheet was spread on the ground for him to lie down, and he repeatedly asked for cold water to drink," wrote the younger Pliny. "Then the flames and smell of sulfur which gave warning of the approaching fire drove the others to take flight and roused him to stand up. He stood leaning on two slaves and then suddenly collapsed, I imagine because the dense fumes choked his breathing by blocking his windpipe, which was constitutionally weak and narrow and often inflamed." At least a few members of the party tumbled into the boats and made their frantic way to safety with the grim story.

Meanwhile, the commander's nephew decided to take his mother from Misenum, where "the buildings were already tottering" and where "we saw the sea sucked away, and apparently forced back by the earthquake. A dense black cloud was coming up behind us, spreading over the earth like a flood. Darkness fell as if the lamp had been put out in a closed room. You could hear the shrieks of women, the wailing of infants and the shouting of men." The young Pliny pulled his mother off the road to avoid their being trampled and waited there in "the belief that the whole world was dying and I with it" until a yellowish sun finally revealed a landscape "buried deep in ashes like snowdrifts."

Both Vesuvius and the surrounding countryside were virtually unrecognizable. The northern wall of the volcano still stood but much of its western slope had been blown away or had fallen into its gaping crater, above which now stood a sharp new cone—Vesuvius reborn. Herculaneum was buried under 45 to 65 feet of pumice-laden mud—which was to harden, gradually, into stone. Pompeii lay under 20 feet of ash.

There is no accurate count of how many people lost their lives: The Romans

The thunderous eruption of Mount Vesuvius in 79 A.D. drives residents from the seaside resort of Pompeii in this painting by 19th Century artist John Martin. Centurions in the foreground use their shields to ward off the shower of hot ash and pumice; behind them, city walls crumble as earthquakes associated with the eruption rip through the area.

took no census of the citizens. It is probable that most of the residents of Herculaneum escaped the relatively slow mud flow. But at least 2,000 Pompeians died under the sudden and overwhelming ash. In any case, both towns were officially abandoned.

Their names persisted through the Dark Ages on European maps—all of which were copies of those drawn for the vanished Roman legions. But the towns themselves were completely forgotten as, over the centuries, the Roman Empire weakened and as the country around Vesuvius was ruled, in turn, by Goths, administrators from Byzantium, Normans, Lombards, Charles of Anjou, and various viceroys of the houses of Aragon and Habsburg. A new town, Resina, rose above Herculaneum. And vineyards grew above Pompeii—Vesuvius permitting.

For the volcano continued to roar fiercely to life every century or so, hurling immense volumes of ash into the heavens and sending rivers of mud and lava down its flanks. Few details of its activity were recorded during the millennium after 79 A.D. But volcanologists studying what records survive, as well as ash and lava layers, have concluded that it erupted heavily in 203 and 472, and so severely in 512 that Theodoric the Goth did not tax the surviving towns. Vesuvius erupted again in 685 and 787, and then, in a burst of activity, spewed forth fiery lava five times between 968 and 1037. The volcano fell silent sometime thereafter for 600 years—at which point it roused itself once again, and has threatened the humans in its vicinity ever since.

Its farmers and villagers have tolerated Vesuvius' fits of cyclic rage as fatalistically as they have tolerated the innumerable rulers of their region. Few groups of people have ever been so willfully unprepared for disaster as were its victims in 1631, and few have been subjected to so awful a display of Vesuvian displeasure. The volcano ended its long period of quiescence—in which lush forests had again grown to its summit—with a violence worse in some ways than that visited on the people of Pompeii and Herculaneum.

A prelate who entered the crater some months before the eruption reported that it measured five miles in circumference and 6,000 feet deep. At the bottom there was a plain on which cattle grazed and large patches of brushy woods that harbored wild boars. In the center of the plain was a rocky depression, which could be reached by a narrow, winding path; the area was barren and held three small pools of water, one hot and tasteless, another hot and bitter to the tongue and the third inexplicably cool but saltier than the sea. This was the mouth of Vesuvius.

The earth began to tremble around Vesuvius in the summer of the fateful year, and the quakes grew in severity with each passing day. By early December the entire vast crater was filled with seething liquid. But the intelligence—as has so often been the case with volcanoes—was widely ignored.

A Stygian darkness fell almost as soon as the eruption began with fearful explosions of ash at 7 a.m. on December 16. Just before noon the next day, two enormous fissures opened in the mountain's southwest side and floods of red-hot lava poured downward. Rivers of hot mud materialized that evening and new lava burst from the volcano's southern slope. Before the volcano finally subsided on December 18, six villages had been destroyed by lava, nine were inundated by mud, and Naples was covered knee-deep with ash. Many villagers had tarried too long before the onslaught of the volcano, seeking to save their animals and other cherished possessions. More than 4,000 people and 6,000 domestic animals died.

For posterity, the Viceroy of Naples ordered a memorial tablet erected at Portici, just south of the city, reading: "Children and children's children. Hear! I warn you now, after this last catastrophe, that you may not be taken unawares. Sooner or later this mountain takes fire. But before this happens there are mutterings and roarings and earthquakes. Smoke and flames and

The volcanic fury unleashed by Vesuvius in a 1631 eruption is graphically illustrated in these before-and-after engravings by a contemporary artist. The tranquil landscape of villages nestled along the base of Vesuvius and nearby Monte Somma is swallowed in lava and mud until, at last, Januarius, patron saint of Naples, extinguishes the eruption with his cape.

lightning are spewed forth, the air trembles and rumbles and howls. Flee so long as you can. For soon the mountain will burst apart and spew out a stream of fire, which will rush down and bar the way for those who are slow to flee. If you despise it, if goods and chattels are dearer to you than life, it will punish your recklessness and greed. Do not trouble about your hearth and home, but flee without hesitation. Anno Domini 1632, in the reign of Philip IV. Emmanuele Fonseca, Viceroy."

By an accident of history, it was this very catastrophe that at last led Neapolitans to the largely forgotten treasures of antiquity lying so long beneath their feet. Among the places demolished by the 1631 eruption was the large town of Resina, which had been built atop the layers of volcanic debris hiding Herculaneum. The vineyards, orchards and gardens flourishing in the fertile layers of ash overlying Pompeii were likewise ruined. And it was dur-

ASHY TOPSOIL

LAPILLI
ASH
LAPILLI

ASH

SANDY ASH WITH PIECES OF
CARBONIZED WOOD

LAPILLI
SANDY ASH

GREENISH-GRAY PUMICE

LIGHT-GRAY PUMICE

WHITE PUMICE

OLD LAVA
FROM PLUG OF CONE

A 12-foot-thick sample exposed during excavation
at Pompeii and diagramed in cross section above
provides a perfect record of the 79 A.D. eruption
in layers of volcanic debris. As read by geologists, the
successive strata of pumice, volcanic sand, small
volcanic fragments called lapilli, and ash confirm
much of the eruption sequence described in
a contemporary account by Pliny the Younger.

ing the long period of reconstruction and rehabilitation of the land that excavators digging civic water systems and irrigation reservoirs came upon clues to the two buried cities.

At first, workers found and pocketed a few Roman coins. In time, as the word spread, numbers of Neapolitans commenced poking around the general area for buried treasure, but discovered other objects: stones inscribed with the word "Pompeii" and some rusty metal objects, including a set of keys. But no one in authority paid much attention until the beginning of the 18th Century, when a well digger stumbled across what appeared to be a large trove of alabaster and marble.

Austria governed in Naples at this point and one Prince d'Elboeuf, the Supreme Officer of the Guard there, hired workmen to bring up more of this elegant stone for a villa he was planning to build. During the excavation, the workers unearthed three lovely statues of women, which were later much admired by the bride of 19-year-old Charles III of Bourbon, who (Spain having forced the Austrians from southern Italy) had just been seated on the throne of the Kingdom of Naples.

The young Queen talked the young King into quarrying for more statues, and in the process his workers found an inscription proving that Herculaneum had been located after more than 1,600 years. Thus, in 1738, began 250 years of archeological exploration that has yielded astonishing insights into Roman civilization—and has made Vesuvius the most renowned volcano in the world.

All through the 18th Century and into the 19th, the rulers of Naples employed gangs of workers to excavate the ruins in search of prizes. Queen Caroline, a sister of Napoleon and wife of the ruler of Naples in 1808, haunted the excavation sites and was so apt to hand out ducats to those who produced rings, coins or pieces of statuary that the workers took to reburying prizes and rediscovering them as she looked on.

This sort of high-level looting, rather than any interest in restoration, prompted most of the early exploration of both Herculaneum and Pompeii. Sir William Hamilton, the British envoy to Naples from 1764 to 1800 and an amateur archeologist, sold artifacts to the British Museum for a small fortune, paid off gambling debts for his nephew, Charles Greville—and was granted Greville's mistress, Emma Lyon, in return. Emma—whom Hamilton married—became the mistress, in turn, of Admiral Horatio Nelson, the hero of Trafalgar, and Hamilton, as a dubious by-product of his scientific interests, became one of history's best-remembered cuckolds.

Engineers who superintended excavation for the various rulers of Naples abetted this disorderly exhumation of the buried cities by ordering the rubble shoveled back into streets and houses once they had yielded their quota of treasure. Pompeii claimed the attention of the world for all that—the German poet Johann von Goethe poked about its streets and so did England's young Queen Victoria—and the digging seldom halted for long no matter who came to power in Naples.

It took a 37-year-old archeologist named Giuseppe Fiorelli, who was appointed in 1860 by King Victor Emmanuel II during the unification of Italy, to bring reason and order to the great project at last. Fiorelli built a little railway to haul away rubble and engaged in no new excavation until he had completed the long and tiresome process of exposing buildings and thoroughfares that had been clogged by his predecessors. He built roofs to protect unshielded frescoes from the weather, drew maps on which he projected the probable courses of streets yet uncovered, and divided unexplored areas into regions or blocks as a means of systematizing excavation in the future.

When serious archeological work began, it was discovered that the airless blanket of ash had served to protect much of Pompeii from the disintegrating processes of time. A sealed bakery oven was found to contain blackened loaves of 1,800-year-old bread. Wall murals had been preserved with their colors still vibrant. The bodies of the victims of Vesuvius had decomposed in the first weeks after burial, but they left their imprints in the hard-packed ash. Fiorelli gave the last hours of Pompeii a tragic immediacy by pumping liquid plaster of paris into these perfect molds, thus reproducing the people they had contained as they had looked at the very moment of death.

Fiorelli's concepts dominated the work of restoration thereafter, and Pompeii came to look, in many areas, very much as it must have looked on the morning of the great eruption. It was a town with stand-up lunch counters and raised stone crosswalks to keep the feet of pedestrians from horse droppings in the streets. Wall paintings celebrated the naked human body as a thing of beauty (and also, at times, an object of ribaldry), and luxurious baths provided men of substance with hours of enjoyment.

Vesuvius had not only preserved the physical aspects of Pompeii but had encapsulated endless clues as to its residents' social organization, political concepts, dress, vocations, intellectual pursuits and appetites. The atmosphere in Pompeii during its final years was one of boundless prosperity, which stemmed in part from seaborne commerce and in part from continuous infusions of money from thousands of wealthy Romans who utilized the services of local merchants, builders and suppliers upon arriving for their seasonal retreats. These Pompeian servitors succeeded so well, in many cases, as to create a noisy and vulgar society of *nouveaux riches* and to horrify the visiting aristocracy by inhabiting villas of their own.

There were 118 bars and taverns in Pompeii, as well as inns that offered food, drink and lodging for traders and merchants from the far reaches of the Roman Empire. Some of the establishments were gaming houses and not a few provided prostitutes. A *thermopolium* (a tavern specializing in hot wine) had walls inscribed with the names of women—perhaps the sort of Andalusian dancing girls who, in the words of Martial, "with endless prurience swing lascivious loins" or, in those of Pliny the Younger, played "antic tricks round the tables." More adorned the walls of the city. "Curses on you, landlord," read one, "you sell water and drink unmixed wine yourself." Wrote a disenchanted man: "Lucilia sells her body." An equally disenchanted Livia told the world what she thought of a certain Alexander: "Do you think I would mind if you dropped dead tomorrow?"

Bakers and fullers were among the busiest of Pompeian tradesmen. No fewer than 10 bakeries have been uncovered; all ground their own flour with crude stone mills turned by a long lever, which a mule or a slave pushed in an endless circle. Twelve fullers' shops have been excavated. These artisans shrank and bleached the heavy wool fabric from which the mandatory white togas of the day were cut; then they laundered them by treading on them in tubs of water and ironed them, after they had been dried in the sun, with a device that resembled an old-fashioned printing press.

Revelations of life in Pompeii had a wide influence on art, literature, history, architecture and fashions in other European countries from the day of the first excavation onward. Two Italian engraver-architects, Giovanni Battista Piranesi and his son, Giovanni Francesco, produced engravings of scenes in Pompeii and Herculaneum, which, in turn, influenced the concepts of the famed Scottish architects Robert and James Adam. The equally famous English potter Josiah Wedgwood was inspired by the shapes and colors of Greek urns unearthed in the buried cities. Pompeian style became the standard for the decorative arts of the early 19th Century; medallions and stucco motifs from the two cities appeared on walls and ceilings everywhere. Painters and sculptors throughout Europe made their pilgrimage to Pompeii, and the superiority of its art was accorded almost the force of law.

Vesuvius, to which all involved in the great project were in such debt,

Perfectly Preserved Treasures from Pompeii

The 20-foot layer of volcanic debris from Mount Vesuvius' 79 A.D. eruption covered the Roman town of Pompeii so completely that its material existence was kept safe from the ravages of time for some 1,600 years. Excavation of this wealth of artifacts during the past 200 years has wrested from the hardened debris a remarkably detailed record of life in a merchant town of ancient Rome. Pompeii has bequeathed to posterity an engaging, occasionally whimsical and often magnificent visual record of itself.

The extraordinary diversity of the artifacts demonstrates that art suffused Pompeian life. In many homes virtually every wall was elaborately painted with scenes from mythology copied from Greek masterpieces, or splendid portraits of the family who lived there. Colorful, intricate mosaics depicting scenes of nature, battle or the theater were set in cement floors. Cupids and gods cavorted across dazzling silverwork imported from the Middle East. Such accouterments of daily life as oil lamps and heating stoves were embellished in marvelous detail with consummate craftsmanship.

Statuary graced the gardens of many homes, and often portrayed the antics of Dionysus, the Greek god of wine and theater. In public areas, grinning stone faces adorned water fountains. More than 70 bronze and marble statues, many immortalizing various civic benefactors, surrounded the Pompeian forum, one of the Roman Empire's architectural wonders.

As bounteous as Pompeii's artistic and historic treasure has already proved to be, its true extent remains unknown; only two fifths of the town has yet to be excavated from the stony depths of its ancient grave.

A delicate lotus-leaf motif graces a lamp of hammered gold. When it was excavated in 1863, the lamp's exquisite craftsmanship caused a sensation.

Hinged eyeshields and an eagle embellish a bronze helmet, the type worn by gladiators who battled to the death before cheering Pompeian crowds.

Ivy leaves decorate this ornately worked silver drinking chalice. Such silver was prized in Pompeii; a service of 118 pieces was found in one villa.

Side handles fashioned in the shape of human hands and elaborate clawed feet impart an air of whimsy to this portable bronze heating stove.

Their futile struggle against Vesuvius' deadly onslaught preserved for centuries by the hardened ash, a group of Pompeians lie at the base of a city wall. Scores of such tragic tableaux have been re-created in remarkable detail by pouring plaster into the cavities left by the victims' decomposed bodies.

gained in ominous eminence with every such new book, engraving, painting and newspaper account. But the mountain spoke thunderously for itself as well. A series of nine violent eruptions between 1766 and 1794 devoured dozens of villages and killed or injured hundreds of hapless peasants. Indeed, during this period it seemed that the Neapolitan sky was never free of smoke from Vesuvius and the ground shook interminably from tremors within the mountain.

A few thoughtful and daring men, most notably Sir William Hamilton, began attempting to understand the volcano's outbursts. Political history may remember Hamilton as an unremarkable minor diplomat whose wife was enamored of an admiral, but volcanologists remember him as a keen observer and one of the first of their breed.

Hamilton was intrigued by the stolidly philosophical attitudes of peasant farmers and villagers who clung to the mountain in such numbers. "The operations of nature are slow," he wrote. "Each peasant flatters himself that an eruption will not happen in his time, or, if it should, that his tutelar saint will turn away the destructive lava from his grounds; and, indeed, the great fertility of soil in the neighborhoods of volcanoes tempts people to inhabit them."

The saint to whom Hamilton alluded was Januarius, patron of Naples. Neapolitans invariably demanded, when terrified by eruptions, that their cardinal order the saint's image paraded through the streets. Scientists had reason to be grateful for this custom, for often the only written clues to eruptions in the Middle Ages were church records noting dates on which Januarius had been hauled into public view.

During a 1767 eruption, Hamilton had noticed from his villa below that repeated "throws of cinders, ashes and pumice stones" had built "a small mountain," or subsidiary cone, within the major crater, and that its top was becoming visible above the rim of Vesuvius. "I had watched the growing of this little mountain," wrote Hamilton, "and by taking drawings of it from time to time, I could perceive its growth most minutely. I make no doubt but that the whole of Mount Vesuvius has been formed in this manner."

Hamilton decided to observe the phenomenon at first hand on the mountain-top. But it was a perilous business, and he was lucky to escape with a whole skin, for "the mountain split, and with much noise from this new mouth, a fountain of liquid fire shot up many feet and rolled directly on toward us. Clouds of black smoke and ashes caused almost a total darkness. My guide took to his heels and I must confess that I was not at ease. I followed close and we ran near three miles without stopping. The earth continued to shake under our feet.

A thoroughfare of ancient Herculaneum, buried under mudflows in the 79 A.D. eruption of Vesuvius and long forgotten along with Pompeii, ends abruptly beneath the village of Ercolano with its forest of television antennas. Excavations were halted when they threatened the modern buildings above.

The pumice stones, falling upon us like hail, were of such a size as to cause a disagreeable sensation upon the part where they fell."

Hamilton remained in Naples 36 years and made more than 200 sorties up the flanks of Vesuvius. Expanding upon his first views of the cinder cone building within Vesuvius, he theorized that the entire mountain—in fact all Mediterranean volcanoes—had been thrown up from the bottom of the sea by successive eruptions. Hamilton found the area devoid of "virgin soil"—as he called sedimentary rock. There was only layer upon layer of volcanic material. And this led him to a flawed but nonetheless fascinating conclusion about geology in general: "Upon the whole, if I was to establish a system, it would be that *Mountains are produced by Volcanoes, and not Volcanoes by Mountains.*" These and other observations Hamilton shared in correspondence with the President of the Royal Society, which in 1774 published the letters in a volume that came to be considered the first modern work of volcanology.

Some 70 years later, in 1841, Italy's King Ferdinand II provided volcanologists with a permanent means of advancing their science by ordaining construction of an observatory high on the northwest shoulder of Mount Vesuvius. The solid stone building, completed in 1845, provided a library and conference hall, space for scientific instruments and living quarters and a study for a director, as well as a splendid view of the volcano's crater nearly two miles away. But royal interest in the project flagged and the observatory was all but abandoned until 1850, when the mountain erupted once again with damaging effect.

Because its elevated position protected it from lava flows, the observatory survived the eruption intact, and it was now decided to make use of it in earnest. A respected physicist from Naples University, Luigi Palmieri, was appointed director in 1856, and for almost 16 years he commuted regularly to the mountain, monitoring its erratic pulse with an array of instruments that included a sensitive seismograph of his own design. But it was all regarded as so much esoterica until 1872, when Palmieri became an Italian national hero and the observatory became a monument to his courage. In March, the volcano's cone opened on the northwest side, in full view of the observatory. Lava poured out and a line of fumaroles sent gas jets into the sky. Palmieri's instruments began to register great activity within the mountain, and the observatory director was at his post on April 25 when Vesuvius erupted violently. For six days, Palmieri staunchly remained at the observatory, choking on noxious gases but nonetheless occasionally venturing outside to study the surrounding lava flows. Crowds of Neapolitans gathered below to view through telescopes the tiny

A Diplomat's Mission to Vesuvius

When Sir William Hamilton set sail for Italy as Britain's Envoy Extraordinary to the Court of Naples in 1764, he had no inkling that he would shortly become one of the first students of volcanology. But Mount Vesuvius, looming as a constant threat over the languid city, fascinated the young diplomat from the moment he laid eyes on it—and the fact that he seemed to be alone in his interest astounded him.

Local chemists had never troubled to examine the composition of the mountain's volcanic rocks and other ejecta, but Sir William did so and sent samples back to London. Hamilton concentrated on recording the daily activity of Mount Vesuvius, and during the decades of the 1760s and 1770s spent many days and nights in perilous observation of the volcano's continual rumblings and frequent eruptions.

During a major eruption in October of 1767, Hamilton scaled the mountain, but the volcano's violent activity forced him to return to Naples, where he kept a daily record of the event from the first "torrents of fire" to the "ashes of pumice stones" that swept a "London fog" over the area. Not content with personal observation, he interviewed peasants and learned from the elderly

and experienced that although the ash was at first gray in color, it eventually fell as white as snow; at that point the spate of volcanic fury was sure to be at its end.

Sir William salted his dispatches to London with frequent news from Vesuvius, but he recorded most of his findings in a series of letters to the President of the Royal Society. Hamilton also hired and trained artist Pietro Fabris, a British subject who was living in Naples, to make hand-colored engravings of the volcanic scenery. At considerable personal expense, Hamilton published the lively and charming illustrations together with his letters in three volumes entitled *Campi Phlegraei (Phlegraean Fields)*. The numerical and alphabetical keys on the works pictured here refer to Hamilton's long and painstaking descriptions.

In later years, Sir William was forced to sell much of his Vesuvian art to defray living expenses, but he was proud of his contribution. "Accurate and faithful observations on the operations of nature, related with simplicity and truth, are not to be met with often," he once wrote. The elegant blend of art and science his folios represent secured for Hamilton a notable position in the history of volcanology.

Mount Vesuvius lights up the night sky on May 11, 1771, to reveal Sir William Hamilton (*left*) pointing out to his guests a glowing lava river winding toward the town of Resina. In the left foreground, artist Pietro Fabris has inserted a figure of himself sketching the scene.

Six sequential drawings by Pietro Fabris illustrate Mount Vesuvius' dramatic increase in height between July 8 and the eruption of October 19, 1767. In the larger view at bottom, Hamilton has had the artist show how "the prodigious quantity of matter erupted in ten days entirely filled up the Valley between the ancient Crater and the Cone." The dotted line E indicates the volcano's initial height.

The Envoy Extraordinary's attention to detail extended to collecting and studying the debris that was blown from Vesuvius. The deep-yellow specimens of lava encrusted with sulfur "I fetched out of the very crater" from "a crevice that was indeed very hot." Sir William observed that salt similar to that evident in the sample at lower right was "such as the Peasants make use of at their tables."

figure on the flaming mountain. And the fact that Palmieri remained defiantly alive gave them heart.

In the next decades, the observatory was manned more or less constantly. But there was little to observe as the mountain sank back into its familiar somnolence. So quiescent was Vesuvius that it was encircled by a little railway that transported tourists up to the 2,477-foot level. There the English travel firm Thos. Cook & Son installed a connecting funicular lift to hoist adventurous pilgrims to the edge of the crater, where they could view the steaming vapors and pools of liquid lava below.

Vesuvius was thus familiar far and wide when it blew up again in 1906—an event dramatized by hair-raising reports sent, as in 1872, from the beleaguered observatory on the upper slopes of the volcano. The reporter was Frank Perret, the soon-to-be-famed American scientist who then was just beginning his studies as a companion of Raffaele Matteucci, resident volcanologist on Vesuvius. And the notes kept by Perret reflect the danger and high drama of the experience as have few such reports since those of Pliny the Younger.

The first phase of this volcanic episode, which began in the spring of 1905, was far less destructive than its violent climax in April of the following year. But it prompted Matteucci to a daring gamble to save the life of a small boy, named Giovanni Olivieri, who became surrounded by rivers of lava while he was seeking a place of refuge in a vineyard below the observatory. Hearing the child's cries for help, the volcanologist summoned a Vesuvian guide named Pasquale Pacifico, and the two men worked their way toward the lad across a fragile crust that had begun forming on the cooling surface of the molten lava. Matteucci later described the traverse: "It may remind you of a treacherous ice crust—but how different and how infinitely more terrible are the conditions with liquid fire below instead of water! The heat was killing. With wet cloths protecting our faces and with burning boots, scorched hands and smoking clothes we made our way across the bending crust and seized the trembling child. We did not dare carry him in our arms but distributed the weight by making him run in front of us on his own account and thus got him to safety."

As the eruption continued to grow increasingly severe, the observatory itself was imperiled by earthquakes, volleys of stones, heavy ashfall and hot gases, which made breathing difficult. Wrote Perret: "Within the building, it was difficult to cross a room without steadying oneself with a hand against the wall." Perret went outside and braced himself against a stone wall to make sure that the motion was not merely an oscillation of the building: "The effect was the same. Like the shell of a humming boiler, the mountain was pulsing and vibrating continuously."

Villages on the northeastern slope of the mountain were buried in ash. The railway and funicular were torn up. Through it all, because of its position and sturdy construction, the observatory remained not only standing but habitable and operational. Matteucci, Perret and six brave Italian *carabinieri* stuck to their posts and made frequent expeditions around the erupting mountain—the scientists in order to study its behavior, the soldiers in order to carry reports to frightened townspeople below.

When the major eruptions began, a mob of 30,000 had gathered in hysteria at the cathedral of Naples. The sacred bust of Saint Januarius was extracted from its resting place and marched through the streets. It had no noticeable effect on the mountain. But the populace took heart thereafter in the knowledge that men were actually staying alive near the crater itself. Matteucci and Perret were meanwhile recording a whole series of astounding phenomena: among them an "electrical wind," wrote Perret, which made metal on the caps of the *carabinieri* "hiss" and created "St. Elmo's fire on every pointed object upon our persons." At one point, a rain of soft mud balls, some as large as eggs, pelted down out of a great ash cloud rising from the volcano; Perret reasoned that the water-saturated ash had condensed and conglomerated as it rose into the cold upper air and had fallen back to earth as a muddy sort of hail.

At another point during his stay, Perret was wakened from his sleep by a faint buzzing sound in one ear—the one that lay on the pillow. Perret raised his head. The noise ceased. He placed his ear back on the pillow. The buzzing resumed. Perret arose and clenched between his teeth an iron rod of the bedstead. Now he could not only hear but feel the tremor—which was, though Perret did not know it at the time, the harmonic vibration set up by great masses of magma in motion.

The next day, Perret told Matteucci of his odd experience, and in an inspired bit of guesswork, added his belief that Vesuvius was readying itself for further eruptions. The professor laughed, saying: "You must have heard them grinding coffee for breakfast."

A few days later, Vesuvius resumed its eruption.

Perret was to shudder for months at the memory of the events of April 18, 1906. On that date, through a break in the suffocating ash clouds, the men in the observatory spotted a large group of men, women and children seeking refuge in a makeshift barracks nearby. As before, the fearless Matteucci set out to rescue the lot. Perret and the admirable *carabinieri* accompanied him. The building was only 60 yards away but the ash clouds had closed in again, worse than before. "Gases made the air almost unbreathable," wrote Perret, "and ashes produced a darkness that was absolute. No compass could be used for it could not be seen." And with all of that, fierce winds blew the volcanic ash about with "such force," reported Perret, "as to make the lips bleed."

When the rescuers reached the barracks, they found that there were 40 terrified refugees in the group. Perret related how "all were placed upon a rope and one end anchored to the barracks door. The head of this human snake would circle about until some familiar spot was found; then the tail drew up and the maneuver was repeated until the observatory was reached. Once inside, more dead than alive, we were forced to endure for eight hours those deadly gases and an atmosphere of floating ashes so thick that a lamp could not be seen across the room. But at midnight the blast subsided and the gases were dissipated. All but one young man survived the ordeal."

Vesuvius did not exhaust itself until the month had passed. It became apparent, as the skies cleared at last, that it had been the mountain's worst eruption since 1631. Naples, Pompeii and other towns on its seaward side were spared,

Terrified peasants pray for divine protection during a massive 1906 eruption of Vesuvius depicted in this contemporary watercolor. Before fleeing their homes near the volcano, residents brandished crosses in vain hopes of halting the torrents of lava.

Ash fills the air and chokes the streets of Ottaviano, a town at the foot of Vesuvius that was devastated in 1906. So great was the accumulation of ash during the 18-day eruption that it prevented cultivation of the land in the vicinity for years.

Fruit-laden apricot trees, grapevines and tomato plants flourish on the slopes of Vesuvius in soil made fertile by the mountain's mineral-rich eruptions. This fecundity born of disaster has over the centuries drawn the people of southern Italy again and again to the dangerous vicinity of the volcano.

but a number of villages on its northern and eastern flanks were buried by ash and other volcanic debris. One hundred fifty people died inside a church at San Giuseppe when the roof collapsed, and scores more perished in their own houses. Great areas of field and vineyard—193,000 acres in all—were ruined by the lava and ash.

The mountain itself had lost as much as 722 feet of its crater rim and the crater had widened by perhaps 1,000 feet; it was now roughly 1,600 feet in diameter and so deep that the bottom could not be seen from the rim. Avalanches continually rumbled down, piling up debris until, in 1909, three years after the eruption, the bottom finally could be seen from the top —at 656 feet down.

The noble Matteucci died in 1909, director of the observatory to the end. He had once written: "I love my mountain. I am wedded to her forever; my few friends say that her breath will scorch and wither my poor life one of these days." And so it was that years of inhaling the fumes of Vesuvius ruined his health until at last he contracted a fatal case of pneumonia.

In the years since, Vesuvius has exhibited its wrath only once—in 1944, when an eruption interrupted flights at American airfields around wartime Naples and sent new armies of homeless refugees down the narrow roads with their farm animals and burdens of furniture and bedding. The decades have mainly been a period of healing on the volcano's slopes. The ground is again green with vines, often cultivated, thanks to the fertility of Vesuvian soil, amid stands of fruit trees and gardens of fennel, beans and peas. Every year the mountain villages ship trainloads of delicious pinkish apricots and $35 million worth of carnations to Germany, Holland and other European countries. New generations of tourists regard the famed volcano with wonder from the streets of Naples below.

However, the mountain still harbors its secrets and musters its strengths. "Vesuvius slumbers," as volcanologist Alessandro Malladra observed in 1913, "but his heart is awake. There is no doubt that sooner or later he will rise from his uneasy somnolence and burst magnificently upon the world once more with banners of fire and plumes of smoke, making the earth shudder and devouring a myriad of humans, demolishing their puny cities and repeating the history of Pompeii and Herculaneum. Vesuvius is a monster not to be restrained by any man's cunning or ingenuity—and, therefore, imperial, awesome, magnificent." Ω

Chapter 5

MONITORING THE EARTH'S HEARTBEAT

Throughout many centuries of affliction, the possibility that humans might pit their puny resources against the titanic forces of volcanism seemed hardly worth contemplating. Instead, wrote American volcanologist Gordon A. Macdonald, the prevailing sentiment was "a feeling of fatalism—the volcano would have its way, and was not to be disputed!" Yet from time to time man has stood fast, and it is perhaps appropriate that the first known attempt to take the measure of a volcano occurred in the Mediterranean region, which had for so many years suffered so much.

Sicily's Mount Etna had been shaken by earthquakes for three days when on March 11, 1669, the volcano finally let loose in the most violent series of eruptions in its long and explosive history. Great clouds of ash fanned out as far as 60 miles, and on March 25 a seething stream of lava surged down the southern slope of the mountain. There, 10 miles below and directly in the path of the flow, lay the ancient city of Catania, protected only by its feudal walls, 60 feet high.

As the molten tide relentlessly approached, demolishing several villages on its way, a Catanian citizen named Diego de Pappalardo, age and occupation unknown, earned a place in volcanic history. The lava streaming down the slope was of a sort, later termed aa, that tended to move through a channel created by levees of cooling substance at the sides of the flow. The dauntless de Pappalardo and perhaps 50 cohorts, clad in wetted cowskins to protect them from the lava's fierce heat and wielding long iron bars, broke down one of the lava levees high on the volcano above their cherished city. Just as they had prayed it would, a tongue of lava moved through the breach, slowing the main stream in its inexorable progress toward Catania.

Unfortunately, the flow from the break in the levee now headed straight for the village of Paterno, 11 miles to the northwest of Catania. Its citizens were understandably outraged. Some 500 strong, and armed with every weapon they could muster, they forced de Pappalardo and his companions to cease their efforts at volcano control. Left unattended, the levee breach soon became clogged and the lava stream, restored to full and formidable volume, continued on its original course toward Catania.

To the astonishment of all—and to the considerable interest of modern volcanologists—the city's old walls held up for several days against the millions of tons of lava, diverting the flow around Catania and into the Ionian Sea. At last, however, a weak place in the barrier gave way, the lava poured through the city and nearly filled the harbor beyond. Today, more than three centuries later, some of Catania's streets are still partly blocked by huge chunks of lava.

A volcanologist using a canvas bag to protect his hand from the heat reaches with a geologic pick through a gap in the crust of a 1972 Hawaiian lava flow to take a sample from the molten interior. By analyzing samples, scientists can estimate the original nature and source of the molten rock.

117

In the rustic wooden building that housed the original Hawaiian Volcano Observatory *(top),* the pioneering American volcanologist Thomas A. Jaggar Jr. *(bottom)* pores over his work surrounded by his photographs of volcanic eruptions. A passionate believer in the need for round-the-clock observation, Jaggar founded the observatory on the island of Hawaii in 1912. He claimed that a scientist living near a live volcano "will learn more in an hour than he ever dreamt of in years at the university."

Nearly 300 years were to elapse before humans again tried to impose a measure of control over the devastation of eruptions. But the effort of the Catanians stayed in mind, and recently bulldozers and hoses and explosives have been used to attack lava flows, not only from within the radius of their immediate environs but from the sea and even from the air. The work has rarely achieved conclusive results—yet it has always held out the promise of future success.

Far more fruitful have been the efforts to forecast eruptions, thereby providing time for people in danger zones to get out of harm's way. Indeed, volcano forecasting has become a discipline with its own array of instruments to record the tremblings of mountains, measure their swelling as they fill with magma from below, trace the movement of molten rock as it forces its way through volcanic systems, and collect gases from surface vents and fissures.

Until these instruments were developed, the science was mainly one of inferences derived from surface activity. It might, said geophysicist Robert Decker, "be compared to medicine before the X-ray. Important diagnoses could be made on symptoms alone, but more accurate diagnoses required data hidden beneath the surface."

Thus, forecasting an eruption, let alone trying to control the forces it unleashes, calls for a special breed of scientist. And it is no coincidence that the volcanologist who renewed man's efforts to manage lava flows also left as his legacy the institution that has taken the lead in forecasting eruptions.

Thomas Augustus Jaggar Jr., son of an Episcopalian bishop, began his long love affair with fire and brimstone at 14 when, on an 1885 European tour with his family, he first saw Mount Vesuvius. Later, as a Harvard professor and then as head of the geology department at the Massachusetts Institute of Technology, Jaggar toiled in the laboratory, trying to imitate volcanic phenomena. He used blobs of mud as substitute lava, and subjected them to pressures and temperature changes. To emulate the lava intrusions that had warped South Dakota's Black Hills, he injected hot wax through the bottom of a tank filled with layers of sand, plaster powder and coal dust. To duplicate volcanic geysers, he rigged a contraption of water-filled bottles, tubes and a Bunsen burner that faithfully shot a pint of water four feet into the air every minute and a half.

Jaggar was bothered not at all by the fact that his experiments had little if any apparent practical application. He sought a basic understanding of the nature of volcanism; putting that knowledge to such uses as forecasting and lava-flow diversion would come later.

But volcanology is a peripatetic profession, and its practitioners can be counted upon to flock to the scenes of fiery fountains and flowing lava. Jaggar had, of course, been in the first wave of scientists to arrive at Martinique after Mount Pelée's 1902 blast, and four years later he hurried to Vesuvius to peer into a crater still fuming from the famed volcano's latest eruption. In the Aleutians in 1907, Jaggar landed on Bogoslof, a volcano whose peak barely broke the surface of the sea, unaware that he was standing on ground that would be shattered by a violent explosion only three weeks after he left.

All the while, however, Jaggar was growing increasingly fretful with the sporadic nature of volcanic examination: fierce interest in periods of crisis followed by apathy in time of repose. What was needed, he believed, were observatories—permanent laboratories on the crests of volcanoes, where scientists could work year round, studying their subject in all its phases. To be sure, the Italians had manned an observatory on Vesuvius since 1845, but they were alone. Jaggar meant to build on their pioneering work—and to build enormously. "The only way to know a crater," he insisted, "is to live with it."

For the site of an American observatory, Jaggar set his heart on the island of Hawaii's Kilauea volcano. Much more accessible than its larger sister, Mauna Loa, Kilauea was—and is—one of the world's most active volcanoes. Yet its effusive eruptions—unlike those of the explosive Vesuvius—generally posed little threat that resident scientists would be blown sky-high.

Jaggar commenced his campaign for a Kilauea observatory in 1909. He hoped for support from the United States Congress, but he found little sympathy for his project among either politicians or the private funding organizations to which he appealed. But Thomas Jaggar Jr. was an exceedingly stubborn individual, and he eventually wangled $25,000 from Boston's newly endowed Whitney Foundation. After sailing to Hawaii at his own expense, he persuaded not only Hawaiian businessmen but the ordinary citizens of Hilo, a city long threatened by lava flows from nearby Mauna Loa, to subscribe to his project.

At last, in January 1912, Jaggar set up shop as head of the Hawaiian Volcano Observatory, its eight-room building perched on the very lip of Kilauea's 400-foot-deep caldera. The new institution's motto was sweepingly Jaggaresque: *Ne plus haustae aut obrutae urbes*—"No more shall the cities be destroyed."

Then, in a modest way, began the work that was to make Kilauea the planet's most heavily instrumented tract of volcanic real estate. "Man is very tiny," Jaggar once wrote, "but if he listens he can hear the earth's heartbeats." One

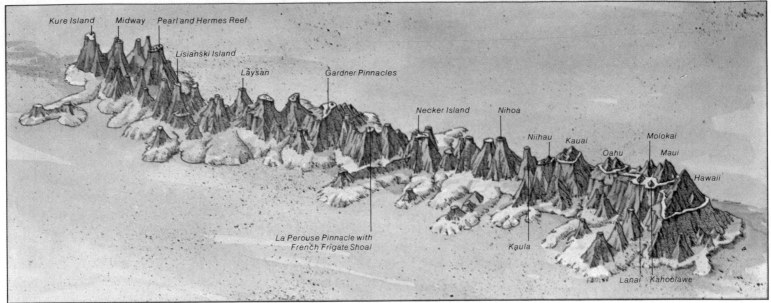

The islands are labeled: Kure Island, Midway, Pearl and Hermes Reef, Lisianski Island, Laysan, Gardner Pinnacles, Necker Island, Nihoa, Niihau, Kauai, Oahu, Molokai, Maui, Hawaii, Kaula, Lanai, Kahoolawe, La Perouse Pinnacle with French Frigate Shoal

of Jaggar's first acts was to blast a crypt in the hot rock almost directly beneath the observatory. In that moistureproof, airtight, solid vault he installed the observatory's seismographs, which traced the mountain's quakes and tremors with tiny needles onto paper sooted by smoke from kerosene lamps.

The weight of a young, active volcano can fracture the rock that lies beneath its overwhelming mass, causing deep-focus earthquakes. More frequent—and much more likely to warn of an impending eruption—are the relatively shallow quakes brought on by the pressures exerted by magma as it forces its way through fissures within the body of a volcano.

As a rule, the greater the number of earthquakes, the greater the chances of an eruption. But every volcano has a different pattern—in some the seismic build-up lasts for years, in others only a few days or even hours—and it would be a long while before the Hawaiian observatory's seismographic records began to make sense as indicators of volcanic activity on Kilauea. Meanwhile, there were more than enough other investigations to satisfy even Jaggar's curiosity.

With volcanology still in its childhood, the process was one of trial and error. Jaggar and his small staff spent many hours recording temperatures within the hot cracks that sundered the surface of Kilauea's summit, but they could find no relationship with the degree of volcanic activity. Similarly, it had been supposed that such climatic factors as rainfall, air temperature, barometric pressure and even variations in the trade winds might affect the volcano's behavior; the observatory's scientists were unable to substantiate the theory.

Working with E. S. Shepherd of Washington's Carnegie Institution, Jaggar devised a method of collecting volcanic gases in glass tubes from which air, a contaminant, had been removed by a vacuum pump. Jaggar and Shepherd ventured onto lava crusts and poked the long, thin tips of the tubes into vents from which gases were issuing. When the tubes were filled, the tips were broken off and the containers sealed with a blowtorch or by thrusting them against molten lava. The results were undoubtedly the best volcanic gas samples collected up to that time—but they were nonetheless unsatisfactory. The composition of gas combinations changes from one environment to another, and gas analysis is a complex and lengthy process. By the time the laboratory work was done, the gaseous mixtures were no longer the same as those taken from Kilauea.

Other projects contributed much more to understanding Kilauea's internal system. In the southwestern sector of Kilauea's 2-by-2½-mile caldera is a circular pit crater named Halemaumau (house of everlasting fire), which has long been a center of eruptive activity. It was here that Jaggar had tested his volcanic gas collectors. Halemaumau ranged at various times between 1,500 to 3,500

The Hawaiian archipelago stretches 1,500 miles across the central Pacific Ocean from Kure Island in the northwest to the island of Hawaii in the southeast. The islands are the tips of huge volcanoes that have slowly built up from depths of 18,000 feet as a result of countless underwater eruptions. Scientists believe the line of volcanoes was formed as the tectonic plate carrying the floor of the Pacific inched northwestward over a fixed "hot spot"—a magma source rising from the earth's interior.

feet in diameter, and within the pit, boiling and bubbling throughout most of the observatory's early years, was a rare volcanic phenomenon: a more or less permanent lake of highly fluid lava. In May 1916, after more than two years of slowly rising in Halemaumau, the lava lake, as Jaggar recalled it, "lowered dramatically during one day, leaving a deep seething puddle of melt." The sudden subsidence was—significantly, as it turned out—coincident with an eruption on Mauna Loa, 28 miles away.

For the next six months the lake's level steadily rose again, and Jaggar decided to discover if the lake had a bottom. As a probe, Jaggar screwed together ten 20-foot sections of one-inch pipe. As 10 assistants fed out the 200-foot length, Jaggar stood on a lava platform at the lake's edge and guided his oversized measuring rod into the caldron at an angle of about 50 degrees. Finally, Jaggar wrote later, "I could feel the pipe encountering the increasing resistance of a pasty bottom." The team kept pushing until the pipe would go no farther: "Its lower end was definitely stuck in the bottom substance of the lake."

Jaggar signaled his helpers to move in the other direction so as to withdraw the pipe. But as they did so, the pipe became mired in a thick lava crust at the lake's edge, which "gripped it like a hot iron." With his contrivance hopelessly stuck, Jaggar had to abandon four of its sections.

Still, by calculating the angle at which the pipe had been fed into the lake and its extension when it reached the bottom, Jaggar was able to estimate the depth of the lava lake at about 50 feet. Subsequent attempts, in which the pipe was kept free by constantly oscillating it back and forth, not only confirmed the initial reckoning but showed that the depth remained generally constant—

The island of Hawaii, known as the Big Island because its 4,030 square miles of area is greater than all seven of the other Hawaiian Islands put together, is the world's largest volcanic island after Iceland. Hualalai and Mauna Loa, two of the three active volcanoes that continue to shape the island, are among the highest mountains in the world, towering more than 30,000 feet above the ocean floor.

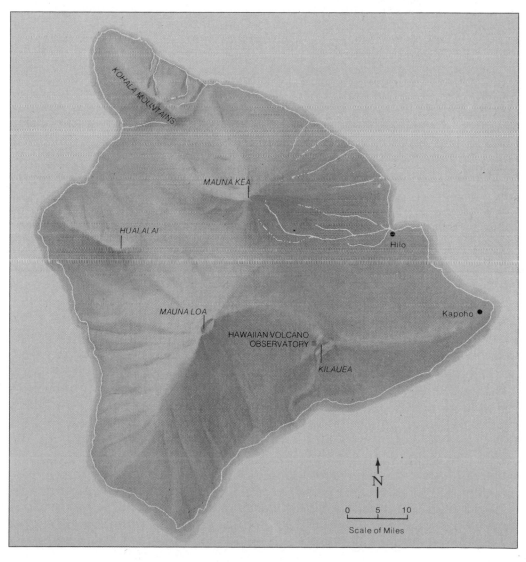

A Novel Scheme to Combat an Age-old Peril

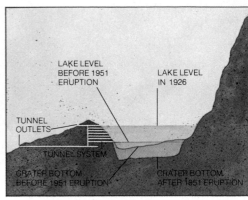

The diagram above shows how Dutch engineers by 1926 prevented overflows from the crater lake in Java's Kelut volcano (*left*). Seven tunnels were dynamited through the crater wall at 30-foot intervals. The tunnels drained enough of the lake to lower it by 185 feet and reduce its water volume from 85 million to four million cubic yards.

For centuries, residents of the area near Kelut volcano on the Indonesian island of Java lived in fear of one of the most destructive volcanic phenomena—mudflows, or lahars. When water from Kelut's crater lake was suddenly ejected by a major eruption, an acidic avalanche of hot water, rock and other debris swept down the mountain's slopes at express-train speeds.

In 1919, after a massive mudflow buried 104 villages, killed 5,110 people and ruined thousands of acres of cultivated land, Dutch colonial engineers came up with a plan to drain off most of the water in the crater lake.

A series of tunnels dug through the volcano's flank was completed in 1926.

The idea worked splendidly. In 1951, when Kelut once again erupted, the much-reduced crater lake simply evaporated. Unfortunately, the eruption wrecked the tunnel system and deepened the crater by 230 feet. More water soon accumulated, and in 1966 an eruption produced mudflows that again killed hundreds of people. The disaster prompted Indonesian officials to build a new, lower tunnel, completed in 1967, and Kelut's crater lake has been carefully maintained at a safe level ever since.

regardless of the lake's surface level relative to the walls of Halemaumau.

From his investigation, Jaggar evolved a theory that is still, for the most part, accepted. According to the volcanologist's hypothesis, the upper end of the conduit leading from Kilauea's magma chamber to the Halemaumau crater was plugged by a thick, pasty substance that he called epimagma. This in effect formed the lake's bottom. Injected through the epimagma by pressure from below was the thin, hot liquid—which Jaggar named pyromagma—of the lake itself. When exposed to air, this liquid congealed to form a denser lava called pahoehoe. The replenishment of the pyromagma from its source, combined with a slow drainage through passages in the epimagma below, kept the lava lake in equilibrium at a depth of about 50 feet.

It also appeared that the lava lake and its semisolid bottom of epimagma moved up and down more or less as a unit within Halemaumau's cylindrical confines. When the magma supply in the conduit under the plug of epimagma was for some reason reduced, the entire lake edifice descended like an elevator.

With that in mind, and recalling the lava lake's plunge during the eruption of Mauna Loa in 1916, Jaggar made an inspired guess. Mauna Loa and Kilauea, he reasoned, might share the same deep magma source. If that were true, then an eruption on Mauna Loa could relieve the upward pressures of magma within Kilauea—with the lowering of the lava lake in Kilauea as a consequence.

Thus, when Mauna Loa erupted in the fall of 1919, Jaggar predicted that the effect would be to "pull down Kilauea lava suddenly, like a siphon." The forecast was fulfilled on November 28, when the surface of Kilauea's lava lake plunged 400 feet in two or three hours.

Jaggar was pleased by the evidence of his increasing ability to postulate volcanic cause and effect. Yet volcanology is a humbling science—and all too soon came an event that was, as Jaggar ruefully admitted, "totally unforeseeable on the basis of earlier experience."

The 1919 eruption had been a last gasp for Mauna Loa: Except for a single brief and relatively mild outburst in the mid-1920s, the volcano would lie in repose for the next 14 years. But no sooner had Mauna Loa subsided than Kilauea, which had been virtually free from major eruptions for almost a quarter of a century, roared to life, erupting in 1919, 1921, 1922 and 1923.

It was part of Kilauea's pattern that each eruption was preceded by a rise in the level of Halemaumau's lake, and in January 1924, the lava stood only 105 feet below the crater's edge. But then it receded, dropping to 370 feet below the lip in February and remaining at that level through March. With the threat of eruption apparently eased, Jaggar felt secure enough to go to New York for a series of lectures—and Kilauea, almost as if on cue, came to life again. Swarms of earthquakes began in April near the caldera, then progressed along a rift zone on the eastern slope. On April 22 and 23, villagers nearly 30 miles east of the summit felt about 200 quakes. In the rift area, gaping cracks split the ground and then closed—but not until one of them had swallowed a cow. Magma was clearly moving into the rift zone, and an eruption there seemed imminent.

It came instead in the Halemaumau crater on May 11 and, far from being of the effusive variety to which Hawaiians were accustomed, it was the first of a two-week series of explosive blasts that spewed ash clouds four miles into the air and sent huge boulders flying in all directions. One of them, weighing about eight tons, was later found a quarter of a mile from the crater rim.

Hawaiian eruptions have always been an attraction for visitors confident that they stand little chance of being harmed. On May 18 a plantation bookkeeper named Truman A. Taylor, one of a group of sightseers on a Sunday outing to the eruption site, ventured close to the caldera for a better look. Just then came an explosion that showered the spectators with hot rocks. Taylor was nearly buried beneath a smoking heap of volcanic debris, both legs crushed and his face horribly burned. His companions dug him out and rushed him down the mountain to Hilo, but it was to no avail. At 11 o'clock that night, Truman Taylor died—the only victim of a Hawaiian volcano in recorded history.

Jaggar, meanwhile, had left New York as soon as he heard that Kilauea was erupting. By the time he arrived, the event was nearly over, and he plunged into the investigation of the rare explosions. It soon became apparent that large amounts of groundwater had seeped beneath Halemaumau through surface ruptures caused by the sinking of the mountaintop as the magma was withdrawn. When the water reached the hot rocks, it turned to steam, generated enormous pressure, and finally blasted its way out of the mountain. One casualty of the explosions was Halemaumau's lava lake, which, though it would reappear briefly and infrequently, was no longer a part of the volcanic moonscape.

The onset of the Great Depression brought difficult years for the Hawaiian Volcano Observatory; the esoteric work of a handful of scientists on a remote

Pacific island held low funding priority. Proprietorship of the observatory bounced from agency to agency, and during the 1930s Jaggar and his staff voluntarily went on half pay. Thus when, in 1935, a chance came not only to arouse great public interest but to prove a scientific point as well, Jaggar was quick to seize it.

On November 21, Mauna Loa erupted high on its northeast rift; the outburst was followed on November 27 by a heavy flow of lava from a new vent at 8,800 feet on the mountain's northeast flank. That lava formed a pond in the saddle created by the juncture of the slopes of Mauna Loa and long-dormant Mauna Kea. It then appeared that Mauna Loa's latest outbreak would—like so many before it—cause little if any harm. On December 22, however, the ponded lava, still fed from its source, broke loose and began moving in a 2,000-foot-wide stream at a rate of more than a mile a day toward Hilo, a city of 20,000 people and the site of the only sheltered harbor on Hawaii's east coast.

It was the first time since the volcano observatory's founding that Hilo had been seriously threatened by lava—and it led to the first major attempt to control a lava flow since the valiant effort of Diego de Pappalardo and his fellow Catanians almost three centuries before. The idea had come in an off-hand fashion from one of Jaggar's nonscientist friends, publisher Lorrin Thurston of the *Honolulu Advertiser*. Might it not be possible, Thurston had suggested in a 1929 article, to disrupt a lava flow with high explosives?

Jaggar was fascinated by the idea and he worked out a scheme based on the known habits of fluid pahoehoe lava. While traversing long distances, pahoehoe tends to form tunnels of its own cooled substance, with sides and roofs composed of thick (up to two feet) but brittle crusts of solid lava—through which run the streams of still-molten lava. Explosives could be used to cave in a tunnel roof, choking the tube with solid chunks of fallen lava; blocked in this manner, the flowing lava would presumably bubble up through the holes in the roof and spread harmlessly across the surrounding terrain. Even if that did not work, the violence of the explosions might stir up and change the nature of the pahoehoe, converting it to more viscous, slower-moving aa lava.

Now, with Hilo menaced by Mauna Loa, Jaggar decided to give explosives a spectacular try—using as a delivery service the U.S. Army Air Corps. On December 26, officers of the 23rd and 72nd Bombing Squadrons from Luke Field, Honolulu, reconnoitered the proposed target area accompanied by "the Volcanologist," as Jaggar was fond of calling himself. As he later described the plan: "The Volcanologist recommended that the uppermost channel of the actual flow be bombarded at elevation approximately 8,500 feet on the north flank of Mauna Loa. The channel about a mile down the lava stream was indicated as a second target."

By next morning, the lava flow was within 15 miles of Hilo. At 8:45 a.m., the first of 10 twin-engined Keystone bombers took off from Hilo Airport carrying two 600-pound TNT bombs and two 300-pound black-powder bombs to mark the targets. The others followed at 20-minute intervals.

Jaggar delightedly watched it all from an observation post on nearby Mauna Kea. "The entire operation," he wrote later, "was spectacular and impressive. Amid the thunder of shattering explosions, masses of rock and sheets of glowing lava were hurled in all directions. Many of the great bombs, dropped from planes traveling at high speed, plunged directly into open channels through which molten lava was flowing, while others crashed upon the roofs of tunnels, blowing them open and releasing the melt imprisoned within, causing it to gush upwards and commence spreading immediately."

Thirty-three hours after the bombing, the lava front stopped moving—only to start again after a few hours. For the next several days, Jaggar watched anxiously as it crept onward. At 2 a.m. on January 2 the stream's last finger, a mere 100 yards wide, came to a halt 12 miles short of Hilo's Kaumana Road.

Indonesia's Brave Band of Volcano Watchers

When the siren wails on the slope above Krintjing, Java, the fate of the mountain village hangs by a thread. The alarm means that Mount Merapi is again spewing clouds of superheated gases and ash from its crater, just four miles away. If a cloud veered toward Krintjing, the villagers would have to flee or face destruction within minutes. And they are not alone in their danger. Scores of villages lie in the shadow of Mount Merapi in densely populated central Java.

For many of the villages, the alarm may be raised by coded beating on drums, part of a primitive yet effective warning system that keeps track of the Indonesian archipelago's 130 active volcanoes—a fifth of the world's total. A force of 70 observers mans 25 stations around the most active and dangerous volcanoes. Understaffed and ill-equipped, the watchers monitor rudimentary seismographs and tiltmeters, and regularly make treks to the mouths of volcanoes to check the temperatures of crater lakes and the composition of volcanic gases.

Familiarity with the volcanoes often fills the gaps left by deficient equipment. Many observers have lived on the volcanoes for years; sometimes the job is passed from father to son. "A stranger cannot predict even with instruments. Each volcano has its moods," says one watcher. "The important thing is to get friendly with the mountain."

A team of volcano watchers rests near the summit of 9,605-foot Mount Merapi following a five-hour climb through forests and boulder fields. The observers make the trip about four times a year, and if the volcano exhibits signs of a possible eruption they keep it under close study.

Crouched over a smoky fire in a tiny wicker enclosure, an observer coats a piece of seismograph paper with soot that will record the tracing of a stylus. Such makeshift techniques help alleviate chronic shortages of equipment and supplies.

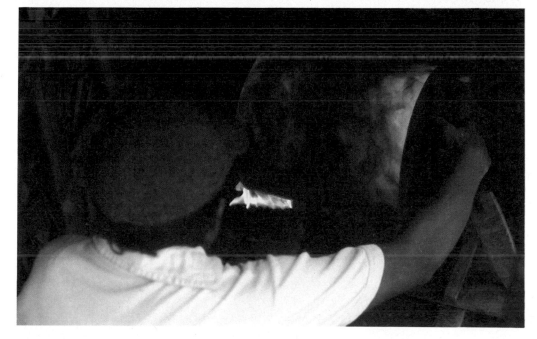

Protected only by an improvised gas mask, an observer uses a temperature probe to measure the heat of escaping gases on Mount Merapi. To ensure accurate readings, observers must brave the sulfurous gases for three or four minutes at a time.

"Thus," Jaggar proclaimed, "terminated the first experiment of its kind in attempting to curb one of the most destructive forces of nature." In later years, other scientists would examine the bombing area and question the actual effectiveness of the attempt. The lava, they argued, had probably stopped because the eruption itself had ceased. But even if that was the case, Jaggar's aerial assault had served another purpose: Thanks in part to the favorable attention attracted by the bombing, the future of the Hawaiian Volcano Observatory was relatively secure when, in 1940, Jaggar retired as its director. He took a post as a research associate in geophysics at the University of Hawaii and, until his death in 1953, combined his work at the university with the pursuit of such interests as astronomy and the measurement of the hardness of minerals.

Jaggar's successors at the observatory mounted a second aerial attack on Mauna Loa during a 1942 eruption that again threatened Hilo with lava flows; they had indifferent success. Nevertheless, in 1975 and 1976 the U.S. Air Force, working with the observatory, conducted bombing tests on ancient lava tubes and on a remnant spatter cone on Mauna Loa's north slope. They found that the cone was especially fragile and was substantially weakened up to 55 yards from the bomb craters. These results, as compiled for a 1980 Hawaiian Volcano Observatory report, led to a highly optimistic conclusion: "Modern aerial bombing has a substantial probability of success."

The search continued for a method of combating lava flows that was certain to succeed; and volcanologists found new hope in an intriguing characteristic of the more fluid basaltic lavas. Although the weight of such lava flows should certainly be enough to bowl over almost anything that gets in their way, they actually exert astonishingly little thrust.

During the 1906 eruption of Vesuvius, for example, a lava stream reached the cemetery of Torre Annunziata, came to a stop against the stone walls and finally divided into two parts that bypassed the enclosed area. At Mexico's Paricutín in 1944, lava filled the inside of the Church of San Juan Parangaricutiro without breaking the walls; when the eruption subsided, the building lay buried—but its bell tower, still intact, rose above the solidified lava.

A variety of factors lies behind the reluctance of lava to sweep aside obstacles it encounters. Molten lava behaves like most other liquids, at least in that it tends to follow the path of least resistance down the steepest available slope. Yet even in its most fluid condition, lava is more than 300,000 times as viscous as water; the farther it travels from its source, the more viscous it becomes, until the ratio of its viscosity to that of water is more than a million to one.

Because of its viscosity, lava moves slowly, at a rate governed mainly by the gravity that impels it downslope. On a reasonably gentle slope, such as those existing on the middle and lower reaches of many volcanoes, the thick, sluggish substance exerts little force. An obstacle standing perpendicular across its path acts as a dam; the lava stops and piles up until, if the flow is of sufficient volume, it laps over the obstruction. But if the barrier is at an angle to the direction of the flow, the lava can be diverted onto another course.

The observed instances of inadvertent diversion inevitably gave rise to speculation about the possibility of erecting man-made barriers to deflect lava flows, and a 1955 Kilauea eruption provided the occasion for some highly impromptu tests. On March 13, nearly two weeks after the eruption began, a tongue of pahoehoe, one of several extending from a larger stream, reached cleared land on the mountain's east flank. Having nothing better at hand, Gordon Macdonald, the observatory's scientist in charge, propped a wooden plank about eight feet long, 18 inches wide and two inches thick on its edge diagonal to the lava flow's path. Reaching the plank, the stream turned tamely aside for about 30 minutes—until the plank, set afire by the lava's heat, was consumed.

On the morning of March 21, a sizable lava stream crept into a valley directly

Lava spurts from a vent that opened in a roadway on the east flank of Kilauea volcano on the island of Hawaii during a 1955 eruption. As the lava fell back and cooled, it built up a spatter cone that reached a height of 20 feet and all but covered the road. Kilauea's four-month-long eruption was accompanied by several similar vents and lava fountains, and provided scientists with a rare opportunity to witness the evolution of such volcanic features firsthand.

toward a small sugar-plantation camp owned by Koji Iwasaki. Working feverishly with six bulldozers in the steaming face of the oncoming lava, Iwasaki and his helpers, supervised by a scientist from the observatory, threw up a wall about 1,000 feet long and 10 feet high. When the lava arrived at the obstruction it was deflected and began moving down the diagonal face of the barrier; it had traveled only about 50 feet when its supply of lava stopped flowing from the source vent. Sadly, subsequent lava streams descended by other routes and wiped out Iwasaki's camp.

Five years later another attempt at wall building also showed mixed results. Still, Gordon Macdonald saw considerable value in them: "A great deal of information was gained on how such walls behave, and how they should be built when they are again needed." Chief among the lessons was that the walls should be built diagonally to the flow so as to divert rather than dam. The base of the wall should be thick—roughly three times the depth of the flow. To enable the lava to move freely down the face of the slanted wall, a pathway should be cleared in front of the barrier, with everything except grass and perhaps small bushes removed. And the slope onto which the flow was to be diverted must be steep enough to ensure that the lava would keep moving.

Those lessons were incorporated in a contingency plan for building barriers to protect Hilo should a lava flow from Mauna Loa menace the city. Bombing remained as a possible backup measure—along with a method once used with dramatic effect, not in sunny Hawaii but in the frigid Atlantic near Iceland.

On January 23, 1973, a fissure near the long-dormant Helgafell volcano on the island of Heimaey, off the southern coast of Iceland, came to life with a vengeance. Vast amounts of ash were hurled aloft and streams of lava issued from scores of fire fountains along the 5,000-foot fissure. The island's 5,300 inhabitants were swiftly evacuated, except for 300 volunteers who remained behind to see what they could do about saving property and preventing the oncoming lava from sealing the narrow mouth of the fishing port (*pages 134-139*).

A wall of lava 120 feet high was advancing along a front that eventually reached 1,000 feet in width, and by February 8 it was within 600 feet of the harbor. Bombing was discussed and discarded; the flow was too near the town to risk a misaimed bomb. Then several Icelandic scientists suggested a technique they had tried, in a small and inconclusive way, during the eruption of nearby Surtsey in 1963. The principle was simplicity itself: If water could be pumped onto the flow, it might cool the lava and cause it to slow or stop.

At first, a few fire engines turned their hoses on the approaching tide of lava. The results were mixed. As little tongues of lava crept from the front of the flow, they solidified under the barrage of water. The solid material began to pile up, forming a dam to which bulldozers added earth. But as the lava continued to flood from its source, the flow repeatedly overlapped the barriers.

In early March the sand dredger *Sandey,* with Iceland's most powerful pumps, began arcing sprays of sea water onto the flow. More high-pressure pumps were rushed from the United States, and it was learned that by piping water to points far behind the flow's front, a series of internal barriers of cooled lava could be created. The Icelanders discovered that easily manageable plastic pipes could be snaked onto the surface of the flow without melting so long as water was kept flowing through them. In all, more than 19 miles of pipes and 43 pumps were used in the operation. Temperature tests indicated that a steady two-week deluge from all the assembled equipment would cool the lava to about 212° F., far below the point (1,472° F.) at which basalt solidifies.

Day after day, week after week, the pumping continued. The water did not halt the lava flow entirely, but did slow it dramatically. Finally, in early July, the eruption subsided, the lava was stopped at its source, and the massive effort came to an end. Heimaey's harbor was saved.

From the forlorn endeavor of Diego de Pappalardo to the remarkable feat of Heimaey, the progress of lava control had been long and fitful. And though scientists, after their experience on Heimaey, could hope to manage the movement of basaltic flows, they remained utterly helpless against the flying debris and numerous other perils of explosive volcanoes. Meanwhile, more rapid progress had been made in the even younger science of volcano forecasting, based on early studies in Italy and Japan and on the experiments of Thomas Jaggar Jr.

"There is no single key to forecasting," said Robert Decker, the scientist in charge at the Hawaiian observatory in 1981. "A variety of factors must be evaluated and interpreted. But past history is certainly one key to the future."

In many places where fairly long and accurate records exist, statistical patterns of volcanic activity began to emerge. But they varied greatly from mountain to mountain, and gleaning from the statistics a pattern suggesting which mountain would erupt when was a complex and frustrating business. Some volcanoes, such as Mauna Loa, seemed to erupt entirely at random—that is, the statistical chances of an outburst remained unchanged, no matter how long since the last eruption. In the case of Mauna Loa, the most statisticians could say was that there was a 20 per cent chance of its erupting in any given year.

In one especially fascinating piece of statistical detective work, the Hawaiian observatory's Daniel Dzurisin studied 52 Kilauea outbreaks since January 1832, and found that the volcano was nearly twice as likely to erupt during a time of high lunisolar tides, which occurred every two weeks, than during a period of low tides. Dzurisin's evidence supported a long-held theory that the gravitational pull of the moon and the sun can trigger an eruption of a volcano already in precarious balance. Dzurisin could not, however, find lunisolar cause and effect in the eruptive history of Mauna Loa.

If nothing else, statistics helped steer volcanologists to the mountains on which they could most profitably concentrate their instruments. And it is in modern instrumentation that volcanology in general and forecasting in particular have made their greatest advances.

By all odds the most useful tool in the volcanologist's inventory is the seismograph, which is used to register the number, measure the intensity and point to the location of the earthquakes that almost always precede volcanic eruptions. In 1912, when Jaggar began work atop Kilauea, the seismographs then in use were relatively crude instruments; they failed to detect the first small earthquakes that often signal the onset of an eruptive period, and they were completely overwhelmed by the shaking of a heavy nearby quake.

But four decades later the state of the art had advanced to the point where the specialized instruments installed on Kilauea could withstand most of the heaviest shakes—yet they were so sensitive that they had to be installed at least a half mile from highways to avoid vibrations from vehicle traffic. Moreover, the number of seismic stations had been expanded from the three with which Jaggar began to a network of 45 on both Kilauea and Mauna Loa.

But the seismographs were not enough. For while eruptions almost invariably were preceded by earthquakes, huge numbers of earthquakes occurred without a subsequent eruption. The Hawaii seismographs recorded as many as 150,000 earthquakes in a single year without a single eruption. Thus accurate forecasting required other instruments giving different sorts of information.

"Active volcanoes almost seem to breathe," wrote volcanologist Howel Williams in 1951. "They are forever swelling and subsiding as the subterranean magma fluctuates in level." The phenomenon of ground deformation—in which volcanoes bloat while being filled with magma and then shrink when the lava is erupted—was first noticed in the early 1900s at Japan's Usu and Sakurajima volcanoes and at Kilauea. The first attempts to measure the tumescence

Hawaiian folklore offered a complete explanation for the astonishing volcanic activity of the islands long before the volcanologists ever arrived to make their analyses. According to ancient songs and stories, a beautiful fiery-haired deity named Pele is responsible for the area's geologic tumult.

Pele, who still commands fear and respect among islanders, is pictured as a tempestuous goddess subject to fits of murderous rage. When angered, Pele extracts a calamitous price from her subjects; she stamps the ground, sending earthquakes reverberating through the land. Then she summons from the underworld a boiling surge of lava, and rides the molten wave, screaming curses and hurling fiery boulders until the lava swallows her hapless target.

In many stories Pele walks the islands in disguise, sometimes as an old woman with blazing eyes, sometimes as an athlete competing with handsome young chieftains. And should she lose such a competition, she unleashes her volcanic fury, and mortals learn too late that they have angered the ill-tempered goddess.

Standing among denuded saplings on the rim of Hawaii's Aloi Crater, a woman prepares to cast an offering to Pele, the goddess of volcanoes. The still-honored tradition is that Pele can be appeased with offerings of gin or sacred ohelo berries.

were made with ordinary surveyor's instruments. But the swelling process can be extremely slow and the degree of tilt is often very small. The huge mass of Kilauea, for example, can take nearly a decade to swell less than four feet at the summit. In such cases, meaningful day-to-day measurements were far beyond the capacity of ordinary tools.

The answer lay in a device called a tiltmeter, developed in 1943 by the Japanese. In one of its basic forms, this instrument consists of two containers of water, spaced several yards apart and connected by tubing; if one pot is elevated above the other by ground deformation, its water flows down through the tube into the other container. The changes in water levels, as measured by micrometers, indicate the amount of tilt. A widely used variation operates much like a carpenter's level, with an air bubble in a water-filled glass tube; when one end is raised, the bubble's motion is gauged by electronic sensors. A number of the Hawaiian observatory's tiltmeters are installed in a 10-by-15-foot seismographic vault, encased by thick concrete and anchored in bedrock—yet they are sensitive enough to register the weight of a man entering the room.

In addition to the tilting of a volcano's slopes during inflation and deflation, a mountain's summit stretches while magma is accumulating in the reservoir and then shrinks after an eruption. To measure such lateral distances, a laser ranging instrument came into use in 1965. It beams a laser light at a prismatic reflector, often several miles away, then registers the time it takes for the re-

The Hawaiian Volcano Observatory, established in 1912, sits on the edge of Kilauea's crater, an unsurpassed vantage point for observing one of the world's most active volcanoes. The continuous, close-in study of Kilauea and neighboring Mauna Loa has paid rich dividends in a broad spectrum of techniques used to monitor volcanoes all around the globe.

flected light to return. By calculating the distance in terms of the speed of light, horizontal measurements can be made to an accuracy of about one part per million. "The idea of one part per million," wrote Robert I. Tilling, formerly of the Hawaiian observatory, "can be visualized in terms of a very dry martini—one drop of vermouth and 16 gallons of gin!"

Used together, with the evidence of one complementing the testimony of the others, tiltmeters and seismographs provided the clues that in 1959 led to timely warning of one of Kilauea's most spectacular—and potentially most dangerous—displays.

One reason the scientists at the observatory had not anticipated the 1955 eruption of Kilauea was that their few tiltmeters occupied permanent positions, providing only the most limited coverage. Hardly had the eruption quieted than the scientists set up a priority project to devise portable tiltmeters that could be moved about according to a developing situation. In the observatory's machine shop, they put together a contraption using ordinary garden hose for tubing and the empty casings of used artillery shells for pots.

Then came the long and arduous task of installing the new tiltmeters on concrete piers set 150 feet apart in triangular formation so that a tilt in any direction would be detected by the instruments. After weeks of jouncing in jeeps across lava fields and slashing trails through tropical thickets to remote sites, the volcanologists discovered to their dismay that their device did not work outdoors—temperature variations expanded and contracted the water and threw the measurements out of kilter. Finally, they decided to make their measurements at night, when environmental changes were less severe.

Meanwhile, Kilauea had awakened from a two-year slumber. In November 1957, the old tiltmeters in the observatory's three vaults detected a slow swelling of the summit, hinting that the volcano was again building toward eruption. But the data were by no means conclusive. As one scientist would recall, the race was now on "between the volcano and the fellows" to see if the new tiltmeter network could be installed before Kilauea made the effort academic.

The "fellows" won—but just barely, and only after two years of labor. By November of 1959, the new tiltmeter network was at last in place. It indicated that the swelling process was accelerating and that Kilauea, its reservoir obviously gorged, was ballooning at a rate three times that of the previous months.

The scientists were ready and civil authorities had been alerted. In midafternoon on November 14, shallow earthquakes—already occurring at a rate of more than 1,000 per day—increased both in number and intensity, and for the next five hours the mountain trembled. At about 8 p.m., seismographs registered the harmonic tremor that Frank Perret had first observed on Vesuvius more than 50 years earlier—steady vibrations caused by magma moving rapidly near the surface in search of a weak spot to burst through.

For years any harmonic tremor lasting more than 10 minutes had set off automatic alarms in the homes of scientists living near the Kilauea caldera, alerting them that an eruption was imminent. This time there was no need: The staffers were already gathered in the observatory, tensely peering into the night through windows overlooking the caldera. In the parking lot outside the low, ramshackle cluster of buildings, every available vehicle was packed with scientific equipment and ready to rush to the scene of the eruption.

Men with asbestos suits were waiting to use the long dippers with which they would gather samples of lava for chemical analysis. Others would be in the field measuring tilt. Still others would be armed with optical pyrometers to measure the temperature and cooling rate of the erupted lava. Resembling a telescope, the pyrometer is equipped with a wire filament passing through its field of vision. As an electrical current is run through the wire it becomes increasingly hot, changing in color from dull to bright red, orange, yellow and white. By matching the color of the wire with that of the lava, the temperature of the molten material can be reckoned from a safe distance.

At 8:08 it happened—fissures split open and 50-foot fountains of lava gushed from Kilauea Iki, a pit crater just east of the caldera and separated from it by a rampart of solidified lava. K. J. Murata, the scientist in charge, picked up a phone and called civil authorities. "Kilauea," he said, "is erupting again."

During the next month, in breathtaking sequence, the volcano subsided, then erupted again no fewer than 16 times. After the Kilauea Iki outburst ceased on December 21, many observers thought the display was over, but the volcanologists knew better: Their new tiltmeter system indicated that the volcano's reservoir, constantly replenished from far below, was even more bloated with magma than at the beginning of the event.

By early January, seismic readings indicated that earthquake activity had shifted from the summit region eastward 28 miles to the vicinity of Kapoho, a village with a population of 300, most of them workers on nearby sugar plantations. Kapoho means "sunken-in place," and the town was appropriately named. It lay in a graben—a long, shallow trough formed by two parallel faults—which provided a perfect channel for the flow of lava.

On the morning of January 13, 1960, as Kapoho's earth shuddered and goods tumbled from the shelves of a Japanese grocery store where he had stationed himself, volcanologist Jerry Eaton placed a telephone call to the island's top administrative official in Hilo. An eruption was imminent, Eaton said, and it was time to evacuate Kapoho. Within minutes, waiting National Guard and plantation trucks were moving out, loaded not only with Kapoho's residents but with many of their belongings, including such heavy items as refrigerators and stoves. By late afternoon, all of the village's inhabitants had been taken to safety. And just as night fell, the sky blazed with the lurid light of eruption. Lava began gushing from a fissure in a sugar-cane field only one-half mile northwest of the village, and lava fountains, one of them more than 300 feet tall, were soon dancing like dervishes over the afflicted landscape. Little Kapoho was doomed. But thanks to the forewarning furnished by the instruments on Kilauea, not a single person had been so much as singed.

Kilauea would remain in a state of almost constant turmoil for the next 15 years. With the success of 1960 bolstering their confidence, and with some 24 new eruptions on which to hone their skills, the scientists at the observatory

Standing on a crust of lava, an observatory scientist jams a stainless-steel pipe into a stream of lava to gauge its depth. His timing is critical; if the pipe is left too long in the 2,100° F. lava, it will soften and bend, making measurement impossible.

steadily improved their forecasting techniques. The Hawaiian Volcano Observatory had by 1975 become an international center for volcanic studies. There were constant interchanges of personnel with the parent U.S. Geological Survey, operator of the observatory since 1948. And there were frequent visits from Japanese, Italian, New Zealand, French, Indonesian and other volcanologists based at permanent observatories that had sprung up on the slopes of mountains around the world. The Russians had established observatories and seismograph stations to monitor the volatile Kamchatka Peninsula. Japan, which had long been a leader in volcano research, boasted several observatories. The first had been set up at Mount Asama in 1934, and in subsequent years several others had been added, notably those at Oshima and Aso. Similar study programs were going on in such far-flung parts of the world as the Philippines, central Africa and New Zealand.

By the 1980s, the Hawaiian observatory had girdled Kilauea, and to a lesser extent Mauna Loa, with networks of nearly 90 tiltmeters and 50 seismic stations. And new studies were under way that held high promise of adding to the mass of information on which forecasts are based.

Geochemists have long been intrigued by indications that eruptions may be preceded by increases in the amount of sulfur dioxide and carbon dioxide in the gases issuing from vents. Such gases are now monitored by a snorkel-like instrument, mounted atop a jeep that is driven through the plumes of vapor. The problem of speedy gas analysis, which so frustrated Jaggar and his colleague Dr. Shepherd, has now been partly solved.

Observatory scientists are especially hopeful that studies of the magnetic and electrical properties of volcanic interiors will also lead to new and effective methods of forecasting. Molten basalt contains no magnetic minerals, but cooled basalt has a small amount of magnetic iron oxide. Conversely, molten rock is a good electrical conductor, while solidified lava is not. Theoretically, therefore, it should be possible to track magma as it moves underground by taking magnetic and electrical soundings.

Yet for all the advances, forecasting can still be endlessly frustrating—if only because the volcanoes themselves keep changing the rules. In 1975, for example, a magnitude 7.2 earthquake and resulting tsunami on Hawaii's southeast coast killed two people (and four horses), triggered a brief eruption

Fountains of lava and clouds of steam erupt from sugar-cane fields near the Hawaiian village of Kapoho in January 1960. This eruption from the flank of Kilauea was unusually explosive for a Hawaiian volcano; rising magma had flashed groundwater into steam, which in its violent expansion shot lava spray and pulverized rock 1,500 feet into the air.

Churning bulldozers push up an earthen barrier against a thick sea of black, encrusted lava creeping toward homes near Kapoho during Kilauea's 1960 eruption. Despite the frantic efforts at containment lava eventually overflowed the 20-foot-high, three-mile-long dam, virtually destroying Kapoho and extending the shoreline half a mile seaward.

in Kilauea's caldera, severely shook up the mountain's internal plumbing—and changed the volcano's pattern of behavior.

Of the 12 major volcanic events in the five years before the 1975 quake, 10 had been eruptions and two intrusions—movements of magma that look like impending eruptions on instruments but that, in fact, peter out before reaching the surface. In the five years after the earthquake, the ratio was reversed, with 10 intrusions and only two eruptions. Said scientist in charge Robert Decker, who, like many volcanologists, tends to personify the subjects of his study: "I don't think the mountain has made up its mind what it wants to do next."

While the scientists in Hawaii waited to find out about their volcano's intentions, an event on the United States mainland dramatically demonstrated how far the science of forecasting has come—and how far it has yet to go. Ω

The fishermen of Heimaey off the south coast of Iceland are of necessity a hardy and self-reliant lot. But nothing in their experience prepared them for the disaster that struck the island early in 1973. At 2 a.m. on January 23, a fiery fissure opened in the land less than a mile from the town of Vestmannaeyjar, and tephra—volcanic ejecta—spewed forth in immense quantities.

Considering Heimaey's tiny size, scarcely 4.36 square miles, and the unpredictability of the eruption, the only prudent course was immediate evacuation. Within six hours, more than 5,000 people had been taken to the mainland. But 300 determined volunteers remained behind to protect the islanders' homes and property from the blanketing tephra and advancing lava. Going from house to house, the volunteers sealed windows facing the volcano, loaded cars and trucks with household goods and drove them to the docks.

Nevertheless, in just over two months, 300 buildings had succumbed to fire, while another 65 had disappeared beneath black tephra. Meanwhile, as the eruption continued, flowing lava threatened to block the entrance to Heimaey's harbor, thus depriving the islanders of their livelihood.

In desperation, the islanders, assisted by Icelandic scientists, began to pump sea water on the lava in hopes of cooling it enough to stem its advance. This did not halt the lava, but did slow its flow. For four months the battle went on, while the lava pushed into the harbor and came within 150 yards of closing its only entrance. And then, mercifully, the volcano fell silent.

The people of Heimaey hurried back to reclaim their island. Nearly one third of the town had been covered by lava; the rest lay under a blanket of ash. Using everything from brooms to bulldozers, the islanders cleared the ash from roofs, gardens and streets; more than 1.3 million cubic yards of volcanic material was cleared away.

The new 735-foot volcano partially compensated the islanders for their ordeal. The ash was used to construct a second runway for Heimaey's airfield, the lava and ash added nearly a square mile of land to the island, and the wall of lava reaching the edge of the harbor provided an excellent breakwater.

A fiery pillar showers ash on Vestmannaeyjar on Iceland's Heimaey island as a volcano is born in January 1973. The eruption transformed farmland into a mountain rivaling in size the cone of extinct Helgafell volcano, half a mile to the southwest.

In a novel attack on encroaching lava, volcano fighters hose the molten material with sea water as it nears the Vestmannaeyjar harbor. The hosing operation was directed at 11 principal locations along the lava front and continued for five months.

A smothering blanket of black tephra, 20 feet thick in places, lies over the tightly clustered homes in the eastern district of Vestmannaeyjar. In some places, ash made heavy by rain caved in roofs, but elsewhere it served to protect buildings from red-hot lava bombs ejected by the volcano.

Islanders pitch in to clear a Vestmannaeyjar roof of tephra after the eruption. In cleaning up, priority was given to digging out and repairing the fish-processing factories, mainstay of the island's economy.

The enormity of the 1973 volcanic eruption comes vividly clear in these before-and-after views of Vestmannaeyjar. In the larger photograph, which was taken in 1976, the new half-mile-wide cinder cone and the 550-acre lava field provide a new investigative site for geologists, biologists and volcanologists.

139

Chapter 6

THE CATACLYSM ON ST. HELENS

One among scores of scientists who flocked to Mount St. Helens when it began to stir in March 1980, British volcanologist Basil Booth studies the mountain from a position 5.5 miles to the northwest. Pressed into service as an observer by the U.S. Geological Survey, Booth communicated with the Survey's base in Vancouver, Washington, using the short-wave radio in the pack beside his chair.

More often than not, the mountain was shrouded in clouds driven inland from the Pacific Ocean. But when it emerged it was magnificent—rising smooth and symmetrical from the surrounding plain, by far the most perfect peak in the entire Cascade Range, which stretches 700 miles south from Canada to California. Upon his first view of the peak in November 1805 from a point near the present site of Portland, Oregon, the explorer William Clark was moved to an uncharacteristic superlative. "Mount St. Helens," he wrote in the log of the Lewis and Clark Expedition, "is perhaps the greatest pinnacle in America." For a mountain just short of 10,000 feet, this was high praise, but Mount St. Helens had that sort of dazzling effect on people.

The mountain had earlier been sighted, logged and named—after a minor diplomat—by another explorer, the British sea captain George Vancouver, who had viewed it from his ship in 1792 as he sailed northward past the mouth of the Columbia River. But the settlers who followed these adventurers to the Pacific Northwest soon found that the Klickitat tribe had two names for the mountain. One, Loo-Wit, referred to a lovely maiden who had been changed by the Great Spirit into an equally beautiful white mountain; the other, everyday, title was Tah-one-lat-clah, or "fire mountain." The more ominous name reflected the obvious respect with which the Indians regarded the mountain—they were reluctant to approach it, though the surrounding forests and waters abounded in fur-bearing animals and fish.

The Indians knew from their ancestors something about this mountain that was not immediately apparent to the newcomers: It was a volcano. The perfect cone and even slopes had been smoothed by lava flows and volcanic ash deposits. The conifer forests at its base had carpeted over the ravages of some devastating eruptions in the geologically recent past. The beautiful Spirit Lake, which mirrored the mountain on its north side, was actually a backup from a natural dam created by a gigantic mudflow sometime between 800 and 1200 B.C. Indeed, the entire area had been structured by violent volcanic action.

As if to remind the settlers of its true identity, Mount St. Helens puffed out occasional clouds of steam and ash and disgorged some lava between 1832 and 1857. Though impressive to behold, these were relatively mild events, and as the years passed succeeding generations of Northwesterners grew to maturity thinking of the Cascade area as a singularly benign environment. For more than a century, the mountain warmly accommodated that view.

The reawakening came with terrible suddenness in the spring of 1980. After a series of premonitory shakes and puffs, Mount St. Helens erupted with incredible violence on the morning of May 18, killing 60 people and turning an area of 232 square miles into a tortured gray landscape. Volcanologists have calculated the force of this explosion as one of the largest in the conterminous United States in the last two centuries: The energy released was equivalent to that of 500 Hiroshima-type atomic bombs, or 10 million tons of TNT.

The white virgin mountain today is a squat, ugly and truncated cone, the color of putty in summer and, under winter's snows, resembling a huge decayed molar, drilled out and awaiting a crown filling. The once-perfect summit cone is gone; in its place, 1,313 feet lower, is a mean-looking amphitheater with sheer 2,000-foot walls opening out toward the devastated area below.

Inside the crater itself on every day of passable visibility, the walls echo to the rattle of helicopters convoying a small army of scientists up over the broken slopes to observe, photograph, sample, measure and mark, poking through the eerie vapors in an exhilarating and dangerous race to find out all that the volcano will tell about itself, and about volcanoes generally, before it subsides for more generations—or erupts again, erasing forever all the new evidence.

The eruption of Mount St. Helens came as an abrupt and stunning reminder of the furnaces that lie beneath the entire Cascade Range, from Mount Garibaldi in the north to Lassen Peak in California. Indeed, except for geologists, scarcely anyone in the Northwest was more than dimly aware of the Cascades' volcanic history, which was both rich and recent. The Cascades are, in fact, a highly volatile stretch of the Ring of Fire that encircles the Pacific Ocean, and there has been, on the average, at least one major volcanic eruption every century since the end of the Pleistocene epoch roughly 10,000 years ago.

In geologic context, the Cascades are an extremely young mountain range, having uplifted only about seven million years ago atop the subduction zone where the Juan de Fuca Plate is being driven, ponderously and irresistibly, underneath the higher-riding North American Plate. Beginning about three million years ago, magma began rising through conduits to the surface to build the modern Cascades.

But by the mid-1960s the lordly volcanoes of the Cascades were known to the public chiefly as scenic landmarks and havens of recreation—and to geologists as formations whose violent origins and dangerous nature deserved further study, if and when priorities permitted.

The clues that something dramatic could happen at any time were present at every hand, but they were not fully understood. The majestic 14,410-foot silhouette of Mount Rainier, 50 miles north of St. Helens, was flawed by ominous signs; it fumed and steamed, and heat from within its massive bulk created

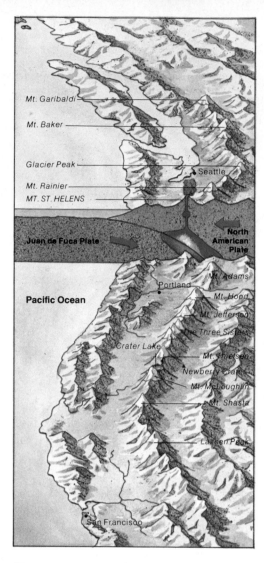

Monuments to the grinding movement of the earth's crust, the mountains of the Cascade Range stretch from southern British Columbia to northern California. The plate movement that has thrust up the mountains has also created enormous pools of magma that feed some 15 volcanoes.

Flathead Indians watch an 1842 eruption of Mount St. Helens from a canoe on the waters of the Lewis River. Canadian artist Paul Kane painted the picture in 1847 from his sketches of the mountain and accounts of the eruption. Though the scene was fanciful—the Indians actually kept a healthy distance from what they called Fire Mountain—the rendering correctly shows the eruption coming from a vent partway down the north face of the volcano.

An explorer gazes in awe at the scalloped formation of a mile-long cave system carved by volcanic steam in the summit ice on seemingly quiescent Mount Rainier. Varying levels of heat emission cause significant changes in the ice caves found on Mounts Rainier, Baker and Hood, and could provide indications of an impending eruption.

spooky caves in the ice and sometimes melted through its gigantic glacier fields. The slopes and crags of Mount Hood, 60 miles south of St. Helens, were dotted with steaming fumaroles, and the smell of sulfur pervaded wide areas.

The clearest evidence of what a Cascade volcano could do was associated with Mount Mazama, in whose caldera was located the famed 2,000-foot-deep Crater Lake—the deepest lake in North America. Mazama's monumental blast almost 7,000 years ago had covered what is now the Northwestern United States with a blanket of ash and had sent avalanches of pumice cascading down the mountain to reach thicknesses of as much as 50 feet 35 miles from the crater.

However, only one Cascade volcano had erupted significantly in the 20th Century. Lassen Peak, 100 miles south of the California-Oregon border, began a series of spectacular eruptions in 1914 that went on sporadically for several years; on May 22, 1915, the greatest blast of the sequence sent a dark gray cloud of debris boiling upward for seven miles, to rain ash on towns 200 miles away. But America's attention was riveted on World War I, and even the pyrotechnics of Lassen Peak failed to intrude the subject of volcanism into the consciousness of the American public.

It remained, oddly, for a drab little volcano in Central America to sound an alarm that would redirect the attention of scientists and politicians alike to the awesome potential of the Cascade volcanoes. In the summer of 1968, with no warning that anyone recognized, Costa Rica's long-dormant Mount Arenal erupted, killing 80 people and inflicting enormous property damage. It continued to erupt intermittently but more quietly in the years that followed, gradually building up a vast lava field.

Arenal bore certain striking similarities to a Cascade volcano. Like the North American range, the Central American volcanoes are part of the Pacific Ring of Fire, and rise directly over a subduction zone where one tectonic plate is driving under another. As data from the Arenal eruption reached the scientific community, a number of volcanologists renewed efforts to begin learning as much as possible about what was going on inside those beautiful Cascade mountains.

It was slow going—the U.S. Geological Survey's volcano studies program was tightly budgeted. But there was general concurrence that priority should be given to the Cascades, and particularly to Mount St. Helens, the youngest and most unstable mountain in the region. Its summit cone was only 1,000 years old, and the oldest known deposits of pumice and ash were less than 40,000 years old. Beyond this, in the past 4,500 years Mount St. Helens had been more consistently explosive than any other volcano in the present continental United States excluding Alaska.

All of which was exceedingly worrisome because of Mount St. Helens' location only 50 miles north of the Portland-Vancouver metropolitan area, second most populous urban concentration in the Northwest. Several rivers, whose tributaries drained the south, west and north slopes of the mountain, entered the Columbia near Portland; there was a strong possibility of heavy flood damage should a debris avalanche temporarily dam the flow.

In 1969, in the wake of the early Arenal eruptions, Dwight Crandell, a Survey geologist, addressed a conference called in San Francisco by the Office of Emergency Preparedness. Crandell's subject was the lack of preparedness for volcanic activity in the Cascades. It behooved public officials at least to develop an awareness of the hazards, Crandell urged, even if it resulted only in visitors "parking their cars headed in the right direction."

Crandell and another Survey geologist, Donal Mullineaux, later published a blunt warning about Mount St. Helens. "Future eruptions of Mount St. Helens are a near certainty," they advised. "Loss of lives and loss or damage to property can be lessened by establishing procedures to be followed if an eruption should occur, and by monitoring the volcano to detect an approaching eruption."

What is more, said the two geologists, St. Helens' behavior pattern suggested that an eruption was "likely to occur within the next hundred years, and perhaps even before the end of this century." This was strong talk from geologists, the nature of whose work generally encourages a cushioning of forecasts within a framework of eras or epochs. Narrowing this prediction struck some colleagues as trying to thread too fine a needle. But it did draw attention to the urgent message: Lovely Mount St. Helens was a live volcano, and failure to take this fact into account was foolishness on the order of nuzzling a grizzly bear.

In 1969, aided by Survey funds, the University of Washington in Seattle set up two small permanent seismic networks, one in western and one in eastern Washington, beginning with approximately a dozen stations. In 1972, the university installed a station labeled "SHW"—for St. Helens West—on the mountain, as well as stations on Mounts Baker and Rainier. Also in 1972, Donald Swanson, who had grown up in the shadow of Mount St. Helens and was now a Survey geologist, borrowed a laser ranging instrument and established the first baseline measurements designed to detect any significant changes in the contours of the mountain's northeast slope.

In 1977, Congress approved funds enabling the Survey to begin a sophisticated seismic monitoring program in cooperation with some of the nation's universities. It was designed for the study of earthquakes but it had tremendous implications for the monitoring of volcanoes, whose seismic disturbances caused by the subterranean movement of magma may escape detection just a short distance away.

One of five institutions chosen to be regional centers for monitored seismic information was the University of Washington, which was within radio telemetry range of the five northern U.S. Cascade volcanoes—Baker, Glacier Peak, Rainier, Adams and St. Helens. The ultimate plan was to place seismometers at stations on and around each of the peaks, and to connect them to the computer by remote-controlled telemetry units.

The first computer feeds went into operation on March 1, 1980. By that time, the seismic network at the University of Washington consisted of 58 stations, 36 in eastern Washington and on the east flank of the Cascades, and 22 in western Washington, primarily in and around the Puget Sound lowlands. But there was still only the one station, SHW, located on Mount St. Helens at about the 4,600-foot level. The next closest station, LMW—Ladd Mountain, Washington—was 33 miles due north of St. Helens.

In the five-year span from 1975 to 1980, the seismic network had identified 44 small earthquakes within 22 miles of the volcano. But at 3:47 p.m. on Thursday, March 20, 1980, the stylus on one of the drum recorders at the university began shivering out a cryptic message from telemetry station SHW that caused immediate concern: An earthquake measuring 4.2 on the scale of magnitude, the strongest tremor since the monitoring system had gone on line, was jarring the St. Helens area. "This was clearly a different beast," said Stephen Malone, a seismologist at the computer center.

As the quakes continued, the seismologists informed the Survey office in Menlo Park, California, and alerted the U.S. Forest Service in Vancouver, Washington, to the possibility of avalanches in the area. On Friday, with no letup in the shocks, Stephen Malone and some colleagues took three portable seismometers to other locations on the mountain to supplement the readings from SHW. The disadvantage of the portable units was that they could not transmit their readings instantly to the computer network; the readings were recorded on magnetic tape, which had to be retrieved every five days.

On Saturday, another magnitude 4 earthquake was recorded in midafternoon. That evening, the seismologists advised the Forest Service in Vancouver that this might be the beginning of a volcanic sequence. The earthquakes were now coming in swarms, mostly small in magnitude but occurring at a rate of more than 15 per hour by Sunday morning. They seemed to be centered at a very shallow point beneath the mountain.

Malone and his colleagues began making plans to add more seismometers if continuing activity heightened their suspicions that molten rock was moving not far beneath the surface of Mount St. Helens. On Monday they relayed their concern to the Geological Survey's hazards center in Denver, Colorado, and a number of volcano experts—among them Mullineaux and Crandell—headed for the mountain.

Until now, the localized earthquakes had caused no damage and raised few alarms. Nevertheless, on Tuesday, March 25, the Forest Service, fearing avalanches, closed the mountain area above the timberline to the public. Seismic activity surged dramatically around noon of that day, with a swarm of earthquakes so numerous that they saturated the SHW drum recorder in Seattle. Not all of these were small quakes. By that evening, magnitude 4 events were shaking St. Helens at the rate of more than three per hour. "We did not see," stated a later report by the group, "how this activity could continue without something dramatic happening."

Shortly after noon on March 27, a day of typical foggy Pacific Northwest spring weather, a thunderous explosion was heard from the direction of Mount St. Helens, conveying a distinct but unverifiable impression that the mountain had erupted. A news team from the Vancouver *Columbian* took to the air immediately, hoping for a break in the cloud cover over the summit. They were about to give up after circling for three hours when the clouds parted. Sure enough, wrote reporter Bill Stewart, "there was a hole in the snow on the north side of the peak. It was smudged with black ash, and the top, especially the north side, was shattered." The newsmen also reported that huge fissures snaked down the snow on the mountain's north face.

The seismic disturbances persisted, as did the cloud cover. On Friday, March 28, a party of scientists was helicoptered in close enough to the peak to establish that the explosion was a phreatic, or steam, eruption caused by subsurface water that had trickled down until it hit hot rock and was vaporized.

Even though airspace was officially closed within five miles of the peak, teams of reporters and cameramen from the national media took to the air in swarms. The authorities tried to control the aerial armada—but to no avail. Shrugged one exasperated official: "What do you do when some guy in a helicopter his company is paying 400 bucks an hour for tells you you're interfering with freedom of the press for trying to keep him alive? Shoot him down?''

The phreatic eruption of March 27 and the continuing earthquake swarm centered under the mountain were only the start of an eruptive cycle—of this the scientists were certain. Yet there was no way of knowing when the next, more explosive phase of the cycle might take place—it could be months—or how severe it might be when it did occur.

Continued bad weather through early April frustrated the newly arrived Survey scientists; although they were able to establish tiltmeter stations, collect rock samples and take gas measurements, they desperately wanted a clear view of what was happening on the mountain. In mid-April, the clouds lifted and it was immediately apparent that on the north face of the cone, just below the summit crater and above an outcropping of lava called Goat Rocks, the slope had begun to rise upward and outward. It was now urgently necessary to install targets on the bulge to enable continuous checking of its dimensions.

Two instruments would provide these measurements: the theodolite, a precision sighting device for determining changes in angles to various targets, and an electronic laser ranging instrument capable of making extremely accurate linear distance measurements. The conventional laser reflector-targets, known as corner-cube prisms, cost about $300 each, and were much too expensive to scatter over an area where they would be highly expendable. The scientists improvised wooden cross boards, painted a fluorescent orange, to serve as the theodolite targets, and attached clusters of plastic highway reflectors to function as targets for the lasers. Each target assembly was secured to a steel post, which could be driven into the ash or snowpack, or wedged between rocks, and then guyed for stability.

The installing teams were lifted onto the trembling bulge by helicopters,

Ringed by dark ash, a crater in the summit area of Mount St. Helens marks the volcano's reawakening on March 27, 1980. The crater, 250 feet across and 150 feet deep, is flanked by fissures up to three miles long, created when the pressure exerted by rising magma deformed the peak. By April 8, the crater was 1,700 feet in diameter and 850 feet deep.

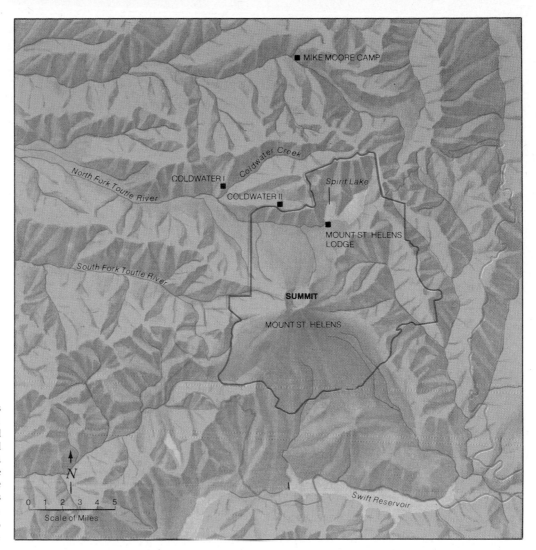

As Mount St. Helens swelled and steamed after its initial eruption, two restricted zones were established to reduce risks to crowds of journalists and sightseers. Only government officials and accredited scientists were permitted within the red zone, a ragged polygon extending three to 14 miles from the summit. Outside this was the blue zone, where daytime entry by loggers and homeowners was allowed. The volcano's largest eruption, on May 18, devastated the two zones and a swath miles beyond, claiming victims up to 16 miles from the summit.

which stood by, engines running, as the reflectors were set up and test readings taken from stations off the mountain. All told, 13 reflector stations were installed on the mountain, eight of which were on the bulge.

From mid-April on, weather permitting, constant readings were taken of the targets on St. Helens' north face. What they showed was astounding: The bulge above Goat Rocks, now a clearly defined area roughly a mile in diameter, was growing at a rate almost discernible to the naked eye. By May 12 the bulge had moved outward nearly 500 feet from its original surface level. The Survey geologists agreed that the area was being pushed out and up by the rise of a magma column inside the mountain; the location of the bulge on the north side indicated that this was the path of least resistance out of the mountain.

As the weather began breaking from mid-April on, the scientists were able to take more extensive photographs of the summit area. Careful analysis of these pictures indicated that the rising magma column had apparently cracked the summit dome, permitting heat from below to escape and melt the snow and ice that had accumulated above the dome. As meltwater had seeped into the mountain, it had come into contact with the hot rock of the interior and had flashed to steam, producing the early eruptions.

The March 27 explosion had excavated a small crater in the center of a new graben, or depression, in the summit ice pack. The graben was about a mile long, east to west, and was situated directly above the bulge and the upper edge of Goat Rocks. By May 12, the crater inside the graben had grown to a volume of perhaps 11.8 million cubic yards, and small lakes and ponds were visible on its floor.

The entire graben, crater and all, seemed to be subsiding into the mountain,

Volcanologist David Johnston relaxes in the spring sun at Coldwater II, a ridgetop observation site five and a half miles from Mount St. Helens' summit. Johnston had a healthy respect for the mountain, comparing it to dynamite with a lit fuse. "We just don't know how long the fuse is," he said of the volcano that would kill him when it erupted.

From his observation point at Coldwater I, photographer Reid Blackburn adjusts a camera aimed at the north slope of Mount St. Helens eight miles away. After nearly three weeks at the site, Blackburn was so attuned to the shaking of the mountain that he could accurately judge the magnitude of the quakes as they happened. Unwilling to risk missing the pictures of a lifetime, he declined an offer of time off a few days before the May 18 eruption and was at his post when the deadly ash engulfed him.

but this subsidence was less than the increased volume of the bulge. When glimpsed through rifts in the cloud, the mountain unquestionably was losing its allure. The snow-capped peak was turning black; the crater, now expanded out near the summit's edges, had begun eroding down the north side as heat from the magma within melted glacial ice and this, mixed with ashfall, caused minor mud slides.

By now, the local authorities considered the mountain so dangerous that they requested that roadblocks be set up 20 miles in all directions from the summit. But this was impossible for various economic and political reasons. On April 30, Washington Governor Dixie Lee Ray compromised by declaring two restricted zones around the mountain: a red zone inside which only accredited scientists would be allowed, and a blue zone, in which daytime access would be allowed by permit only (page 147).

Spirit Lake fell within the red zone on the north side, and property owners there were expected to get out. But Harry Truman, the gregarious elderly proprietor of the lakeside Mount St. Helens Lodge, adamantly refused—even

In the company of four of his 16 cats, Harry Truman expounds on his favorite subject—Mount St. Helens—in the kitchen of his lodge at the edge of Spirit Lake. The 84-year-old Truman, who regarded the mountain as a friend after having spent a lifetime on its slopes, refused to leave when it began to act up and was never found after its eruption.

after a magnitude 5 earthquake shook the mountain on May 12. The tremor jarred loose the lower part of an ice field above Spirit Lake in an ice avalanche that stopped just short of the lake. Truman, though admittedly "scared all to hell," took a harder grip on his bourbon glass and refused to leave his lodge and his 16 cats. "I am part of that mountain," he told a friend. "The mountain is part of me." The authorities finally capitulated and made Truman a deputy sheriff of Skamania County, thereby giving his obstinacy the cover of legality.

Loggers also remained on the mountain despite the emergency. To the consternation of the scientists, most of the vast private and state-owned timberlands near the mountain had been included in the blue zone. The logging companies, taking the position that their people knew the mountain and were equipped to cope with emergency situations, went on with the timber harvest.

The volcanologists, who were in the best position to know the dangers, were also in the worst position to avoid them. "By any measure," said Donald Peterson, who would become scientist in charge of the St. Helens project, "this is the opportunity of a lifetime. Very little, really, is known about these mountains and how they act. If you are going to learn, you get on with it."

But resoluteness and audacity did not pay the bills. Vastly underbudgeted for an emergency of this dimension, the Geological Survey had to economize stringently. The $10 targets up on the bulge were a fair example of an economy measure; but there was no substitute for expensive helicopters when it came to getting them up there. Economies in helicopter expenditures had to be invoked, however, in the movement of personnel between the mountain measuring stations and Vancouver. And while two of the stations on the mountain could be reached only by helicopter, the other two—Timberline Turnaround, two and a half miles northeast of the summit, and Coldwater II, five and a half miles northwest of the summit—were manned in shifts of several days by scientists who drove to the observation sites over Forest Service and logging roads, and slept in campers.

The government scientists showed no resentment over their assignments—though all seemed aware of the perils. "This parking lot is an extremely dangerous place to be," David Johnston had told some reporters at an informal press briefing the day after the March 27 eruption. The 30-year-old volcanologist had just circled the crater taking vapor samplings from a helicopter, which had put down at the Timberline Turnaround parking lot, about 5,000 feet below the

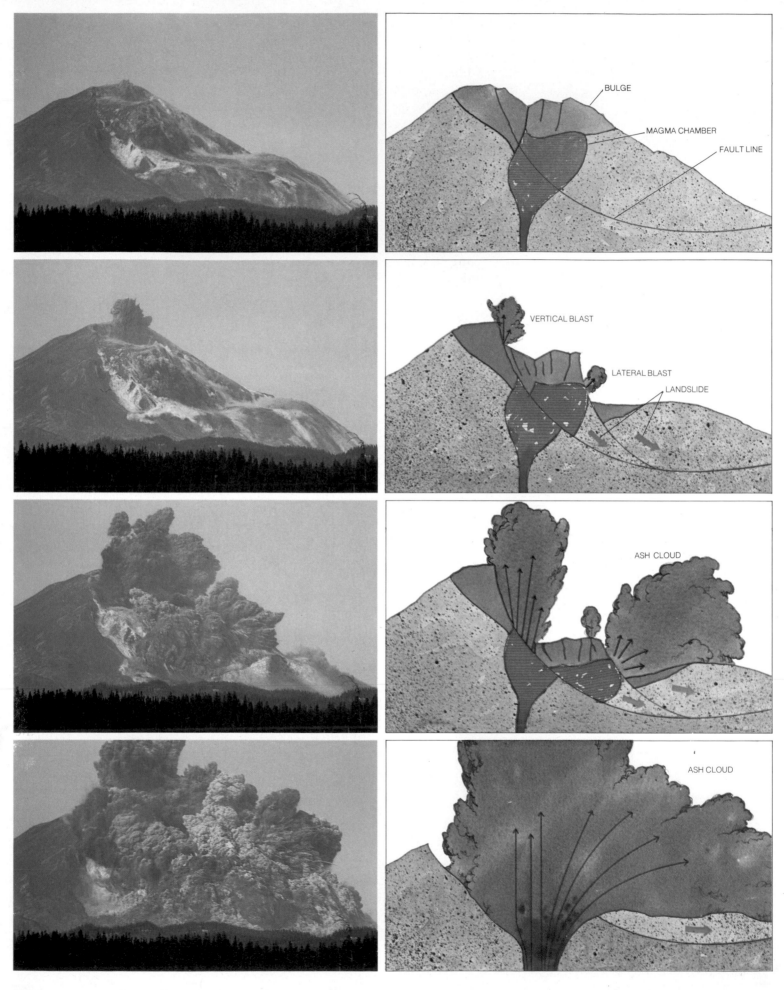

The mechanics of the eruption of Mount St. Helens, diagramed at left, are evident in the photographs at far left. For more than a month before the 1980 eruption, pressure of the magma chamber caused the north face of the mountain to bulge upward and outward (*diagram*). At 8:32 a.m. on May 18 an earthquake broke the unstable bulge loose, starting the landslide under way in the photograph; the slumping mass of the north face is already dusted with a haze of rock and ice thrown up by the churning slide.

Huge quantities of rock and ice slide down the north face of the volcano, suddenly reducing the pressure on the rock remaining over the magma chamber. Superheated water in the rock, kept liquid by the pressure, flashed to steam and exploded laterally from a fissure midway down the slope (*diagram*), then upward from the summit. This photo, taken five seconds after the first, shows the emerging plumes of steam and pulverized rock.

Fifteen seconds after the first photograph was taken, the landslide and steam explosions uncover the magma chamber. Its power redoubled, the explosive release of steam jets upward from the collapsing summit, while the magma itself blasts a high-velocity cloud of superheated debris horizontally from the shattered north face (*diagram*). In this photograph the ash cloud is overtaking the landslide.

Clouds of ash and debris obscure the entire north face of the volcano just 25 seconds into the sequence of photographs. As the eruption continued, magma welled up through the volcano and ran down the north face (*diagram*), leaving a crater 1.2 miles wide and 2.4 miles long when the volcano quieted a day later.

summit. "If the mountain were to erupt right now," Johnston told the reporters, "we would die. I'm genuinely afraid of it."

Early in the afternoon of May 17, Johnston drove up to Coldwater II station, from which the encamped scientists could look straight up the mountain at the bulge and the steaming summit just above it. Johnston relieved geologist Harry Glicken, who had been monitoring the mountain from the trailer station for two weeks. On this day there would be 41 quakes greater than magnitude 3, which was about average for the preceding three to four weeks. "On a time scale of hours," noted seismologist Stephen Malone, "there was no apparent seismic precursor to the major eruption."

David Johnston was not alone in the Coldwater sector. Reid Blackburn, a 27-year-old photographer on leave from the Vancouver *Columbian,* was camped about three miles west of the Survey trailer at a station called Coldwater I. Blackburn had aimed two cameras at the volatile north slope. If and when something happened, he planned to trigger one camera manually, and a second, at a remote location, by radio signal. A few loggers were also working on the mountain through the weekend, but most had the weekend off. It was a rare clear day, sunny and warm.

In view of the relatively harmless quaking, a group of Spirit Lake property owners had been escorted to the lake this Saturday afternoon to bring out some of their belongings. While the loading was going on, four of the escorting officers from the Washington State Patrol and the Skamania County sheriff's office dropped by to pay their respects to Harry Truman, who was setting sprinklers on the lawn in front of the lodge. The officers asked the old gentleman one more time to consider leaving. "No damned chance," said Truman.

The drum recorders at the University of Washington's seismic monitoring center were watched around the clock, mostly by earth sciences undergraduates. At 11 seconds after 8:32 on Sunday morning, May 18, geology student Steve Bryant watched the stylus on the St. Helens monitoring graph begin oscillating crazily. Bryant reached for the phone and called Stephen Malone, who jumped on his bike and headed for the office, arriving about 20 minutes later—just as the sound waves from Mount St. Helens hit Seattle.

In the time lapse between the first spasm of the stylus and the sound of the explosion in Seattle, the north side of Mount St. Helens had seemed to slump and then blow completely apart. Several people, most of whom should have been much farther away, were looking toward the peak when a small plume puffed up from high on the north face near the top of the bulge. Then, as some remarkable photographs would confirm (*page 150*), the whole upper north side of the mountain simply let go and began sliding like an enormous carpet in the general direction of Spirit Lake.

Seconds later, a huge plume of black smoke and ash shot laterally from the north face, and then another plume, also black, boiled straight up from the summit. In less time than it takes to relate it, Mount St. Helens reverted to its volcanic origins.

There is general agreement among volcanologists now on the details of the St. Helens eruption. Photographs have been arranged in sequence, time-keyed, projected, reversed in sequence, reprojected; ejecta samplings have been analyzed from every point in the eruption sequence; and all this information has been studied in the context of the known geological history of the mountain.

At the outset, one important clue to an understanding of the violence and direction of the May 18 explosion was the fact that, beneath its recently serene façade, Mount St. Helens was obviously "rotten." The interior of much of the volcano's cone was not rock, as it was commonly thought to be, but a very wet, sticky clay. "When rock is surrounded with water," explained William Melson, a senior volcanologist at the Smithsonian Institution, "and subjected to

high temperature over a period of time—particularly where the water is rich in things like hydrochloric acid—the rock will essentially be turned into clay." The rise of the magma column intensified both the temperature and the pressure inside the volcano. As the magma sought a yielding path to the surface, the mountain began to bulge. At last, when a convulsive 5.1 magnitude earthquake shook the mountain at 8:32 a.m., the bulge simply let go from the summit and began slipping down toward the lake.

The removal of all that weight caused the pressurized water in the surrounding magma column to flash to steam in a tremendous lateral explosion directed outward from where the bulge had just slipped away. The force of this sideways explosion immediately broke up the overlying rock of the summit and produced a second explosion, this one straight up.

Scientists studying the volcanic sequence are now satisfied that the rock and

A sparkling panorama of one of the world's most beautiful mountain landscapes lies transformed into an unearthly gray wasteland following the explosion of its volcanic centerpiece, Mount St. Helens. "Nothing was left," said a shaken logger of his first view of the devastation, pictured here four months after the eruption. "It's like a huge vacuum just sucked everything out of there."

ash ejected during the early hours of the May 18 eruption consisted partly of rock from the old cone and partly of solidified, extremely hot gray dacite, which had been the carapace of the rising water-rich magma. It was not until around noon on May 18 that the ash clouds boiling out of the mountain changed from dark gray to near-white, signaling that most of the carapace and old rock had been blown from the conduit, and that the rising magma column was erupting in pure form. The ejected material now was a light pumice, formed when the liquid dacite of the magma column "foamed" with the final release of pressure above it, liberating the entrapped gases and vapor.

The enormous force of the lateral blast was directed out across a fan-shaped 140-degree area to the north, knocking down timber over a 232-square-mile expanse as it blew right over and past the slower-moving debris avalanche. This roiling cloud of ash, steam and hot gases moved downslope from the new crater

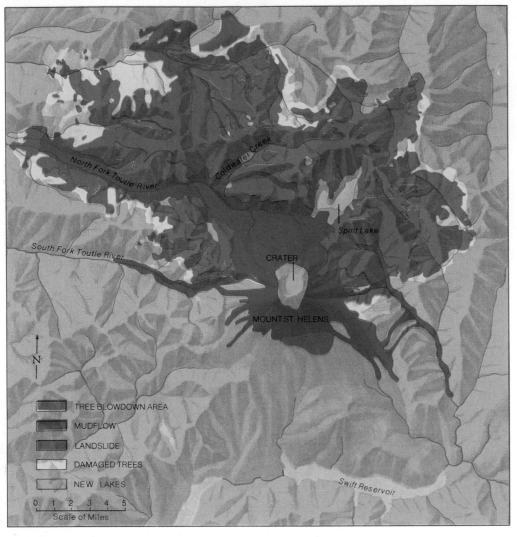

TREE BLOWDOWN AREA
MUDFLOW
LANDSLIDE
DAMAGED TREES
NEW LAKES

0 1 2 3 4 5
Scale of Miles

with three times the destructive force of the worst conventional windstorm. Temperatures in the cloud rose as high as 500° F.—hot enough to inflict serious burns and ignite vegetation.

The ash cloud reached the high ridges and Spirit Lake ahead of the debris flow, overtopping the ridges on the far side of the lake and the north fork of the Toutle River. The huge stands of evergreen timber that lay in the cloud's path were stripped of branches and bark, and either snapped off just above the ground or uprooted.

When the debris avalanche arrived, it pushed the downed timber ahead of it into the lake or the river valleys. All told, the avalanche moved some three billion cubic yards of mud, ash, rock, ice and other materials into the upper 17 miles of the North Fork Toutle River valley. When the debris flow struck Spirit Lake, the monstrous intrusion of new materials sloshed the water out of the lake and up the ridge on the far side. By the time the water rushed back down the ridge, the lake was shallower by 80 feet and its surface was covered with logs and steaming ooze.

The portion of the debris avalanche that flowed west of the lake into the North Fork Toutle River valley left deposits as thick as 600 feet, increasing the height of the old Spirit Lake debris dam by some 200 feet. But even as the mighty north-face avalanche came to rest, a nasty epilogue was in progress. The heat from the eruption had caused rapid melting of snow and glacial ice; more water condensed from the eruption cloud itself, and all this liquid mixed with volcanic debris to form a huge mudflow that was sliding over the avalanche debris and heading down the North Fork Toutle River valley. Flowing with the consistency of very fluid mortar, the mud destroyed trees, homes and bridges

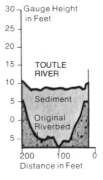

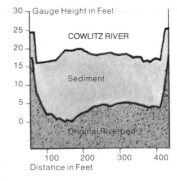

In both the lower Toutle and Cowlitz Rivers, the mudflows from Mount St. Helens' May 18 eruption buried the original riverbeds beneath 15 feet of sediment, which reduced their water-carrying capacity to ¹/₁₀ of normal. Hydrologists feared that severe floods during the winter rainy season would be virtually inevitable, but round-the-clock dredging by the U.S. Army Corps of Engineers averted the threat, removing 28 million cubic yards of mud within a six-month period.

Smudged with ash, Mike Moore and his four-year-old daughter, BonnieLu, pause during their arduous trek out of a forest devastated by the eruption of Mount St. Helens. The picture above was taken by Lu Moore. "The magnitude of the eruption became apparent almost at once," said Moore. The enormous ash cloud *(right)* that rolled toward the family's campsite was an "overpowering" sight.

One of the more dramatic stories to come out of the May 18 eruption of Mount St. Helens was that of Mike and Lu Moore and their two children, who were camped only 13 miles from the north face of the volcano when it blew, and yet survived unharmed.

Moore, a graduate in geology, was fascinated by the activity on St. Helens but was careful to camp well outside the danger zone that had been established by authorities. He selected a site shielded from the volcano by three tall ridges, a decision that saved the lives of his family.

At 8:32 a.m. a low rumble reverberated through the forest surrounding the Moores' campsite. The family stared in awe at the immense billowing ash cloud racing toward them. Mike Moore grabbed his camera and snapped a dozen pictures (including the one above) of the cloud looming overhead. Lu Moore quickly packed and carried the children, BonnieLu, four, and Terra, three months, to a nearby hunter's shack. "Once we saw the cloud coming our way, I never looked back," she recalled.

While the cloud smothered the shack in ash and a pelting rain of small rocks, the Moores covered Terra with a blanket and dampened socks for themselves and Bonnie-Lu to breathe through. "We were afraid," said Lu. "But we didn't panic."

Darkness enveloped the shack, accompanied by earsplitting thunder. The mountain sounded, said Lu, like "a giant cement mixer tumbling rock, popping and banging with incredible volume and intensity."

As the ash storm ended, the Moores ventured outside, where their flashlight revealed a powdery gray world. By 10, it became light enough for them to attempt their two-and-a-half-mile hike through the eerie, ash-covered forest to their car.

They had scarcely gone a mile before they came on a number of huge trees ripped up by volcanic wind and strewn across the trail. It took them five more hours to cover another mile, to a point where suddenly both the trail and the forest were totally obliterated.

The Moores camped for the night, and the next day were spotted by a rescue helicopter. The family made their way to a small island in the Green River; from there the helicopter lifted them to safety. Later they learned that the eruption had claimed 60 lives. The experience left them stunned. They had gone to the area for a vacation. "We never expected the mountain to act that way," said Lu Moore.

and wiped out a midriver logging station. Thinning with distance, it traveled another 28 miles down the Toutle to deposit more than one billion cubic feet of sediment in the Cowlitz River, and enough mud flowed on through the Cowlitz to block the shipping channel of the Columbia River itself.

The damage inflicted by the May 18 eruptions was unbelievable—"made to order," noted a Forest Service report, "for those who enjoy calibrating the stupendous." The north slope was a vista of unearthly, ash-caked devastation of a scale to stagger the senses. The timber blowdown represented 3.7 billion board feet of lumber, enough to build nearly a quarter of a million homes.

Within the context of this mind-stretching destruction, the human death toll of 60 was astoundingly low. Most of those who died had perished almost instantly of asphyxiation, their lungs clogged with hot ash. Photographer Reid Blackburn had reached his automobile only to have the windows blown in by the force of the blast. The roof of Blackburn's vehicle was spotted by a search helicopter, and his body was found in the driver's seat, buried up to the shoulders in ash.

David Johnston had completed and radioed in his early laser ranging measurements of the bulge just 90 minutes before the triggering 8:32 a.m. earthquake. His excited call—"Vancouver, Vancouver, this is it . . ."—was heard instants later, but nothing more. No trace could be found of Johnston or his car; nor was there any but circumstantial evidence of the fate of Harry Truman, whose lodge lay under 40 feet of ash and debris.

In all assessments of casualties, there were strong suggestions of how much worse the St. Helens cataclysm might have been. Had it happened a day later, the destruction zone would have been abuzz with the chain saws of hundreds of logging crewmen. Had it been later in the day, another caravan of property owners would have visited Spirit Lake. In only another hour or so, other Survey scientists would have been up on the mountain to check the bulge. Had the authorities not stood fast for weeks at the roadblocks, there might have been thousands of Sunday picnickers and hikers in the zone of destruction. Had the mountain erupted toward the south, it would have topped the reservoir dams on the Lewis River and endangered the lives of tens of thousands of residents of the valley area.

It was also fortunate from a scientific standpoint that St. Helens picked such a nice day to erupt. Had the earthquake occurred at night, or when the mountain was hidden by clouds, the entire eruption sequence would have been a mystery, with no eyewitness reports and no photographs.

Wild creatures, long believed by many to have some sixth-sense forewarning of volcanic eruptions, appeared to have been taken more by surprise than humans. The carcasses of elk and deer in the blast area were found time and again curled in their ruminating beds. Wildlife on the north slope of Mount St. Helens was almost totally erased. According to the Washington State Department of Game, 5,000 black-tailed deer, 200 black bear and 1,500 elk had died in the disaster along with all the birds and small mammals in the devastated area. Songbirds especially had been hard-hit even outside the blast area, where ashfall had smothered food sources. Over these thousands of ruined acres, nothing seemed to move or make a sound.

The Northwest was slow to recover from the sudden eruption of its Fire Mountain. But there seems to have been a gradual acceptance of the fact that it was a pure act of nature, which, as Aristotle insisted more than 2,300 years ago, does nothing uselessly. Mount St. Helens exemplified not only the destructive power of a volcano, but also the manner in which nature responds to it.

Within 10 days of the awful destruction of David Johnston's Coldwater II station, some of his cohorts noticed the first signs of regeneration: fresh deer tracks in the ash, from animals that survived on the south side of the mountain.

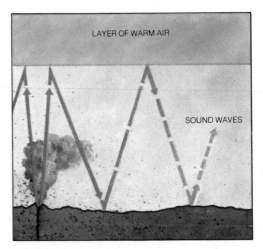

The diagram above illustrates why the explosion of Mount St. Helens was heard as a loud boom that rattled windows at a distance of 100 miles while people near the mountain heard only the crash of falling trees and rocks and the hiss of a hot, dust-laden wind. The sound waves were directed upward rather than outward; a layer of warm air at an altitude of 150,000 feet reflected some of the sound waves back to earth, where they were heard more than 500 miles from the volcano.

The lightning-streaked cloud rolling northeast from Mount St. Helens at nearly 60 miles an hour looked exactly like a towering thunderhead—but it was bigger and blacker than any in memory. Most people in its path, as yet unaware of the volcano's eruption, braced for a storm.

But no rain fell. Instead, the cloud descended like a shroud, cloaking the landscape in a blackness of volcanic ash that even automobile headlights could not penetrate. The choking 12-hour ashfall blanketed the Northwestern United States and southern Canada with as much as three inches of ash.

In Washington State, Idaho and Montana, wind-borne ash short-circuited electrical transformers, causing power failures. Ash deposits clogged automobile air filters and contaminated oil systems, disabling half of the emergency vehicles in eastern Washington. Like microscopic shards of glass, ash particles scratched and pitted whatever they touched: windshields, furniture, machine bearings, airplane engines. Clouds of ash made breathing difficult; residents had to improvise face masks from coffee filters and rubber bands.

At first, no one knew quite how to cope with the appalling mess that was deposited by the ashfall. A makeshift method eventually evolved. After fire fighters dampened the ash to keep the dust to a minimum, snowplows pushed it into piles and dump trucks hauled it to landfill sites. The scale of the cleanup was staggering: In Yakima, Washington, with a population of 51,000, city crews removed 600,000 tons of volcanic ash; the job took 10 weeks to complete and cost $2.2 million.

But the scientists' worst fears about the St. Helens ashfall never materialized. Although ash shot up 14 miles into the stratosphere and circled the globe several times, most of it soon dropped to earth. The ash did not affect global weather patterns—apparently because it contained little sulfur, a chemical that can linger at high altitude in droplets of sulfuric acid, blocking solar radiation and cooling the atmosphere. And residents of the Northwest could actually be thankful that, by historical standards, they received only a light dusting. In 4600 B.C., Mount Mazama (now Crater Lake), 200 miles south of Mount St. Helens, spewed out nearly 30 times as much ash in one cataclysmic explosion.

The day after the eruption, traffic 85 miles northeast of Mount St. Helens creeps through clouds of ash at 15 miles per hour, an emergency speed limit imposed to prevent collisions in poor visibility.

Dust mask hanging at his neck, a farmer 90 miles from the volcano shakes ash from his grapevines. Despite man's best efforts and heavy rains, the clinging ash coated plant leaves for months, blocking sunlight needed for photosynthesis and ruining an estimated 7 per cent of the affected crops.

Guarding his gutter with cardboard, a homeowner sweeps a torrent of ash from his roof into a wheelbarrow. Even dry, ash on a 2,500-square-foot rooftop weighed as much as 15,000 pounds. Wet, it might weigh up to twice as much.

Exploiting a break in winter storms, parka-clad scientists measure Mount St. Helens' dark lava dome with a laser range finder from this bench mark on Harry's Ridge, five miles north of the summit. By measuring distances to laser reflectors around the dome from several sites, the scientists were able to monitor the growth of each new dome to the inch.

Barely a month after, a fireweed blossom was discovered on a ridge behind Spirit Lake. Here and there, the surviving roots of fireweed plants whose tops had been sheared off by the blast found moisture and began sending up shoots in search of daylight. Their final burst through the cement-like crust of ash was a triumph of nature: Alongside each fireweed shoot lay a plug, a cap, of packed ash about the size of a nickel, that had been pushed straight up and laid over, like a manhole cover.

"Fireweed is mostly it right now, a lot of fireweed," observed Bill Ruediger, a wildlife biologist for the Gifford Pinchot National Forest. "In the next five to ten years you can expect to see the whole mountainscape almost a sea of fireweed."

As the fireweed spread, animals moved into the area to browse on it and thus disturbed the ash crust, making a more hospitable seedbed. Decaying plant matter and animal excretions added much-needed organic matter to the ash. The march back up the mountainside was under way.

To everyone's astonishment, a few small animals survived in the devastated area. Amphibious creatures, chiefly frogs and salamanders, were either in the mud or under the water when the blast reached them, and were observed moving about very shortly after the eruption subsided. So were a few crayfish. There were unmistakable tracks and feeding evidence in two areas where beavers were known to exist before the blast. They owed their survival to their habit of burrowing 20 or 30 feet into the banks of rivers and streams, usually below the water line.

"I think people need to put all this devastation into perspective," said Ruediger. "Although it's totally unique as far as our lifetimes are concerned, it's the way nature is: every couple thousand years she cleans the slate again. What we have here right now is almost a genesis situation."

Ruediger's scholarly awe was echoed by the geologists and geophysicists moving through the caustic vapors of the St. Helens crater, elated to be present at the downbeat of one of nature's most majestic cadences. "It took some time getting used to all the devastation," reflected Donald Swanson. "But I've really come to appreciate the scene. It's a hard thing to get across to people, but I'm able to see lots of beauty now, kind of a desert beauty. From a scientific standpoint, of course, it's a fantastic opportunity. This is a classic example of how the earth rebuilds itself, of how life returns. It's happened before and it's going

A U.S. Geological Survey technician checks a recording seismograph at the edge of the Mount St. Helens blast zone. Such portable, battery-powered machines supplement the permanent network of 12 telemetered seismographs, letting scientists alter their instrument array to test new theories or to monitor changes within the volcano.

To amass data about Mount St. Helens—and to warn of eruptions—the Geological Survey command post in Vancouver, Washington, monitors a steady stream of telemetered reports: Drums trace seismograms, tapes record readings from magnetometers and tiltmeters, and on clear days the TV screen at rear shows the volcano itself.

to happen again; but still, not many get to be around to see it happen." By September, four months after the eruption, the Geological Survey had established a permanent office in Vancouver and had commenced work on a monitoring network covering not just St. Helens and its neighbors but the whole file of Cascade peaks from Canada to California.

But learning from Mount St. Helens remained the primary goal, and on every day of acceptable visibility, a flying squad of youthful scientists swarmed to the mountain. The blast had revealed, on the steep interior walls of the crater, a fascinating geological record of the volcano's history. However, the focus of their concern was a lava dome about the height of a 40-story building that hissed and steamed on the crater's floor. The scientists, wearing gas masks and protective clothing, leaped out of helicopters and hurried gingerly across the crater toward the dome, where sizable fissures—stress tears caused by the continued upward thrust of lava from the magma chamber within the mountain—radiated out across the crater floor. The fissures were from one to three feet wide, and their rock walls just a few feet down were glowing hot, in some cases reaching 1,300° F. "Those fissures are the main problem in working up there," observed William Melson. "It's real hot to walk around them and risky to jump over them. They give off a gas that can rot clothing and wreck equipment; if there were no gas masks, they could give your lungs a hard time."

Daily progress reports on the status of the fissures were priority items on the scientists' checklists. Measurements were taken at preset points to see if there had been any change in the width of the cracks, if there had been any faulting—uplifting or downward movement of one side of a fissure—or whether any of the cracks had extended farther out from the dome. Any acceleration in the growth of the cracks or fault movement was regarded as a possible precursor to an eruption. The scientists also studied a ridge of volcanic tephra, which they called the rampart, located just beyond the north side of the dome; they theorized that any movement of the ridge was associated with subsurface magma expansion, and thus was another possible indication of impending eruption.

Targets were placed for laser ranging instrument readings being taken at stations off the mountain. But no one camped at these stations anymore; they were serviced by helicopter.

Other laser readings were shot by instruments inside the crater, to determine whether the dome had grown, and if so how much, to check for any bulging or subsiding in the crater floor itself, and to measure any contour changes on the crater walls. The prevalence of hydrogen fluoride so etched the prism reflectors that the crews had long since abandoned any idea of setting up permanent reflector stations inside the crater. Someone carried a target to a given station and held it each time a measurement was to be taken. Sulfuric, hydrochloric and hydrofluoric acids also ate the finish off the radios that kept the crews in touch with one another and with Vancouver; the acidic vapors stung the eyes and turned the steel rims of eyeglasses green.

The whole array of instrument checks and collections of samples within the crater was accomplished at the pace of a swift walk or a dogtrot. The helicopters' engines were always idling, ready for a fast take-off at a radioed order from Vancouver, where a change in the seismic pattern or perhaps merely the sudden approach of a bad storm system could result in the terse command: "Let's get out of there."

On May 18, 1981, the first anniversary of the big explosion, the crater dome measured roughly 350 feet high and approximately 2,000 feet in its long north-south dimension. This was the third dome—the others had blown out in smaller eruptions in July and October. It was much larger and appeared far more stable than the rest, and if it held fast, the expectation among a number of geologists was that within a space of six months to two years Mount St. Helens would move into another phase of the eruptive cycle: a lava flow.

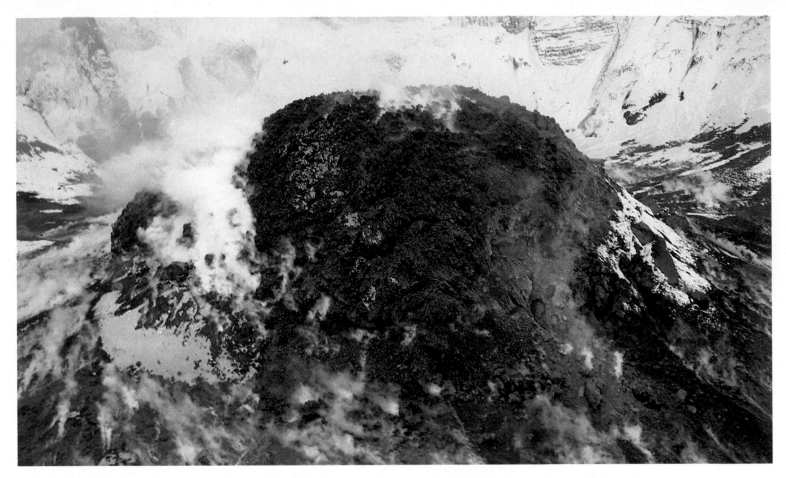

According to this theory, with the dome firmly in place, an andesite lava, much thinner than the stiff pasty magma now being extruded from the top of the vent, would begin oozing out of the crater. It would probably come from some spot at the base of the dome, and eventually would pour out of the crater through the notch in the north side and down the slope, perhaps as far as Spirit Lake. "And of course, then again," said one of the geologists, "maybe not."

"Prediction is still in a very primitive state," said Donald Peterson. While serious volcanological studies were going on in Italy, Indonesia, Japan and elsewhere, the state of the art had reached its highest level in Hawaii. And yet the experience of the volcanologists in Hawaii was inherently limited in value. The Hawaiian volcanoes, which provided the Survey monitors with most of the training and historical background upon which the St. Helens studies were built, were "very different in their degree of explosiveness," Peterson pointed out, "so we have to be cautious in any assumptions we make in the St. Helens studies."

On the evidence, they were getting closer to solutions at St. Helens. On March 30, 1981, the Survey had issued a press statement predicting that there would be another minor eruption within two weeks. On April 10, 11 days later, the eruption occurred.

Perhaps 25 Geological Survey staffers made their headquarters at Vancouver after the 1980 eruption. Once St. Helens became stabilized, intense studies were to begin at Hood, Rainier, Baker, the Three Sisters and a number of other Cascade volcanoes. Beneath the habitual calm of scientists accustomed to taking the geologic—which is to say the long, long—view, there was a certain urgency to their approach to the work.

The St. Helens episode stimulated considerable speculation among earth scientists concerning which of the Cascade volcanoes might erupt next. There was, in fact, an informal "priority" list on which the Cascade volcanoes were rated alphabetically according to their perceived likelihood of erupting in the rela-

Within the snow-draped walls of Mount St. Helens' gaping amphitheater, more than a mile wide, a hissing dark lava dome 600 feet high and 2,000 feet in diameter bulges over the volcano's vent, dwarfing the U.S. Geological Survey helicopter flying behind the dome at upper left. Although minor explosions sometimes blow apart such a crinkled plug of magma, the pressure created by underlying gases soon extrudes a new one in its place.

tively near future, and by Roman numeral according to the jeopardy each posed to population and property.

An A-I, for example, would be a mountain viewed with the greatest potential for eruption and situated where it could do extensive damage. On the list were Mount Baker, where gaseous emissions and internal heat remained high following a 1975 scare, and Mount Shasta, because of its eruptive history and the presence of fumaroles. The remaining A-I volcanoes, in no special order, were Mount Rainier, Mount Hood and the Three Sisters.

Lassen Peak was an A-II—likely to erupt, but less threatening to people and property. Also rated A-II was Mount Mazama—Crater Lake—which many geologists had long felt certain would erupt again at some point in the future. Another cleverly camouflaged volcano, Newberry Crater, was an A-III—dangerous, but far enough out in the high central Oregon desert to endanger few people and little property.

Mount Adams was on a B list—geologically less dangerous, but warily regarded because so little was known about it—and so were Glacier Peak, Mount Jefferson and Mount McLoughlin.

The list was drawn up by the Geological Survey for planning purposes only, and at best it represented only an educated guess until the Survey scientists had much more detailed information about the Cascade Range. "It's a disconcerting thought," said Donald Peterson, "but there might very well be a volcano rated C-III on the list that could be the next one to blow up. Arenal should have taught us that.

"The sad truth," he added, "is that we know very little about some of these Cascade peaks, and not nearly enough about any of them. We're only seeing part of one volcanic system here—we're trying to find out what goes on underneath the mountain by watching what happens on the surface. But if we're clever enough, we can learn a great deal." **Ω**

Until the morning of May 18, 1980, the Cascade country in the vicinity of Mount St. Helens in Washington State ranked among the most majestic wilderness areas on earth, with its lush forests, verdant meadows and jewel-like lakes. But then came the cataclysm. In a single day, 232 square miles of breathtaking beauty were transformed into an eerie, lunar landscape that seemed utterly devoid of life.

The awesome dimensions of the volcanic inferno that had cremated the countryside emerged only gradually, as scientists and photographers cautiously returned to the blasted terrain. The mountain had hurled out 275 million tons of airborne ash and rock, nearly a ton for every person in North America. Superheated ash at 500° F. shot from the volcano's vent at 230 miles an hour, igniting widespread fires that burned for months. The ash-laden blast killed people 16 miles from the summit, and the avalanche of mud and debris that followed swept away everything in its path—trees, bridges, bulldozers, entire hillsides—filling valleys 17 miles from the mountain with a stupendous rubble hundreds of feet deep.

The blast leveled every living thing within a fan-shaped area extending as far as 15 miles from its source, and the hot gases mortally seared anything that was still standing within another mile. Subsequent eruptions further entombed the lifeless landscape at the base of the mountain beneath a layer of ash 600 feet deep.

Remarkably, the first signs of reemergent life appeared on the barren volcanic slopes almost immediately. Within a month a few perennial wildflowers appeared in the ash fields, sprouting from rootstock that had been protected by the winter snowpack. Insects and small animals soon gained a foothold, feeding on the rotting debris from the eruption; and healing rains washed away much of the ash layer, exposing the fertile underlying soil.

The scars of the holocaust will endure for millennia, but if the volcano remains relatively quiet, U.S. Forest Service ecologists predict that within a century the new contours around the mountain will again be clothed in forests and teeming with wildlife.

Hovering over a bleak, monotone landscape blanketed by 10 inches of ash, a U.S. National Guard helicopter checks a battered pickup truck nine miles north of Mount St. Helens. The volcano's blast blew out the truck's windows and gashed its aluminum camper top, instantly killing both occupants.

An enormous crater yawns in the 300-foot-thick ash bed near the barren shores of Spirit Lake. Many similar craters hundreds of feet in diameter were gouged out when pools of lake water were heated by the layer of searing ash until they exploded in 2,000-foot plumes of scalding steam. Later, small chunks of explosively vaporized ice scooped out smaller dimples within each of the craters.

A rotting scum of blasted logs overlies Spirit Lake, whose crystal waters once reflected the glory of Mount St. Helens. The landslide of May 18, emanating from the notch clearly visible in the mountain's crater, deposited 300 feet of rock and ash in some places on the lake's bottom and dammed its outlet *(upper left)* with a 200-foot ridge of volcanic debris; the lake was nearly doubled in size and its former shoreline was submerged under 200 feet of mud and water.

As if cut by a giant scythe, the ash-scoured trunks
of thousands of 200-foot trees, their bark and branches
stripped away by the volcano's blast, lie strewn
across mountain terrain. The superheated windstorm
of ash from the summit snapped off trees up to 17
feet in diameter with such force that their stumps
shattered into splintery apparitions (*below*).

Only four months after the devastating eruption, a colorful vanguard of returning life dots the bleak landscape near Mount St. Helens. Shoots of wild lupine peek through a six-inch blanket of ash *(above)*, while pink clumps of hardy fireweed *(right)* flourish undaunted by the catastrophe. The wandering elk that left the tracks near the rivulet at right broke the crust of ash and created a fertile bed for airborne seeds—whose germination will be the next step toward the mountain's renewal.

ACKNOWLEDGMENTS

For their help in the preparation of this book the editors wish to thank: **In Belgium:** Brussels—Professor François Lechat, International Center for Disaster Epidemiology, Leuven University. **In France:** Chamalières—Hervé Chaumeton; Gif-sur-Yvette—François Le Guern, C.N.R.S.; Meudon—Daniel Cavillon; Paris—Gérard Baschet, Éditions de l'Illustration; Claude Daney; Dr. Jacques Fabriès and Professor Théodore Monod, Muséum National d'Histoire Naturelle; Haroun Tazieff. **In Great Britain:** Edinburgh—Douglas Grant, Scottish Academic Press Ltd.; London—Marjorie Willis, BBC Hulton Picture Library; R. Williams, Department of Prints and Drawings, British Museum; Elisabeth Moore, *Illustrated London News;* John Falconer, Royal Commonwealth Society; Alan Clark, Sally Grover, L. P. Townsend and N. H. Robinson, The Royal Society Library; York—Barbara Pyrah, Keeper of Geology, The Yorkshire Museum. **In Greece:** Athens—Professor Christos Doumas, National Archaelogical Museum. **In Iceland:** Reykjavik—Omar Ragnarsson; Sigurdur Thorarinsson, University of Iceland. **In Italy:** Catania—Romolo Romano, Istituto Internazionale di Vulcanologia; Genoa—Nicoletta Morello, Istituto di Storia Moderna e Contemporanea, University of Genoa; Naples—Paolo Gasparini and Antonio Nazzaro, Osservatorio Vesuviano; Professor Fausto Zeri, Soprintendenza alle Antichitá della Campania; Nicolosi—Filippo Cataldo, Biblioteca Comunale; Pisa—Franco Barberi, Roberto Santacroce and Mauro Rosi, Instituto di Mineralogia e Petrografia, University of Pisa; Pompeii—Stefano de Caro, Soprintendenza alle Antichitá della Campania; Rome—Vitorio Cagnetti, CNEN; Countess Maria Fede Caproni. **In Japan:** Fukushima Prefecture—Fukushima Prefectural Library; Kagoshima Prefecture—Kagoshima Prefectural Library; Tokyo—Takeshi Mizukami; Dr. Joyo Osaka, Tokyo Institute of Technology; Dr. Daisuke Shimozura, Earthquake Research Institute of the University of Tokyo. **In Martinique:** Fort-de-France—Lois Hayot; Bib Monville, Radio Martinique. **In the Netherlands:** The Hague—Dr. M. Neumann Van Padang; Leyden—Dr. H. J. W. G. Schalke, Leyden University; National Museum of the History of Science and Medicine; Royal Institute of Linguistics and Anthropology; Rotterdam—Mrs. G. Sttehn. **In Peru:** Lima—Instituto Geofisico del Peru; Julio Kuroiwa, National University of Engineering of Lima; Gonzalo de Reparaz. **In Singapore:** Michael W. Quearry, American Overseas Petroleum, Ltd. **In the United States:** Arizona—(Flagstaff) Susan Kieffer, United States Geological Survey; (Tucson) Tad Nichols; California—(La Jolla) John S. Shelton; (San Francisco) Janice Miller, Pacific Gas and Electric Co.; (Santa Barbara) Mary Lou Bevier, University of California; Colorado—(Denver) Peter Lipman, United States Geological Survey; (Golden) Marge Dalecheck and Phyllis Dennis, United States Geological Survey Photo Library; Connecticut—(New Haven) Timothy Goodhue, Yale Center for British Art; Washington, D.C.—Hatten S. Yoder and David Singer, the Geophysical Laboratory of the Carnegie Institution of Washington; Vivian Sammons, Library of Congress; Richard Fiske, Smithsonian Institution; Hawaii—(Hawaii National Park) Robert Decker, Daniel Dzurisin, J. D. Griggs, Fred Klein and Reggie Okamura, United States Geological Survey; Harry Wills, United States Park Service; (Honolulu) Susan Yasutake, Amfac, Inc.; John C. Wright, Bishop Museum; (Kailua) William Bowles; (Volcano) Jeffrey B. Judd; Maryland—(Greenbelt) Nicholas M. Short, Goddard Space Flight Center; Massachusetts—(Salem) Mark Sexton, Peabody Museum of Salem; New Hampshire—(Hanover) Richard W. Birnie, Richard Stoiber and Stanley Williams, Dartmouth College; New Jersey—(Princeton) Hollis D. Hedberg, Princeton University; New York—(Ithaca) Larry D. Brown, Cornell University; (Poughkeepsie) Rhoda Rappaport, Vassar College; (Syracuse) John Sloan Dickey, Syracuse University; Oregon—(Portland) Clara Fairfield, Oregon Museum of Science and Industry; Orvid Ellson, United States Department of Agriculture; Virginia—(Arlington) William C. Buell; (Reston) Roy Bailey, Barbara Chappell, John Filson, Al Kover, Robert Tilling, Richard S. Williams and Thomas L. Wright Jr., United States Geological Survey; Washington—(Cheney) Eugene P. Kiver, Eastern Washington University; (Olympia) Patricia M. Baron, Office of the Attorney General; Lora Murphy, Washington Department of Emergency Services; (Seattle) Stephen Malone, University of Washington; (Vancouver) John Johnson, Bill Ruediger and Eugene Smith, Gifford Pinchot National Forest; Dave Olsen; Philip Carpenter, Thomas Casadevall, Katharine Cashman, Norman Dion, Willie Kinoshita, Norman MacLeod, Donald Peterson and Donald Swanson, United States Geological Survey. **In West Germany:** Bensberg—Professor L. Ahorner, Erdbebenstation; Bochum—Dieter Knippschild, Ruhr-Universität; Köln—Dr. Martin Schwarzbach, Bensberg Bei Köln; Dr. Horst Noll, Geologisches Institut der Universität zu Köln; Munich—Christine Hoffmann, Bayerische Staatsgemäldesammlung; Rudolf Heinrich, Deutsches Museum; West Berlin—Dr. Roland Klemig and Heidi Klein, Bildarchiv Preussischer Kulturbesitz; Axel Schulz, Ullstein Bilderdienst.

The editors also wish to thank Mirka Gondicas, Athens; Enid Farmer, Boston; Brigid Grauman, Brussels; Katrina Van Duyn, Copenhagen; Robert Kroon, Geneva; Tomas Loayza, Lima; Martha de la Cal, Lisbon; Jane Walker, Madrid; John Dunn, Melbourne; Laura Lopez, Mexico City; S. Imai, Tokyo; Martha Durham, Westport.

The index was prepared by Gisela S. Knight.

BIBLIOGRAPHY

Books

Alfano, G. B., and I. Friedlaender, *Die Geschichte des Vesuv.* Berlin: Verlag Dietrich Reimer (E. Vohsen), A.-G., 1929.

Bailey, Edward B., *James Hutton: The Founder of Modern Geology.* Amsterdam: Elsevier Publishing Co. Ltd., 1961.

Bates, D. E. B., and J. F. Kirkaldy, *Field Geology in Colour.* Poole, Dorset: Blandford Press, 1979.

Bennett, Ross, *The New America's Wonderlands: Our National Parks.* The National Geographic Society, 1980.

Bolt, Bruce, et al., *Geographical Hazards.* Springer-Verlag, 1977.

Brilliant, Richard, *Pompeii A.D. 79: The Treasure of Rediscovery.* Clarkson N. Potter, 1979.

Brion, Marcel, *Pompeii and Herculaneum: The Glory and the Grief.* London: Elek Books, Ltd., 1960.

Bullard, Fred M., *Volcanoes of the Earth.* University of Texas Press, 1976.

Bunau-Varilla, Philippe, *Panama: The Creation, Destruction, and Resurrection.* McBride, Nast & Co., 1914.

Clerk, John (of Eldin, Esq.), *A Series of Etchings, Chiefly of Views in Scotland.* Edinburgh: Bannatyne Club Publications, 1855.

Conrad, Katia, et al., *Volcans et Tremblements de Terre.* Paris: Deux Coqs d'Or, 1975.

Corti, Egon C., *The Destruction and Resurrection of Pompeii and Herculaneum.* London: Routledge & Kegan Paul, 1951.

Craig, G. Y., et al., *James Hutton's Theory of the Earth: The Lost Drawings.* Edinburgh: Scottish Academic Press, 1978.

Crandall, Hugh, *Yellowstone: The Story behind the Scenery.* KC Publications, 1978.

Crandell, Dwight R., *Potential Hazards from Future Eruptions of Mount St. Helens Volcano, Washington.* United States Government Printing Office, 1978.

The Daily News (Longview, Washington) and The Journal-American (Bellevue, Washington) combined staffs, *Volcano: The Eruption of Mount St. Helens.* Longview Publishing Co., 1980.

Decker, Robert and Barbara:
Volcanoes. W. H. Freeman, 1981.
Volcano Watching. Hawaii Natural History Association, 1980.

Donnelly, Ignatius, *Atlantis: The Antediluvian World.* Dover Publications, 1976.

Fairbridge, Rhodes W., ed., *The Encyclopedia of Geomorphology: Encyclopedia of Earth Sciences Series,* Vol. 3. Dowden, Hutchinson & Ross, 1968.

Fenton, Carroll L. and Mildred A., *Giants of Geology.* Doubleday, 1952.

Fotherhill, Brian, *Sir William Hamilton: Envoy Extraordinary.* Harcourt, Brace & World, 1969.

Francis, Peter, *Volcanoes.* Harmondsworth, Middlesex: Penguin Books Ltd., 1978.

Furneaux, Rupert, *Krakatoa.* Prentice-Hall, 1964.

Galanopoulos, A. G., and Edward Bacon, *Atlantis: The Truth behind the Legend.* Bobbs-Merrill, 1969.

Geikie, Sir Archibald, *The Founders of Geology.* Dover Publications, 1962.

Gillispie, Charles Coulston, ed., *Dictionary of Scientific Biography,* Vol. 1. Charles Scribner's Sons, 1981.

Grant, Michael:
The Art and Life of Pompeii and Herculaneum. Newsweek Books, 1979.
Cities of Vesuvius: Pompeii and Herculaneum. Harmondsworth, Middlesex: Penguin Books Ltd., 1979.

Green, Jack, and Nicholas M. Short, eds., *Volcanic Landforms and Surface Features: A Photographic Atlas and Glossary.* Springer-Verlag, 1971.

Gribbin, John, *This Shaking Earth.* G. P. Putnam's Sons, 1978.

Gunnarsson, Arni, *Volcano: Ordeal by Fire in Iceland's Westmann Islands.* Reykjavik: Iceland Review, 1973.

Hamilton, Sir William, *Observations on Mount Vesuvius, Mount Etna, and Other Volcanos in a Series of*

Letters. London: T. Cadebe, in the Strand, 1772.

Harper, J. Russell, *Paul Kane's Frontier*. University of Texas Press, 1971.

Harris, Stephen L., *Fire & Ice: The Cascade Volcanoes*. Pacific Search Press, 1980.

Hearn, Lafcadio, *Two Years in the French West Indies*. Harper & Brothers, 1890.

Heilprin, Angelo:
The Eruption of Pelée: A Summary and Discussion of the Phenomena and Their Sequels. J. B. Lippincott, 1908.
Mont Pelée and The Tragedy of Martinique. J. B. Lippincott, 1903.
The Tower of Pelée: New Studies of the Great Volcano of Martinique. J. B. Lippincott, 1904.

Herbert, Don, and Fulvio Bardossi, *Kilauea: Case History of a Volcano*. Harper & Row, 1968.

Hughes, Patrick, *American Weather Stories*. United States Department of Commerce, 1976.

Hutton, James, *Theory of the Earth, with Proofs and Illustrations*, Vol. 1. Codicote, Hertfordshire: Wheldon & Wesley, Ltd., 1972.

Jaggar, Thomas A.:
My Experiments with Volcanoes. Hawaiian Volcano Research Association, 1956.
Volcanoes Declare War. Paradise of the Pacific Ltd., 1945.

Johnstone, Christopher, *John Martin*. London: Academy Editions, 1974.

Kaye, Glen, *Hawaii Volcanoes: The Story behind the Scenery*. KC Publications, 1976.

Krafft, Katia and Maurice, *Volcanoes: Earth's Awakening*. Hammond, 1980.

Lacroix, A., *La Montagne Pelée et Ses Eruptions*. Paris: Masson et Cie, 1904.

Lambert, M. B., *Volcanoes*. University of Washington Press, 1980.

Lovell, John W., *Martinique, St. Vincent*. John W. Lovell, 1902.

McCullough, David, *The Path between the Seas*. Simon and Schuster, 1977.

Macdonald, Gordon A., *Volcanoes*. Prentice-Hall, 1972.

Macdonald, Gordon A., and Agatin T. Abbott, *Volcanoes in the Sea: The Geology of Hawaii*. University Press of Hawaii, 1977.

Macdonald, Gordon A., and Douglass H. Hubbard, *Volcanoes of the National Parks in Hawaii*. Tongg Publishing Co., 1974.

Man against Volcano: The Eruption of Heimaey, Vestmann Islands, Iceland. United States Department of the Interior Geological Survey, 1977.

Mather, Kirtley F., *The Earth beneath Us*. Random House, 1964.

Mavor, James W., Jr., *Voyage to Atlantis*. G. P. Putnam's Sons, 1969.

Miller, J. Martin, *The Martinique Horror and St. Vincent Calamity*. National Publishing Co., no date.

Palmieri, Luigi, *The Eruption of Vesuvius in 1872*. London: Asher & Co., 1873.

Perret, Frank A.:
The Eruption of Mt. Pelée: 1929-1932. Carnegie Institution of Washington, 1935.
The Vesuvius Eruption of 1906: Study of a Volcanic Cycle. Carnegie Institution of Washington, 1924.
Volcanological Observations. Carnegie Institution of Washington, 1950.

Phillips, John, *Vesuvius*. Oxford: Clarendon Press, 1869.

Playfair, John, *Illustrations of the Huttonian Theory of the Earth*. Edinburgh: Cadell and Davies, 1802.

Press, Frank, and Raymond Siever, *Earth*. W. H. Freeman, 1978.

Raffles, Sophia, *Memoir of Sir T. Stamford Raffles*. London: John Murray, 1830.

Reader's Digest, ed., *Scenic Wonders of America*. Reader's Digest Assoc., 1973.

Rittmann, A., *Volcanoes and Their Activity*. John Wiley & Sons, 1962.

Rodwell, G. F., *Etna: A History of the Mountain and of Its Eruptions*. London: C. Kegan Paul & Co., 1878.

Schneer, Cecil J., ed., *Toward a History of Geology*. M.I.T. Press, 1969.

Scrope, George P.:
The Geology and Extinct Volcanos of Central France. London: John Murray, 1858.
Volcanos: The Character of Their Phenomena. London: Longmans, Green, Reader, and Dyer, 1872.

Seymour, Jacqueline, *The Wonders of Nature*. Crescent Books, 1978.

Sheets, Payson D., and Donald K. Grayson, *Volcanic Activity and Human Ecology*. Academic Press, 1979.

Shelton, John S., *Geology Illustrated*. W. H. Freeman, 1966.

Stone, Scott C. S., *Volcano!!* Island Heritage, 1977.

Thomas, Gordon, and Max Morgan Witts, *The Day the World Ended*. Stein and Day, 1976.

Trevelyan, Raleigh, *The Shadow of Vesuvius: Pompeii A.D. 79*. London: Michael Joseph Ltd., 1976.

Van Bemmelen, R. W., *The Geology of Indonesia*, Vol. IA, *General Geology of Indonesia and Adjacent Archipelagoes*. The Hague: Martinus Nijhoff, 1970.

Van Rose, Susanna, and Ian Mercer, *Volcanoes*. London: Her Majesty's Stationery Office for the Institute of Geological Sciences, 1977.

Verbeek, R. D. M., *Krakatau*. Brussels: Institut National de Géographie, no date.

Vitaliano, Dorothy B., *Legends of the Earth: Their Geologic Origins*. Indiana University Press, 1973.

Von Zittel, Karl, *History of Geology and Palaeontology*. Codicote, Hertfordshire: Wheldon & Wesley, Ltd., 1962.

Ward-Perkins, John, and Amanda Claridge, *Pompeii A.D. 79*. Museum of Fine Arts, 1978.

Warmington, E. H., ed., *Pliny: Letters and Panegyricus*. Harvard University Press, 1969.

White, George W., ed., *James Hutton's System of the Earth, 1785; Theory of the Earth, 1788; Observations on Granite, 1794; Together with Playfair's Biography of Hutton*. Hafner Press, 1973.

Williams, Chuck, *Mount St. Helens: A Changing Landscape*. Graphic Arts Center Publishing Co., 1980.

Williams, Howel, and Alexander R. McBirney, *Volcanology*. Freeman, Cooper & Co., 1979.

Yoder, Hatten S., Jr., *Generation of Basaltic Magma*. National Academy of Sciences, 1976.

Periodicals

Andrews, William P., "Vesuvius in Fury." *Century Magazine*, August 1906.

Asimov, Isaac, "Kamchatka: Blazing Jewels in a Fiery Ring." *Geo*, September 1979.

Bullard, Fred M., "Studies on Parícutin Volcano, Michoacan, Mexico." *Bulletin of the Geological Society of America*, May 1947.

Cook, R. J., et al., "Impact on Agriculture of the Mount St. Helens Eruptions." *Science*, January 2, 1981.

Crandell, Dwight, and Donal Mullineaux, "Mount St. Helens Volcano: Recent and Future Behavior." *Science*, February 7, 1975.

De Beer, Sir Gavin, "The Volcanoes of Auvergne." *Annals of Science*, 1962.

Decker, Robert and Barbara, "The Eruptions of Mount St. Helens." *Scientific American*, March

1981.

"The Destruction of St. Pierre." *Harper's Weekly*, June 7, 1902.

Douglas, Marjory Stoneman, "He Talks with Volcanoes." *The Saturday Evening Post*, December 25, 1937.

Dzurisin, Daniel, "Influence of Fortnightly Earth Tides at Kilauea Volcano, Hawaii." *Geophysical Research Letters*, November 1980.

Earthquake Information Bulletin, July-August, 1980.

Eaton, J. P., and D. J. Murata, "How Volcanoes Grow." *Science*, October 7, 1960.

"Eruption of Mt. St. Helens: Seismology." *Nature*, June 19, 1980.

Eyles, V. A., "Sir James Hall, Bt. (1761-1832)." *Endeavor*, October 1961.

Finch, Ruy H., and Gordon A. Macdonald, "Bombing to Divert Lava Flows." *The Volcano Letter*, October-December, 1949.

Findley, Rowe, "Mount St. Helens: Mountain with a Death Wish." *National Geographic*, January 1981.

Francis, Peter, "The Blast That Moved a Mountain." *Geographical*, August 1980.

Gannon, Robert, "Volcanoes: Geologists Watch, Probe—and Wait." *Popular Science*, November 1978.

Heilprin, Angelo, "Mont Pelée in Its Might." *McClure's Magazine*, May-October, 1902.

Hill, Robert T.:
"Report by Robert T. Hill on the Volcanic Disturbances in the West Indies." *National Geographic*, July 1902.
"A Study of Pelée." *The Century Magazine*, September 1902.

Hoblitt, Richard P., et al., "Mount St. Helens Eruptive Behavior during the Past 1,500 Years." *Geology*, November 1980.

Hovey, Edmund Otis:
"The Eruptions of La Soufrière, St. Vincent, in May, 1902." *National Geographic*, December 1902.
"Martinique and St. Vincent; a Preliminary Report upon the Eruption of 1902." *Bulletin of the American Museum of Natural History*, October 11, 1902.
"A Wonderful Change in Pelée." *The Century Magazine*, September 1903.

Hoyt, Joseph B., "The Cold Summer of 1816." *Annals of the Association of American Geographers*, June 1958.

Jaggar, T. A., Jr.:
"The Bombing Operation at Mauna Loa." *The Volcano Letter*, January 1936.
"The Eruption of Pelée." *Popular Science Monthly*, January 1904.
"Field Notes of a Geologist in Martinique and St. Vincent." *Popular Science Monthly*, August 1902.
"Initial Stages of the Spine on Pelée." *American Journal of Science*, 1904.
"Protection of Harbors from Lava Flow." *American Journal of Science*, 1945.

Kennan, George, "The Tragedy of Pelée." *The Outlook*, June-August, 1902.

Kennedy, Robert A., "Ash From Mt. St. Helens." *Nature*, October 16, 1980.

Kieffer, Susan Werner, "Blast Dynamics at Mount St. Helens on 18 May 1980." *Nature*, June 18, 1981.

Kilburn, Christopher, "Shaken Not Stirred." *The (London) Guardian*, July 23, 1981.

Kiver, Eugene P., "Washington's Geothermal Ice Caves." *Pacific Search*, December/January 1975-1976.

"The Last Days of St. Pierre." *The Century Magazine*,

August 1902.
McCormick, M., "Monitoring Mt. St. Helens." *Nature,* March 12, 1981.
Macdonald, Gordon A.:
"Barriers to Protect Hilo from Lava Flows." *Pacific Science,* July 1958.
"The 1959 and 1960 Eruptions of Kilauea Volcano, Hawaii, and the Construction of Walls to Restrict the Spread of the Lava Flows." *Bulletin Volcanologique,* 1962.
Macdonald, Gordon A., and Jerry P. Eaton, "The 1955 Eruption of Kilauea Volcano." *The Volcano Letter,* July-December, 1955.
MacGregor, A. G., "Eruptive Mechanisms: Mt. Pelée, the Soufrière of St. Vincent and the Valley of Ten Thousand Smokes." *Bulletin Volcanologique,* 1952.
McKee, S. S., "Most Fatal and Frightful Disaster of Our Times." *Leslie's Weekly,* June 12, 1902.
McTaggart, K. C., "The Mobility of Nuées Ardentes." *American Journal of Science,* May 1960.
Maiuri, Amadeo, "Last Moments of the Pompeians." *National Geographic,* November 1961.
Marinatos, Spyridon, "Thera: Key to the Riddle of Minos." *National Geographic,* May 1972.
Matteucci, R. V., "My Life on the Vesuvian Lid." *Cosmopolitan,* October 1905.
"Mount St. Helens: Special Report." *The Oregonian,* October 27, 1980.
Parsons, Willard H., "Kilauea Volcano." *The Explorer,* Winter 1974.
Peck, Dallas L., et al., "The Lava Lakes of Kilauea." *Scientific American,* October 1979.
Perret, Frank A., "The Day's Work of a Volcanologist." *World's Work,* November 1907.
Petroeschevsky, W. A., "A Contribution to the Knowledge of the Gunung Tambora (Sumbawa)." *Koninklijk Nederlandsch Aardrijkskundig Genootschap,* November 1949.
Sadler, Cindi, "Stanford Alumni Document Largest Known Landslide." *The Stanford Observer,* February 1981.
Sigurdsson, Haraldur, and Stephen Sparks, "An Active Submarine Volcano." *Natural History,* October 1979.
Sigurgeirsson, Thorbjorn, "The Battle of Heimaey." *Welcome to Iceland,* 1974.
Stocking, Hobart E., "The Greatest Explosion of All Time." *Natural History,* May 1943.
Stommel, Henry and Elizabeth, "The Year without a Summer." *Scientific American,* June 1979.
Strother, French, "Frank A. Perret, Volcanologist." *The World's Work,* April 1915.

"A Sunday Holocaust: Mount St. Helens Diary." *The Columbian,* May 1980.
Thomas, Lately, "Prelude to Doomsday." *American Heritage,* August 1961.
Thorarinsson, S., et al., "The Eruption on Heimaey, Iceland." *Nature,* February 9, 1973.
Tilling, Robert I., "What Does HVO Do?" *Orchid Isle Magazine,* December 22-28, 1974.
Verbeek, R. D. M., "The Krakatoa Eruption." *Nature,* May 1, 1884.
Voorhies, Michael R., "Dwarfing the St. Helens Eruption: Ancient Ashfall Creates a Pompeii of Prehistoric Animals." *National Geographic,* January 1981.
Waesche, Hugh H., and Dallas L. Peck, "Volcanoes Tell Secrets in Hawaii." *Natural History,* March 1966.
"Wenn die Erde Uberkocht." *Stern Magazine,* December 27, 1972.
Wentworth, C. K., et al., "Feasibility of a Lava-diverting Barrier at Hilo, Hawaii." *Pacific Science,* July 1961.
Williams, Howel, "Volcanoes." *Scientific American,* November 1951.

Other Publications

Anderson, Tempest, and John S. Flett:
"Preliminary Report on the Recent Eruption of the Soufrière in St. Vincent, and of a Visit to Mont Pelée, in Martinique." Smithsonian Institution Annual Report, 1902.
"Report on the Eruptions of the Soufrière, in St. Vincent, in 1902." *Philosophical Transactions of the Royal Society of London,* Series A, Vol. 200, 1903.
"Catalogue of the Active Volcanoes of the World, Including Solfatara Fields, Parts I-XXII, 1951-1975," International Association of Volcanology and Chemistry of the Earth's Interior, 1975.
Cummans, John, "Mudflows Resulting from the May 18, 1980, Eruption of Mount St. Helens, Washington." Geological Survey Circular 850-B, 1981.
Decker, Robert W., "State of the Art in Volcano Forecasting." *Geophysical Predictions,* Geophysics Study Committee and Research Board, National Academy of Sciences, 1978.
Doumas, C., ed., "Thera and the Aegean World II." Papers and Proceedings of the Second International Scientific Congress, Santorini, Greece, August 1978.
"Geology, 1888-1938, Fiftieth Anniversary Volume." Geological Society of America, June 1941.

Girod, Michel, "Le Massif Volcanique de l'Atakor (Hoggar, Sahara Algérien)." Centre de Recherches sur les Zones Arides, Série: *Géologie,* No. 12, 1971.
Gonzalez, Jenaro, "The Birth of Parícutin." Annual Report of the Smithsonian Institution, 1946.
Hall, Sir James:
"Accounts of a Series of Experiments Modifying the Action of Heat." *Transactions of the Royal Society of Edinburgh,* Vol. 6, 1812.
"Experiments in Whenstone and Lava." *Transactions of the Royal Society of Edinburgh,* Vol. 5, 1805.
"Indonesia, Comparable with the Plinian Outburst of the Volcano of Thera (Santorini) in Minoan Time." Paper presented at the 1st International Scientific Congress on the Volcano of Thera, September 1969.
Klein, Fred W., "Patterns of Historic Eruptions at Hawaiian Volcanoes." Paper submitted to the *Journal of Volcanology and Geothermal Research,* September 1980.
Lipman, Peter W., and Donal R. Mullineaux, "The 1980 Eruptions of Mount St. Helens, Washington." Geological Survey Professional Paper 1250, 1980.
Lockwood, J. P., and F. A. Torgerson, "Diversion of Lava Flows by Aerial Bombing; Lessons from Mauna Loa Volcano, Hawaii." U.S. Geological Survey, no date.
Lockwood, John P., et al., "Hawaiian Volcano Observatory—An Expanding Research Effort." U.S. Geological Survey, no date.
"Monitoring Active Volcanoes." USGS Yearbook, 1977.
"Mount St. Helens Land Management Plan." U.S. Department of Agriculture Draft Environmental Impact Statement, 1981.
Olson, Robert A., and Mildred M. Wallace, "Geologic Hazards and Public Problems." Office of Emergency Preparedness Conference paper, May 1969.
Shulters, Michael V., and Daphne G. Clifton, "Mount St. Helens: Volcanic-Ash Fall in the Bull Run Watershed, Oregon, March-June 1980." Geological Survey Circular 850-A, 1980.
"The Surveillance and Prediction of Volcanic Activity; A Review of Methods and Techniques." UNESCO, Paris, 1971.
Symons, G. J., ed., "The Eruption of Krakatoa, and Subsequent Phenomena." Report of the Krakatoa Committee of the Royal Society of London, 1888.

PICTURE CREDITS

therthur, 1885. 62-71: Art by Lloyd K. Townsend. 72: Robert I. Tilling, courtesy U.S. Geological Survey. 75: Library of Congress. 76-79: U.S. Geological Survey. 81: Fred M. Bullard—art by Richard Schlecht. 82: Library of Congress. 85: Sidney Horenstein. 86, 87: Map by Bill Hezlep. 88: Stella Snead from Bruce Coleman, Inc. 90, 91: Paul Chesley. 92, 93: Art by Richard Schlecht; John Buitenkant; Heather Angel, London (2)—Sandro Prato from Bruce Coleman, Ltd., London. 94, 95: Paul Chesley. 96: Janice L. Miller, courtesy Pacific Gas and Electric Company. 97: Art by Richard Schlecht. 98: George Rodger for *Life*. 101: Art by Richard Schlecht. 102: Library of Congress. 104: University of Manchester: Tabley Collection, England. 106: Joseph Natanson, courtesy Osservatorio Vesuviano, Naples. 107: Art by Richard Schlecht. 109: Mondadori, Milan—Scala, Florence; Aldo Durazzi, courtesy Museo Archeologico Nazionale, Naples (2). 110: I.G.D.A., Milan. 111: Leonard von Matt from Photo Researchers. 112, 113: Library of Congress. 114: Painting by Achille Beltrame, courtesy Domenica del Corriere, Milan—Library of Congress. 115: Professor Giuseppe Pugliano, Istituto Di Coltivazioni Arboree, Università degli Studi, Portici, Naples. 116: Robert I. Tilling, courtesy U.S. Geological Survey. 118: Courtesy of the Geophysical Laboratory of the Carnegie Institution, Washington. 120: Art by Bill Hezlep. 121: Art by Bill Hezlep and John Britt. 122: Royal Institute of Linguistics and Anthropology, Leyden; art by Richard Schlecht. 124, 125: Arthur Zich. 126: N. R. Farbman for *Life*. 129: U.S. Geological Survey. 130, 131: Robert I. Tilling, courtesy U.S. Geological Survey. 132: Camera Hawaii. 133: Robert Wenkam. 134, 135: © Mats Wibe Lund, Reykjavik. 136, 137: © Pete Turner; Sigurgeir Jonasson, Westman Islands, Iceland. 138, 139: © Mats Wibe Lund, Reykjavik, except right, Sigurgeir Jonasson, Westman Islands, Iceland. 140: Vince Streano. 142: Art by Richard Schlecht—courtesy of the Royal Ontario Museum, Toronto, Canada. 143: Eugene P. Kiver. 146: © Al Hayward. 147: Art by Bill Hezlep and John Britt. 148: U.S. Geological Survey—Steve Small. 149: Roger Werth. 150: Gary Rosenquist/Earth Images (4); art by Richard Schlecht (4). 152, 153: Michael Lawton/Cirama. 154: Art by Bill Hezlep and John Britt; art by Richard Schlecht. 155: © 1980 Lu Moore; © 1980 Mike Moore. 156: Art by Richard Schlecht. 157: Bill Thompson/Earth Images—Bill Thompson © 1980/Earth Images; Kurt E. Smith, Visions Photo Group. 158: Tim Harmon from Eyelights Photography. 159: Ralph Perry from Black Star—Tim Thompson. 160: Tim Thompson. 162, 163: Ralph Perry. 164: Roger Werth. 165: Gary Braasch © 1980. 166, 167: Ralph Perry; Russell Johnson from Silverlight Studio. 168, 169: Gary Braasch © 1981; John Marshall.

INDEX